THE FATHERS OF THE LATIN CHURCH

THE FATHERS OF
THE LATIN CHURCH

BY

HANS von CAMPENHAUSEN, D.D.

PROFESSOR OF ECCLESIASTICAL HISTORY
IN THE UNIVERSITY OF HEIDELBERG

TRANSLATED BY MANFRED HOFFMANN

ADAM & CHARLES BLACK
LONDON

FIRST PUBLISHED 1964

A. AND C. BLACK LIMITED
4, 5 AND 6 SOHO SQUARE LONDON W.I

FROM THE GERMAN 'LATEINISCHE KIRCHENVÄTER'
© 1960 W. KOHLHAMMER GMBH, STUTTGART

ENGLISH TRANSLATION © 1964 A. AND C. BLACK LTD

PRINTED IN GREAT BRITAIN
BY R. & R. CLARK, LIMITED, EDINBURGH

VENERANDO ORDINI THEOLOGORUM
UNIVERSITATIS OSLOENSIS
HOC LIBELLO GRATIAS TESTATUR MAXIMAS AUCTOR
PIE MEMOR
PRIORIS COMMERCII QUO CUM ILLO AMICE ERAT
CONIUNCTUS HONORISQUE SUMMI QUO FACTUS EST
THEOLOGIAE DOCTOR

TRANSLATOR'S NOTE

PROFESSOR VON CAMPENHAUSEN is well known in the academic world as a leading expert in patristics, and as one of the outstanding Protestant scholars in Germany, but his major works have not until recently been available in English. A beginning has been made to remedy this situation by the publication in translation of two of his books, on the Greek and the Latin church fathers, which are highly esteemed both by scholars and by the educated laity. Although the author expressly renounces 'learned quotations, notes, explanations, marginal citations, footnotes, and appendages of that sort', the expert will recognize behind these biographical sketches a background of exact knowledge of the literary work of the church fathers, of their historical setting, and of their theological impact.

As translator, and a former pupil of the author, well acquainted with his methodological and theological approach, I have endeavoured to preserve faithfully the spirit of this work, and the individuality of the author in it. I acknowledge my indebtedness to my colleagues and friends, Professor John Lawson of Atlanta and Dr. Jack H. Wilson of Athens, Tennessee, as well as to the Rev. L. A. Garrard of Oxford for his editorial work. Above all I owe thanks to the author himself for his intellectual inspiration, and for his warm interest in my own work also.

M. H.

Emory University
Atlanta, Georgia

CONTENTS

CONTENTS

THE LATIN CHURCH FATHERS
AND THE GREEKS

AN earlier volume in this series was devoted to the Greek church fathers. What was said there about the expressions 'church father' and 'patristics' will not be repeated here. The present volume may be read independently, although in subject-matter it is a continuation of the earlier one. The Latin patristic literature originated almost one hundred years after the Greek. The Latin fathers were the younger pupils of the Greeks, who were their first teachers in Christian faith and thought, and indeed in their whole theology. This relationship is not made sufficiently distinct by the usual purely chronological arrangement of the Greek and Latin church fathers. Through the early church, as through the whole world of ancient culture, flowed a constant stream of intellectual stimulus from the East to the West. There was no comparable counterflow from West to East to correspond to the large amount of literature translated into Latin. Nevertheless, in the Western world there very swiftly developed a new, vigorous, and independent form of ecclesiastical life and Christian theology, which was ultimately to prove not inferior to the Greek, and probably surpassed it in its effect on world history. The rise of this Latin ecclesiastical phenomenon is noteworthy because it marks the first transformation into a new intellectual mould which Christianity underwent as a whole.

Although Jesus and His first disciples did not speak Greek, but Aramaic, Christianity is no 'Jewish religion'. The church consisted of 'Jews and Greeks'; and the Greek fathers rightly understood their faith as a new truth transcending Judaism as well as Hellenism. The New Testament was written in Greek and, as always, the language is more than an external clothing. The Greek spirit touched and to some extent determined Christianity even in its inception. This factor increasingly and rather one-sidedly influenced the further development at the expense of the Hebraic Old Testament foundations. Even where the ancient church in its missionary activity pushed beyond the frontiers of the empire into the East and apparently reorientalized itself, the Greek presuppositions of the text of the Bible, the creeds, and theological thinking generally remained and proved to be ineradicable. To be sure there were also Oriental church fathers; yet they fell far short of the Latin fathers with respect to independent power and importance.

The 'Latin' West, which alone need really be taken into account for the history of the ancient church, had long been influenced and permeated by Greek culture and Hellenistic thinking when Christianity entered the scene. In fact it was only this that made the rapid intellectual development of the Western church possible. However, if the Roman spirit did not simply dissolve into Hellenism, but preserved its identity throughout the constant interchange with it, and only thereby attained its own intellectual character, the same is true to an even greater degree of the Latin church and its theological independence. As has already been said, the Latin church fathers were instructed and educated by their Greek teachers; but they possessed from the very beginning their own approach to the Bible, especially to the Old Testament. In opposition to the philosophical trend, and the metaphysical and speculative tendencies of Hellenism, they display a restraint and reserve which were overcome only at the end of the fourth century. This led to the Golden Age of theology of the Latin fathers, as exemplified above all in Augustine. Even this new 'philosophical' theology, however, did not lose its foundation in Latin thinking. Not by chance was it linked with a rediscovery of Paul, and with a taking up of the question, so characteristic of Paul, of the opposition of faith to 'law'. This is an aspect which was scarcely ever considered by Greek theology and which in its original meaning, at any rate, remained completely foreign to it. The peculiar affinity which existed between the Roman character and Judaism enabled the Latin church, just because of its sobriety and practical legalism, to understand what the 'gospel' meant.

However, we shall not speak of these things in detail in this volume, which presents only a series of biographical sketches and which does not set out to be a substitute for a history of theology and doctrine. The selection of the personalities portrayed is again strictly limited and does not range beyond the end of the old classical culture, the decline of which marks an epoch for church history too. Yet behind my endeavours lies the conviction that historical life is realized primarily through human personalities, or at least that in them it can be grasped most directly and comprehended most distinctly.

CHAPTER I

TERTULLIAN

A CHRISTIAN congregation already existed in Rome at the time of the apostle Paul, but it was then not yet a Roman congregation. The metropolis contained immigrants from all over the world, and not least from the Greek-speaking Orient, from which also came the first missionaries and adherents of the new faith. The language of the Christians throughout the West was exclusively Greek and remained so for a hundred years. This was not only because the church had originated in the East, but it reflected also the general conditions of the empire, which had become one united empire of the Mediterranean area and its culture. Greek was not only the language of the intelligentsia (as French was at one time in Germany), it was likewise the prevalent language of commerce and travel. In every large town of the West, Greek was not only understood but spoken, probably as the ordinary language of the people. For a religion of townsfolk, a faith which at the very outset dissociated the individual from national ties and placed him in a new community as Christianity did, Greek was the obvious religious and ecclesiastical language.

When this situation slowly began to change toward the end of the second century, we can observe the broadening of this intellectual and social basis and the growing popularity and stability of the Western church. The members of the congregations began to speak Latin among themselves and Greek at most only with the higher clergy. Sermons were preached for the first time in Latin; and we also come across the beginnings of a modest Latin-Christian literature for practical use in the church: translations of the Bible, accounts of martyrdoms, and a cata-

4

logue of the Canon have been preserved. Yet when and where did the independent intellectual development begin? The first Latin document of importance is considered by some scholars to be the dialogue 'Octavius', which significantly is an 'apology' written with an eye toward non-Christian readers. Its author is a Roman lawyer by the name of Minucius Felix. In the old quarrel about chronological priority it at least looks as if the scale is tipping in his favour, and against the precedence of his fellow-lawyer, Tertullian. Despite this, we start off with Tertullian and can set aside without misgivings the otherwise unknown Minucius. In any event, the first Latin theologian whom we really know in the West as a distinct personality is Tertullian. Tertullian elucidates through the abundance of his vigorous and original writings the whole world in which he lived and worked. To this extent he stands at the beginning of the entire Latin church history.

Tertullian was an African, i.e. a citizen of Africa, the province colonized by the Romans, which is the modern Tunisia. Here in the capital, Carthage, Quintus Septimus Florens Tertullianus was born soon after the middle of the second century. His father was a subaltern in the army. The Roman outlook is taken for granted, although it is a characteristically African form of the Roman spirit which tends to combine discipline with criticism and a sense of order with scorn and passion and which prefers self-sufficiency even to the point of rebellion, rather than blindly to follow and obey. The young Tertullian, having received a sound education in rhetoric and law, lived for a time in Rome and may have begun a practice as an attorney. That he is identical with the famous lawyer Tertullianus, mentioned in the Digests, is very unlikely. Tertullian was no deep scholar, although he had read and knew much and liked to startle his reader with obscure facts. He was, in Harnack's phrase, a 'philosophizing advocate' in whose mouth the precise language of the lawyer has become a means of rhetoric. His keen intellect was constantly in motion; yet he was unfitted for a contemplative life. Everything Tertullian thought, said, and did was directed toward the real world and pressed for a practical decision. This was the determinative factor also in his intellectual and spiritual life. Tertullian was impetuous, hot-blooded, at times intentionally reckless; he himself complained that he could never learn the precious virtue of patience. Jerome, who had in many respects a similar nature, once called him a man always afire (*vir ardens*). Yet his manner was not primitive; he never lost control of his temper. On the contrary, the more he spoke in anger, and the more passionately and personally he threw his weight behind what he thought was right, the more polished were his thoughts and his style, the more subtle his tactics and the more sparkling his cruelly biting wit. Roman restraint, legal clarity, and military discipline were transmuted into an intellectual and moral force in the ardent, aspiring mind and heart of Tertullian.

We do not know the circumstances which led Tertullian to Christianity. Usually one thinks above all of the effect of the Christian martyrs which, according to his own testimony, exercises the strongest persuasive force, and also of the moral impact of the Christian community generally, imperturbable and united in the midst of the world of urban licentiousness. In addition to this, however, the spiritual impact of Christian teaching and preaching must not be overlooked. The message of the one God, Creator and Sovereign—who is no mere idea but directs the whole course of the world—who has overthrown the demons through Christ, and who now calls all men to the ultimate decision, was the source of the decisive experience in Tertullian's life. Contrasted with this, the artificially constructed theories and wisdom of the philosophers were exposed as vain and ineffectual babble. The truth of God cannot be denied in principle by any intelligent being, and yet obviously it is really revealed and truly made known only to the Christians. They know God's Son and through Him, His teaching, and His word, they know the entire will, nature, and law of God. Tertullian must have come upon the Bible quite early, and he adhered to it throughout his life. He knew it inside and out and referred to it expressly on every possible occasion, not hesitating to interpret it independently, when necessary according to the original Greek text. In hearing the direct voice of God throughout—in the words of the prophets, of the Saviour and of His disciples—Tertullian was, of course, not original. He shared this belief in 'the Scripture' with the Christians of his time. But far more than all of his contemporaries he also had an immediate sense of the unique character of the Bible. He knew and stated time and again that it is absolutely different from the spirit and noble wisdom of the world. His blunt, rough-hewn realism discovered through a natural affinity the unclassical ardour and stern sobriety of the Holy Scripture, its concrete, paradoxical character, unapproachable by any religious-aesthetic idealization. And by accepting it in this particularity and loving it in its strangeness he became the most original and in many respects the most penetrating exegete of the whole ancient church, whose detailed accuracy and understanding was outdone by none of the later theologians. The limitations which finally defeated him were the limits of his own comprehension of the faith, namely the limits of his proud and mercilessly rigid nature.

When we first become acquainted with Tertullian, he was already a respected member of the Christian congregation of Carthage. He was in the prime of life, happily married, and although perhaps not wealthy, in an independent and secure position economically. Thus he made himself available for the instruction of the catechumens, the candidates for baptism, and the newly converted. Moreover, he may have 'preached' occasionally, i.e. delivered spiritually instructive speeches before the congregation. Above all, however, Tertullian was active as an independent writer, acting as advocate before Christians and pagans for the best aspects of Christianity. In part he did his literary work in Greek—'for the sake of our theatre-aesthetes' as he ironically remarked (*De Cor.* 6)—but it is characteristic that none of his Greek writings have been preserved. The transition to Latin was most appropriate for an author who, like

Tertullian, aimed at a direct effect and confrontation, and by
appeals and lectures tried to reach primarily his nearest brethren
and fellow-citizens. But what Latin it was that Tertullian suddenly dared to write! It was without precedent in the literary
field. In Tertullian's writings, we come across the living language of the Christians of that time, the Latin of the growing
Latin church, a language which accordingly is filled with loan-
words and new coinage to describe the new facts and ideas of
the Christian daily life. It observes and adopts at the same time
even in grammatical details the language actually spoken by the
society of Carthage, and by the people whom Tertullian knew,
observed and sought out. But above all it was Tertullian's own
language, an expression of his violent creative power which
left nothing unattempted in order to obtain the new self-
imposed goal.

Tertullian well knew what he was doing. He renounced no
trick of approved rhetoric, which he knew how to combine
with the most telling of surprises, puns, rhymes, alliterations,
and rhythmic clauses, and all the peculiarities and idiosyn-
crasies of the contemporary school of writers. In this respect
he seems to show a kinship with his older contemporary and
African fellow-countryman, Apuleius. At any rate Tertullian
had nothing to do with the polished classical elegance of Minucius Felix, who presents his apology in the style of Cicero. He
wanted to strike and unmask the reality of his time; he wanted
above all to grip, enchain, and captivate his hearers. Hence he
expressed himself in a lively and vivid way which often violently exceeds the bounds of good taste. Nevertheless, his
colloquialism is never simply crude, because it is demanded by
the subject-matter—i.e., as Tertullian sees it, it is demanded by
the truth itself. This gives to the crudeness and apparent vul-
garity of his language the dignity of a higher mission and the
consecration of real sincerity. This impression of an inflexible,
heroic realism even intensifies the intended close-clipped phrase-
ology, the volcanic eruption of his sentences. According to a
statement made by a critic in the ancient church, almost every

word of Tertullian becomes an aphorism. And this aphoristic sententiousness, this rough conciseness occasionally reminds one of Tacitus. But 'the fervour which Tacitus holds in check with an aristocratically restrained indignation, becomes in him [Tertullian] a tidal wave which carries with it, whirling and swirling, everything in its path'. No other ancient author, says Eduard Norden in this connection, has so incessantly violated the 'highest law of the ancient conception of art, the subordination of individuality to the traditional' as has Tertullian, to whom Christ revealed Himself, as he once said, precisely 'not as tradition but as truth' (de Virg. Vel. 1, 1). Even in ancient times complaints were raised concerning the difficulty of his writings. And another consequence of his style for us is that Tertullian's sentences cannot possibly be directly translated into a modern language, not even into English. Only the original Latin preserves the hard stroke and sound of the metal, the sparks flying as he forges it.

There was scarcely a problem in the church of that time about which Tertullian did not express his view, or in some way offer his opinion. The thirty or so different writings we possess today are as varied as can be imagined. Tertullian liked to arrange a topic thematically and treat it exhaustively without becoming verbose. He did not adopt the literary form of a continuous Biblical commentary which was originating at that time. His publications range from the short, crisp, and clever, pamphlet or essay to voluminous theological treatises which are 'books' even in a modern sense, and are thoroughly scholarly. They are well-organized, and always keep in focus his intended purpose. They skilfully put the reader in the picture and anticipate his possible objections; they draw his attention to the bearing and importance of certain ideas and irresistibly carry him with them. Tertullian possessed an ability rare among theologians: he is incapable of being dull. This is true also of treatises written for purely edifying and instructive purposes which mainly represent the result of his teaching of catechumens. Thus he wrote the famous tract on prayer—'which alone defeats God'—containing a beautiful and impressive exposition of

2

the Lord's Prayer. He instructs his readers about the meaning and right use of baptism and repentance. He describes what a Christian marriage should be; and in a short tract praises patience—which he himself sorely lacked. What he expounds is not always new; but it is always independently considered, handled in a new way, and so presented that everyone can realize the significance of the problem. Even when using other authors he was no mere plagiarist, but adapted himself to the actual reader. And this makes his writings an incomparable source of material on the church life of his time.

Most of his writings, however, are of a different nature. They are polemical in approach and pugnaciously directed outwards against the enemies and persecutors, the heretics and seducers of the church. And it is in these that his gifts and superior talents fully unfold. Tertullian knew how a rhetorician convinces his hearers, wins them over to himself and incites them against others. In every situation he appears as the one who really knows, while his opponents are all malicious, stubborn, and ignorant fellows who scarcely need refutation before a competent audience. But simultaneously he liked to act the role of the noble controversialist who holds his punches because he does not want to condemn someone without examination, and is first willing to give every opponent his due and more than his due. He presents his evidence gradually; he knows how to add to it impressively while leaving the impression that he is offering only a selection of what he has available. Often he releases an already defeated adversary, apparently granting him a new chance by still accepting with reservation a thesis already proven as false in order to crush his position a second, third, and fourth time under this and any other imaginable presupposition, and finally to expose him to disdain and complete ridicule while the victorious truth rises unharmed like a phoenix from the ashes. It is not surprising that such a technique of argument sometimes overreaches itself. Since Tertullian was forever rearranging his very sharply formulated, allegedly incontrovertible statements in different ways, the reader who looks for the logical, hermeneutical, and theological principles which are really determinative easily becomes bewildered. His brilliant subtlety tempts one to take him more seriously and regard him as a deeper thinker than he really is. Nonetheless, this does not means that Tertullian is not in earnest about what he defends. As a rule, ancient rhetoric considered much in polemics legitimate which today would appear as unfair or mere shadow-boxing. Tertullian made radical use of the possibilities given to him by his education and his incomparable talent. He was no cynic; but he was a master of the most cunning dialectics and pointed irony. Each time when, after such invectives, he returns to his actual subject with a passion often splendid, never bombastic, even the modern reader has the feeling that the whole man stands heart and soul behind his testimony. And he realizes too why Tertullian stands up for his conviction so harshly and fervently, with such wild vehemence.

The earliest writings which we possess by Tertullian are aimed at the defence of Christianity against pagan suspicion, against defamation and bloody persecution. This was the first, the classic task, so to speak, of a Christian writer in that period. From the middle of the second century onward, the Greek 'apologists' had composed their more or less voluminous 'apologies' addressed to the emperors. These were in reality, like any such literature, naturally read much more by the Christians than by the pagans for whom they were intended. Minucius Felix had already joined himself to this group. Tertullian obviously had studied his various predecessors intensively and had discovered immediately the reason for their failure: they were not really directed to their opponents; they all tried to accomplish too much at once and did not concentrate on the factually and psychologically decisive points. Moreover, they did not attain the literary and intellectual level necessary for such a debate. We can still pursue the stages through which Tertullian endeavoured to cope with his task in a new style. We see a first attempt in the work in two parts: *To the Heathen*, which he later abandoned. Then follows the great

Apologeticum in an earlier draft followed by another, perhaps revised by him, and no longer addressed to an inaccessible emperor, but to his unintelligent governors and government officials. Finally there are original variations on specific topics dating from a later time.

The great *Apologeticum* is justly considered to be the unexcelled masterpiece of early Christian apologetics. It was even translated at once into Greek, a distinction which even in later times fell to the lot only of a very few writings of the Latin church fathers. Tertullian advisedly chose for the apology the form of a speech before the tribunal, something which it had long been impossible for the Christians actually to make. This situation itself, he suggests, shows how altogether objectionable the proceedings against the Christians were. 'Truth makes no appeal on her own behalf, because she does not wonder at her present condition. She knows that she plays the role of an alien on earth, that among strangers she readily discovers enemies, but she has her origin, abode, hope, recompense, and honour in heaven. Meanwhile, there is one thing for which she strives: that she be not condemned without a hearing.' This surely could not threaten the prevailing legal system, he adds sarcastically, for the authorities would be able to have an even higher opinion of themselves if they could hear the truth and then nevertheless condemn it (*Apol.* 1, 2 f.; *FC*, 10, 7).

So begins his defence. Tertullian, in his own way, tears apart the whole legal proceedings, and demonstrates that it is insane to prosecute the most trustworthy citizens of the empire in the name of a religion which, itself founded on falsehood and deceit, is no longer really followed or taken seriously anywhere. He is never tired of pointing out that all the atrocities and crimes falsely attributed to the Christians have long been perpetrated and tolerated by the pagans. Yet he now abstains from the clumsy attempt to connect these polemics with positive propaganda for Christianity and conversion. This conclusion may be drawn by the reader himself when he has learned of the teaching, rules of morality, and behaviour of the Christians as they actually are. The necessary evidence and proofs for such a conclusion are to be offered at their proper place. Tertullian has not abandoned any of the traditional material of the old apologetics; he has even materially amplified it. Yet by holding on to the last to the framework of a simulated court-speech, everything now appears much more concise, more clearly arranged, exciting, and distinct. Holding his breath, the reader follows the surprising demonstrations and disclosures and, before he is aware of it, he has reached the summary with which Tertullian, seemingly all too soon, breaks off the speech for the defence as though he regarded all further efforts as pointless: 'But, carry on, good officials; you will become much better in the eyes of the people if you sacrifice the Christians for them. Crucify us—torture us—condemn us—destroy us! Your iniquity is the proof of our innocence. For this reason God permits us to suffer these things. . . . Yet your tortures accomplish nothing, though each is more refined than the last; rather, they are an enticement to our religion. We become more every time we are hewn down by you: the blood of Christians is seed (*semen est sanguis Christianorum*).' We are just thankful to you that you end the trial so rapidly. It seems as if two courts confront each other in God's and man's fight, and 'when we are condemned by you, we are acquitted by God' (*Apol.* 50, 12 ff.; FC, 10, 126).

The decisive thought with which Tertullian turns upside down the state's proceedings is consequently not of juridical but theological origin. It is the conviction of the emptiness of polytheism and of the reality of the one, revealed God. What the authorities and the crazy masses venerate is based upon a lie, upon man-worship, and vain folly; behind this, however, stand the dangerous demons as the really operative, beguiling, and misleading force. These are the natural enemies of the truth, and they have for that reason set off the insane actions against the Christians. Therewith at a single blow the combination of religion and politics, the present state religion, until then unquestioned, collapses. How can one possibly still demand pernicious sacrifices to idols and demons by those who have come to know the true, almighty God? How can one reproach those with the charge that they lack loyalty and fidelity, who wish only to avoid participation in the falsehood perpetuated by the state, and instead of harming the emperor with a devilish adoration wish rather for his sake to invoke the true God, and who are truly devoted to him in every respect? This is why the good rulers have all along been well-disposed towards the Christians, and only the bad ones have persecuted them. This old tendentious legend, which tries to make real an unfulfilled wish of the Christians, attains, as stated by Tertullian, a little more probability and importance. For out of loyal sentiment he is able to appeal over the heads of the local authorities to the good emperors who may not have been informed about the actions of their executive agencies and the malpractice done in their names.

All these tactical declamations, however, bear in addition a more far-reaching and basic significance. Here we find ourselves at the beginnings of a new understanding of the state, and of obedience to it, which had not existed in the world prior to Christianity and which points to a distant future, at that time completely unattainable. The rulers and the state as such lose their direct religious power. There arises instead a concept of a concrete, this-worldly obedience to the state which becomes, in a new sense, binding and inevitable because it is carried on in the name of the true God. 'What betters man is the worship of God' (de Paen. 2, 7). Despite a liberal interpretation in practice the state was still in principle considered sacred. The essentially religious understanding of the state, which had existed until then, appears now simply as untruth and hypocrisy. It sheds its demonic elements in the light of the new radical faith and the obedience flowing from it. Who, asks Tertullian, really regards the emperor as a god in a serious, i.e. in the radical Christian sense? And who still is faithful to him if not the Christians? He does not shrink from alluding to the constant Palace-revolutions and murders, and suggests that if the breasts of the citizens

and politicians were made of transparent glass, some thoroughly
undesirable things would doubtless be seen! And is it not after
all an absurdity to dictate religious convictions by order of the
state? Is faith not free by its very nature? The attempt to demand
worship by force is against human and natural law, 'and it also
is not religious to wish to enforce religion' (*ad Scap.* 2, 2). We
sense here contact with ideas of philosophical enlightenment.
Yet the new faith in a revealed God acting in this world not
only liberates the individual from the external authority of the
'tyrant'. It also threatens to arouse doubt regarding the entire
combination of religion and politics, and to change it radically
in a manner which philosophical teaching on politics and
criticisms could neither have sought nor effected.

Furthermore, Tertullian presents the fact in such a way as to
indicate that the recognition of the Christians by the empire
would impose no practical problem at all. They are not surely
—as suggested—'the enemies of mankind', but rather enemies
of 'error' (*Apol.* 37, 10). Therefore, there are no better subjects
than they. Christians do not commit crimes, not even those not
punished by law. They obey any just order, pay taxes without
defrauding, and do not join in subversive activities. Quite
childish are the fancies regarding the social and economic
dangers of their way of life. The Christians participate in all
civic activities of commercial and economic life like everybody
else. They are to be found everywhere—except in the temple!
'We are neither Brahmins nor Indian gymnosophists, nor hermits of the forests, nor cranks who run away from life.' He who
believes in the Creator does not despise his gifts but only excess
and debauchery. 'We are supposedly destroying your commerce although we live with you and are dependent on you,
this somebody else may understand' (*Apol.* 42, 1 f.). Theologically those sentences are interesting; yet in the concrete political
situation, they reveal Tertullian—as apologist. In reality, he
knows very well that this living together with the pagan society of which he speaks is by no means so easy. Indeed, strictly
speaking, it is impossible for Christians. Pagan life is the

domain of the demons; one cannot participate in it without encountering their influence, cult, and symbols everywhere. When Tertullian addresses the Christians, he is the first to arouse their consciences as much as possible against all compromise, unfortunately so often attempted, and does not draw back from any consequence. Only in the case of pagan education does he make a characteristic exception. 'The emergency serves here as the excuse.' Christians cannot avoid secular instruction, because even religious culture cannot manage without it, and also because they will refute the pagan poison all the better since they are at the same time being instructed about the true God. Yet this excuse is valid only for the pupils, not the teachers, who could not possibly deal with the pagan religious mythology and everything connected with it (de Idol. 10). The limits to what may be allowed are set as narrowly as possible. A Christian craftsman or businessman must not manufacture or sell anything which in one way or another could be used to the possible advantage of idolatry, votive offerings, or even the immoral and luxurious pagan way of life. In no circumstances whatever is one allowed to accept a public office; for how could anyone in such a position escape the prescribed ceremonies and festivities, the libations and smoke of incense always connected with it? Moreover, how could a soldier avoid honouring the idolatrous banner? A judge, in addition, has to inflict tortures and decree capital punishment. Tertullian does not want to say that these offices are simply unjust and should be either reformed or abolished. The world must be as it is, and 'the Romans, i.e. the non-Christians' (Apol. 35, 9) naturally need their administration, their civil officials, and their emperors. But what has this to do with Christians who do not become Caesars, just as the Caesars of necessity are not Christians? (Apol. 21, 24). One may continue to persecute and martyr them; it will be evident on doomsday who has made the more prudent decision and sworn his allegiance to the better flag!

These are the old, primitive Christian views of believers as strangers here, and of the necessity of their affliction in this world, and of the all-determining future of God. These notions spring to life in Tertullian with new vigour—only that they attain now a one-sided tone, polemical, grim, and irreconcilable, and an accent which cannot be missed and is almost politically threatening. This is partly intended—Tertullian would like to deter the persecutors by his warnings if he can; yet it also at the same time conforms to his inner nature which fights rather than loves, breaks rather than bends, and which has accepted with joy the 'service', the *militia Christi*. He loves to conjure up military metaphors just because it is not a matter of agreement but of decision. Paganism is to Tertullian no foolishness to be enlightened, no prejudice or mistake to be dispelled or brought to reason. It is the 'world', and as such a great demonic unity to be recognized in its entirety, and to be rejected and condemned.

It is therefore no mere accident that in the last chapters of his *Apologeticum* Tertullian comes to speak expressly of philosophy, the highest and seemingly ideal embodiment of ancient spirit and life. Even at this point where the Greek apologists had almost without exception taken pains to indicate a certain appreciation and willingness to bring out a positive common basis for ethical criteria and the recognition of truth, he sees only the differences, and the increased danger of a deception and confusion in the essential matter. For Tertullian philosophers are 'Sophists', who are not seeking the truth but rather their own glory and success. Their dialectical and rhetorical tricks are vain, and result continually in contradictions and inconsistencies. Their knowledge is deceitful, and their conduct of life defective. Even the holiest symbol of philosophical independence and freedom, the death of Socrates, does not arouse Tertullian's admiration. The equanimity of his alleged wisdom was artificial and did not come from the certainty of a real possession of truth (*de An.* 1, 2 ff.). There is no common ground 'between a philosopher and a Christian, between a disciple of Hellas and a disciple of Heaven' (*Apol.* 46, 18;

FC. 10, 114) or, historically speaking, between 'Athens and Jerusalem, Academy and Church' (de Praescr. 7, 9).

Of course, Tertullian does not overlook the correspondence every educated Christian of the day seems to detect between his convictions and many traditional teachings, particularly the Platonic. He does not wish to deny them (de An. 2, 1) and is much too much of an apologist not to refer to them occasionally. However, he then explains them, in conformity with an older, originally Jewish, theory as due to the use of the Old Testament by the philosophers, the 'theft' of God's wisdom by the Greeks. Alternatively, like the Stoics, he traces them back to the sensus communes, to the elements of reasonable insight in which everybody participates by nature. The result in any case is a new confirmation of the Christian revelation, and by no means a recommendation of the philosophers or of philosophy. The philosophers always have blended the truth with their faults and errors. It would surely be a wrong and dangerous détour to try to find right understanding from their conjectures, instead of accepting it where the truth is given complete and pure. He who wants to talk about God must be instructed by God. A Christian, therefore, should build his faith 'not on a foreign foundation, but on his own' (de An. 26, 1).

What puzzles the modern reader time and again is the fact that Tertullian, in spite of his radical rejection of philosophy, again and again still makes use of his own philosophical education, even when he moves on to thoroughly theological ground. He refers to 'reason' and 'nature'; he speaks of the substance, accidents, and 'status' of a thing; he establishes methodological principles and makes dialectical distinctions—not to mention the countless instances in which he takes the presuppositions of his proof consciously or unconsciously from philosophical, and especially from Stoic, traditions of his time, and considers them more or less self-evident. For instance, he takes up the Stoic teaching of the physical nature of all reality, God's 'person' not excluded. This apparent contradiction, however, is based on a misunderstanding of what Tertullian understands by philosophy. Faith and philosophy designate to Tertullian the possession of fundamentally analogous knowledge distinguished primarily with regard to their content, which is sought and adopted in different ways. Faith clings to what God has revealed, while the philosopher lives under the illusion that he is able to solve by himself even those problems which lie beyond the human horizon. What Tertullian demands is not really a *sacrificium intellectus* but an appropriate limitation of the intellectual *hubris* of man according to the criterion of God's word. God certainly never acts unreasonably (*de Paen.* 1, 2); but he has made man to hear and obey (*ibid.* 4, 4 ff.). The question is that of the relationship of revelation to philosophy, but not yet that of the later formal distinction between faith and reason, or the issue of 'believing and thinking'. By acknowledging the divine revelation, the believer does not think less logically, reasonably and 'scientifically' than a philosopher; it is only that, as a matter of fact, he reaches the goal in his own way. To that extent Christianity can be called the true or 'better philosophy' (*de Pall.* 6, 2), although Tertullian generally avoids this conception, which is so common in the writings of the apologists. On no account, however, can a philosophy which is not willing to accept God's wisdom be equated with 'natural reason'; for unspoiled nature agrees entirely with Christianity in acknowledging God. Tertullian tries to illustrate this in a little apologetic essay on *The Testimony of the Soul*, the most charming piece he ever wrote. It is possible, he thinks, to demonstrate readily from those things which are 'self-evident' to human common sense, and also from spontaneous exclamations and expressions, that the 'soul' truly knows only one God, and that it fears his judgement and tries to find refuge with him against the power of demons. For that reason it testifies more effectively to faith than any erudite apologetics. It should, however, be noted: this is true only of the soul 'in its natural state, plain, uncultivated and simple' a schooled and educated soul which 'belches' the academic wisdom of Attica is no longer Christian, and there is nothing that can be done to make it reasonable (*Test. An.* 1, 6 ff.).

To understand these views it is useful to remind oneself that Tertullian was a Westerner; philosophy never obtained in the Latin West the publicly approved position and independent activity it had in the Greek world. Here, it could easily appear in fact as dead book-learning and mere rhetoric, as superficial culture without content, and as mere entertaining small talk. But to understand Tertullian's anger fully we must not stop here. We must envisage the actual theological adversaries of whom he instinctively thinks as soon as he talks of the useless hollowness of philosophy. They are the heretics, pompous heads of schools who believe in the fantasy of an 'educated', allegedly higher wisdom and knowledge, which leads even Christians astray and corrupts all true belief. The philosophers are 'the patriarchs of the heretics' (*de An.* 3, 1); only when one recognizes this is the full abomination of philosophical nonsense revealed once for all.

As a mere matter of bulk, the fight against heresy occupies the largest part of the works left behind by Tertullian. These are at the same time the writings which more clearly present his earnestness and objective interest, despite the polemical strife and exaggeration. Of course, the modern reader easily takes offence at his immoderate polemics. Tertullian does not take pains to understand his opponents from the point of view of their own presuppositions or to do justice to their 'concern' at the moment; he seeks to expose them and time and again pours forth against them his biting sarcasm. Yet he would hardly have seen anything blameworthy in this fact. Precisely because he is really concerned about the cause, the truth, and existence of the Christian faith, he seeks to fight and destroy the heretics with every available weapon. The only question which matters to him in these circumstances is whether the caricature of the heretics which is what he undoubtedly gives is 'right' as such, i.e. whether it unveils and strikes at the essential weakness of the hostile position, and so attains a deeper and basic significance.

The answer must be 'yes'. Tertullian is no slanderer, no mean pamphleteer inventing cheap reproaches. He has understood the essential common elements of the heretical position, presented and combated them in their general aspects, long before modern scholarship brought the countless groups and currents of the heresy of the period together under the single designation of 'Gnosticism'. What is Gnosticism to Tertullian? It is a destructive syncretism appealing to man's innate spiritual nature, his inclination to overestimate his own spiritual and idealistic nature, and obliterating the fixed boundary between creature and deity. It is at the same time a 'nihilistic' hostility to the God of reality who has created the world and has revealed himself concretely in the flesh.

As was the case with his Greek predecessors, what stands out is the strong emphasis on the ecclesiastical and doctrinal instability, the permanent inconstancy and fluctuation of the Gnostic congregations and their speculation. The heretics rely only on their own whims and not on God's word. The basic factor of insatiable curiosity and conceit, *curiositas*, establishes the inner relationship and connection with philosophy. Already with good cause Paul had forewarned Christians of philosophy (Col. ii. 8). They should 'seek the Lord with sincerity of heart', as Solomon had taught (Wisdom of Solomon, i. 1), and not invent a new 'Stoic, Platonic or dialectic Christianity' (*de Praescr.* 7, 11). The fantasies which follow are worse than all philosophy. It can be positively painful to see how Plato is forced to 'season' each soup of the heretical kitchen with his thoughts (*de An.* 23, 5). Because of what he reasonably says, Seneca also does not belong to them but rather, as so often, 'to us' (*de An.* 20, 1). There is no New Testament passage which the heretics are so fond of quoting as Christ's advice: 'Seek, and ye shall find' (*de Praescr.* 8, 2). Yet they only refer to it to spread their 'endless fables and genealogies' (I Tim. i. 4), their unproductive questions, and their talk which crawls at a crab-like gait to confuse innocent hearers (*de Praescr.* 7, 7). The heretics will not listen and understand that a search is sensible only when one does not yet know the truth, and that with Christ and His gospel we have reached the end and goal of our seeking. True faith is always simple (*adv. Marc.* V, 20). Tertullian is indignant at the speculative and problematical basis of heresy which is unable to hold on to the one thing that matters. 'Any Christian workman' knows precisely what is at stake, and on what everything for him really depends. 'He finds God, makes him known and then puts a practical seal on all theoretical questions about God with his action' (*Apol.* 46, 9). Obviously Christ was gravely mistaken when He 'commissioned simple fishermen rather than sophists to proclaim his gospel' (*de An.* 3, 3).

Relate to
answers or
ask too
many Q's.

T telling Xans not to seek

The heretic does not know what it means to believe. He takes pride in understanding. He wants to know instead of letting himself be taught by God, and would rather follow human teachers than be satisfied when God does not want to speak any more and is silent. He thinks always that he knows in advance who God is, what God does, can, and ought to do, and what is appropriate for God, and what is not. Therefore, he also fails to understand the meaning of God's Son becoming man. Tertullian comes to the decisive point of the contemporary discussion: Gnostic spiritualism denies the incarnation. It seems to it unnecessary and unworthy of God. The Gnostic can concede only an apparent ('docetic') acceptance of the flesh by Jesus; for he knows only of an imagined, unreal, 'God of the philosophers' —this expression originates from Tertullian (*adv. Marc.* II, 27, 6)—who changes and saves nothing but remains distant and transcendent. He takes offence at the ugly, humiliated, inglorious figure of the Saviour; he considers this kind of revelation and immanence an insult to the divine majesty. He does not see that in no other way would God really have reached us and that his dignity is of a kind different from human honour. 'Nothing is so worthy of God as man's salvation' (*adv. Marc.* II, 27, 1).

The incarnation, and no less the crucifixion, which embarrass the docetic theologians, are the real mysteries of our salvation. With reference to these doctrines, and not, as he makes plain, the general proclamation of God and his commandments, Tertullian is therefore quite justified in appealing to the Pauline expressions of God's 'foolishness' which frustrates human 'wisdom'. His famous statement *'credo, quia absurdum est'* is usually not quoted accurately and still less understood in the context which he envisages: 'God's Son was crucified—this is not a matter for shame, because it is a disgrace; and God's Son has died—this is credible because it is a foolishness; and he was buried and is risen—this is certain, because it is impossible' (*de Carn. Chr.* 5, 4). These forceful paradoxes are intentionally so formulated to be provoking; the Christians know and want their God like this—and this God does not forsake them, least of all when they must confess Him in an apparently hopeless situation and the 'outward man' perishes under tortures.

Religion is for Tertullian nothing other than life in the sphere of reality. For the heretic, on the other hand, it is the realm of self-satisfied speculation and pious dreams. Faith can make nothing of this. He who will follow Christ in life as in death asks for a God who is real and encountered in history; a God who has died and lives forever. The human existence, the full reality of Christ's 'flesh', is the guarantee of the actuality and seriousness of our redemption, as our bodily existence at the same time determines the inescapable necessity of our personal responsibility in this world. As for the man who denies the reality of Christ's flesh, and wants to think of himself as being not flesh, but as existing in the unfettered state of an other-worldly spirituality, he is forced because of his own nature to compromise with this world in the actual situation of temptation and affliction—to compromise with the wisdom and immorality, the deities and demons of the world. The reluctance to undergo martyrdom shown by so many sects is the crucial test. Tertullian composed a writing *The Antidote Against the Scorpion's Sting* in which he rebuts the various excuses wherewith some try to depreciate martyrdom in favour of a transcendant or inner testimony of the spirit! To him every Gnostic

is a potential denier, a lax shirker, and an arrogant despiser of
the church's command. This is indeed an exaggeration and an
unfair generalization. Yet the history of Gnosticism shows that
Tertullian's contention was not so wrong, after all. Almost all
their societies perished in the course of time in a vague syncretism, which corresponded to the vagueness and boundless-
ness of their impersonal and unhistorical concept of revelation.

The Catholic church has received the revelation also in externally clear and binding fashion. She lives by the one, certain,
and real principle ordered by Christ and contained in the Holy
Scripture. She possesses the two-edged sword of God's word
in law and gospel, the divine wisdom, 'the enemy of the devil,
our armour against spiritual foes, all malice, and carnal lust, the
sword which can cut off from us for the sake of God's name
even those whom we love most' (adv. Marc. III, 14, 3). He who
does not want to understand the truth will not be disputed
with. The church knows God's word and does not need to
fight with Marcionites, Valentinians, and other Gnostics about
its meaning, which they distort. Tertullian has attempted to
form this thought into a strictly juristic mould in a monograph,
Prescriptions Against the Heretics. This has had a far-reaching
effect on the later development of Catholicism. The Catholic
church, according to the work, received its teaching as well as
its Scripture directly from the apostles at a time when all present heresies had not yet arisen. She has preserved the original
truth faithfully and is also able to prove it against later aberra-
tions; for she stands even today in undisturbed communion
with the old churches founded by the apostles in Asia Minor,
Greece, etc., or in the West, with Rome. And whence should
the harmony of all orthodox Christians in the whole world
derive, if it was not originally given? Against this the favourite
Gnostic insinuation regarding the apostles avails nothing, that
Christ had not entrusted everything to them or they had mis-
understood or falsified his teaching. They could not all have
confused the truth in the same manner. 'What in so many
congregations always is recognizable as the very same cannot

be erroneous: it must be tradition' (*de Praescr.* 28, 3). It thus suffices if we remain faithful to the ecclesiastical teaching and understand the Bible in a sense which corresponds with the Creed. (In Tertullian, the Apostles' Creed occurs for the first time in this normative sense, as a 'rule of faith' binding the congregations.) The heretics, on the other hand, have no place in the church, and no right to appeal to the Scripture. 'Who are you, when and whence do you come? What are you doing on my property without belonging to me? Who gives you the right, Marcion, to cut my timber? Who gives you permission to divert my springs, Valentinus? Whence your claim, Apelles, to remove my landmarks? . . . The property belongs to me; I have always possessed it, I have possessed it prior to you and have reliable title-deeds from the actual owners to whom the estate belonged. I am the heir of the apostles' (*de Praescr.* 37, 3 ff.).

This is typical of the way Tertullian goes to work; he proves his point from every possible point of view. Tertullian first claims every right for himself alone and denies everything to his opponents. Yet we should not be concerned with Tertullian if he had been satisfied with such an external, formal assurance. So he closes the already 'summary' plea with the assurance that he would, if God wills, return again in detail to the heretical doctrines, and during the course of his life he energetically fulfilled this promise. Above all, his major five-volume work, *Against Marcion*, must be mentioned in this connection. Tertullian has here summoned all his strength and ability, for he has found in Marcion his most dangerous enemy. It is admirable how he understands the way to combine in this polemical masterpiece the keenest logic and dialectic, all the arts of rhetoric and irony, the most earnest, embittered passion, and the finest accuracy and exhaustive thoroughness in dealing with the subject-matter. To Tertullian Marcion is the arch-heretic. As a matter of fact, he had in the middle of the second century founded his own church, which had now spread everywhere. Marcion's nature was similar to Tertullian's in that he

3

likewise regarded the most radical solutions and the strictest positions as the best and most genuinely Christian. Like the Catholics he despised the unconfined indiscipline and fantasy of the ordinary Gnostics, and for his part aspired to be nothing other than a faithful disciple of Jesus and student of his greatest apostle, Paul. Yet Marcion and the Marcionites denied any connection between the Christian message and the previous revelation to the Jews in the Old Testament, behind which he saw another God, strict and hostile, the moralistic 'just' God of this world with whom on this account the true gospel by its very nature has nothing at all to do. According to these principles, Marcion drew up his own Bible, consisting only of texts of Luke's gospel mutilated in accord with his principles, and of the Pauline letters. In opposition Tertullian demonstrates the impossibility of this piece of editing with a clarity which would do credit to any modern theologian. In his usual manner he declares forthwith his willingness to show that even the falsified Marcionite Testament still contradicts Marcion and testifies to the Christian truth. He also systematically consolidates his own position and confession of God's unity by proving that God's righteousness and grace, the sovereign transcendence of the creator and his merciful descent into the world, are not to be separated within the Christian understanding of God.

We cannot examine in detail the anti-Gnostic writings of Tertullian. The question they deal with has become unfamiliar to us, in so far as Gnostic thought takes up and answers the problem of reality and divine revelation from the side opposite to that to which we are accustomed, so to speak. The Gnostics as a group do not deny the transcendence and reality of the divine spirit, but the reality and significance of the material, earthly world. They do not question the necessity of redemption, but the divine origin of creation, and similarly they do not deny the divine but the human nature of the Saviour, his corporeality and his flesh. This way also leads finally to the ethical consequence of a certain 'nihilism', and we can easily understand that Gnosticism could hardly have

found a more bitter enemy than Tertullian. To Tertullian anything merely intellectual and theoretical, poetic and aesthetic,
i.e. anything he cannot directly come to grips with practically
and morally, is as such an abomination. As we have seen,
he is a materialistic thinker and as a Christian predomi-
nantly a man of law, of the divine command, and of unconditional obedience. What he defends is the Catholic church and
the Christian demand of faith in its inflexible reality; yet we
can easily understand that the harsh rigorism of such a personality was, just because of its intellectual superiority, not always
comfortable and easy to endure even to his fellow-believers.
This was bound to lead in the course of time to friction,
especially in practical questions of church discipline and of
everyday morality.

We have already come across Tertullian's difficult attitude
where he deals with the Christian's relationship to the world
and its sins. 'Everyone is a denier who does not show himself
openly upon every occasion and who lets himself be taken for
a pagan' (de Idol. 22, 4), and everyone, likewise, who profits in
any way whatsoever from pagan worship and pagan immorality. We are bound to ask what profession a poor Christian
could possibly take up without being reproached by Tertullian
with indirect assistance to idolatry, which is the fount of all
vice. He storms in the same way against all pagan pleasures, the
civic prize-fights, the circuses, and the theatre, which not only
was founded in honour of false deities, as he demonstrates with
archeological scholarship, but in his day still remained the
breeding place of all immorality and excess. A Christian should
likewise renounce all luxury, cosmetics, finery, and costly
adornments. If God had pleasure in colourful garments, why
did he not then create purple and sky-blue sheep? The Christian theatre-goers seem to have been especially stubborn in
their resistance. They even tried to find Biblical support: where
is it written that God condemns plays, since he tolerates them
and lets them go on? Did not even David dance in front of the
Ark of the Covenant? And did not Elijah drive to heaven in a

fiery chariot? But there is no getting round Tertullian with such *ad hoc* exegesis. He tears them apart with caustic irony and approves in the end one play only, which will reward the Christians for all earthly abstinence. This is the spectacle of the last judgement! 'What a panorama of spectacle on that day! Which sight shall excite my wonder? Which, my laughter? Where shall I rejoice, where exult—as I see so many and so mighty kings, whose ascent to heaven used to be made known by public announcement, now along with Jupiter himself, along with the very witnesses of their ascent, groaning in the depths of darkness? Governors of provinces, too, who persecuted the name of the Lord, melting in flames fiercer than those they themselves kindled in their rage against the Christians braving them with contempt? Whom else shall I behold? Those wise philosophers blushing before their followers as they burn together, the followers to whom they taught that the world is no concern of God's, whom they assured that either they had no souls at all or that what souls they had would never return to their former bodies? . . . Then will the tragic actors be worth hearing, more vocal in their own catastrophe; then the comic actors will be worth watching, much lither of limb in the fire; then the charioteer will be worth seeing, red all over in his fiery wheel.' And then the Lord appears in His glory amidst angels and risen saints, before the false Jews and other persecutors, the Lord who was ridiculed, beaten, spit at, given gall and vinegar to drink! Such a spectacle no praetor, consul, or priest in the world can produce, and today already we have it in a sense before our eyes even before 'what no eye has seen nor ear heard' (I Cor. ii. 9) begins in the eternal realm of God, 'things of greater delight, I believe, than circus, both kinds of theatre, and any stadium' (*de Spect.* 30, 3 ff.; *FC*, 40, 106 f.).

Only Tertullian writes like this. No Greek, nor even a medieval Christian, has ever put on paper such a description, wild to the point of sadism, dreadful and grandiose. Nothing can shock Tertullian. He likewise dismisses offhand the economic worries of those whose livelihood is endangered by his rigorous demands. 'What do you say: "I am being reduced to penury?" But the Lord praises the poor as blessed . . . the disciples he called never declared: "But I cannot make a living!" Faith does not fear hunger; it knows that for God's sake it must despise death by starvation even as any other kind of death' (de Idol. 12, 2, 4). Such cutting answers reduce the hearers to silence; but their apathetic resistance nevertheless cannot thereby be overcome. Tertullian himself feels this. He complains ironically and bitterly of the fate 'peculiar to him', to which he has grown accustomed, that he has no success with his books. And yet he fights for nothing to which truth itself does not point, and against the witness of truth no difference in the times, no human authority, and no local custom have any sanction! (de Virg. Vel. 1, 1). Yet the worst he cannot even express; Tertullian himself is too good a dialectician not to see the gaps in his proofs, not to anticipate the objections which can be raised against his arguments, if anyone is unwilling to accept the right teaching because of laziness, cowardice, or lack of understanding. Tertullian is attempting something fundamentally impossible; he wants to decide on the basis of a legalistic standard the ultimate questions of credal obligation and spiritual obedience. Hence he becomes ever more stringent in his demands, and finally would like to declare everything prohibited that the Scripture does not explicitly allow (de Coron. 2, 4). But he himself feels that not even the strictest interpretation of the Scripture, nor adherence to the creed and tradition of his church, much less still the knowledge of 'natural law' not yet illuminated by revelation (de Spect. 2, 5) can ever reach the point of that complete certainty which a Christian needs, if he is to take and maintain a firm stand in the difficulties of daily life which arise anew each hour. This agonizing experience 'peculiar to him' forms the background of the last portentous change in Tertullian's life.

In the second half of the second century there burst forth a revival movement, enthusiastic and apocalyptic, in Phrygia deep in the hinterland of Asia Minor. Its prophets, Montanus and the women who accompanied him, thought of themselves as instruments of a new outpouring of the Holy Spirit, the 'Paraclete' promised in John's gospel, and they preached the speedy coming of the kingdom of God on the mountains of their homeland. They demanded repentance, renewal, and the surpassing of the current morality. They distinguished themselves particularly by their eager readiness to be martyred. The movement spread abroad speedily and had reached Africa by the beginning of the third century. Tertullian joined it and soon became the most ardent pioneer of the 'new prophecy'. Like many whose nature inclines towards rationalism and drives them to action, he had from the beginning a special liking for the parapsychological, visionary, and ecstatic phenomena of the religious life. In the revelations, exorcisms, and other miraculous signs of the Montanists he now believed that he had encountered anew in increased strength the living spirit of early Christianity. And here, in the Montanist circles, he finally arrived at a complete determination to stand for God's cause without reserve. He found unrelenting severity against all sinners and lax members in the congregation, new regulations for the ethical conduct of life, and above all an ultimate spiritual authority able to secure all this by its inspired testimony. The oracles of Montanus and of the prophetesses were even then collected, and had an unlimited and virtually canonical validity for their followers.

When Tertullian joined the Montanists, their ecclesiastical position was not yet clearly decided. The Western church still hesitated until first the bishop of Rome, and then also the bishop of Carthage and the remaining African bishops followed the example of their colleagues in Asia Minor and pronounced the 'Cataphrygians' a sect. This decided their fate for the future. The movement did not possess enough religious content and originality to prevail by its own strength. It was henceforth a sectarian church gathering together members of morally intransigent reactionary circles—the first of such phenomena, which were to accompany from now on the popular development of the ancient Catholic church. Tertullian of course remained faithful to the movement. External failure did not matter to him, and he soon made the Montanist conventicle the basis of a new, even more definite attack against his old enemies. Only through him and his writings did Montanism gain something like a theology and an 'intellectual profile'.

As a Montanist Tertullian did not become other than he had always been. We can see this from the themes with which he now deals, and equally from the conclusions at which he arrives. From this second period of his activity comes, for example, his famous polemic treatise *Against Praxeas*. As a 'Monarchian', Praxeas had gone so far in emphasizing the divine unity in his refutation of Gnostic speculation that he denied altogether the difference between God the Father and the Son. In opposition to this Tertullian advances Scriptural proof and, above all, effectively disarms his opponent in respect of his appeal to the 'Monarchian' sounding passages in the gospel of John. In this connection he now attempts to clarify the systematic conceptions of the developing Trinitarian theology more precisely, and frames the symbols and ideas which have become determinative for the further Christological and Trinitarian controversies, especially in the West. His formulae turned out to be so useful and convenient just because they remain entirely formal in the legal and logical precision of their definitions and distinctions. Yet they never get to the real root of the theological and metaphysical problems which are bound to arise here. Tertullian deals exclusively with the unity in the Trinity, but not with the later problem of the equality of rank between the divine persons; and to that extent his rough draft is still deficient, compared with the final dogma. Nevertheless, his teaching on the Trinity represents for his time an achievement for orthodoxy. The incidental combination attempted by Tertullian of the anti-Monarchian with the Montanist polemic remains wholly superficial, and was no obstacle to the spread of his thoughts.

It is, moreover, also Tertullian's personal conviction, which he repeats time and again, that the Paraclete never changes the old doctrines of the church, but only endorses them and thereby adduces proof of his legitimacy. Real progress is made—even as earlier from the Old to the New Testament—only in regard to ethics, inasmuch as the new revelation now finally demands the ultimate sanctity and unqualified fulfilment of all commandments. This is a condition which at the beginning of the church the apostles could not yet demand. Tertullian outlines on this basis a new scheme of salvation in three phases and not two. As the New Testament revelation is prophesied in the Old Covenant, and then simultaneously confirms and transcends it, so 'the new prophecy builds on top' of the older order and at the same time brings it to its goal. So we come to the typical idea of a third revelation and a 'third Dispensation' of the church, such as was brought up again in the High Middle Ages by Joachim of Flora and since then has often been repeated. This is always possible only when one envisages as the essential point a higher, 'spiritual' order (or knowledge) of life and when the belief in the saving deed of Christ by itself no longer seems to suffice. This is obviously also the case with Tertullian.

Looking through his Montanist writings we frequently come across praise of the revelations and miracles provoked by the new spirit—'to the infidels a testimony, to believers salvation' (*Pass. Perp.* 1). In a lost tract *On Ecstasy* Tertullian takes expressly under his protection the spirit of the 'new prophecy' against opponents from Asia Minor (hence the tract is written in Greek). For the rest, however, it is still a matter of questions of moral decision. Now finally Tertullian is sure that a second marriage, which he had always advised against, is positively forbidden for the Christian, and must be identified flatly as adultery. The new Montanist orders of fasting must be observed, since they restrain excessive appetite, which even in paradise was the cause of the fall and of original sin. Tertullian had previously approved of evading persecution as such; yet 'nobody is ashamed if he makes progress' (*de Pudic.* 1, 12). Now such an attitude means only cowardly denial and escape. All these claims are asserted with the excited emotion of constant moral indignation. Tertullian wrote—as he once claimed of Paul—'no more with ink but with gall' (*de Pudic.* 14, 4). The foil for the new, 'spiritual' ideal was an almost sordid, caustic caricature of a decadent Catholic life where love seems to boil only in the cooking-pot, where faith and hope are intended for the menu, where the indolent let themselves be petted and fattened as though they were martyrs, and brethren and sisters spend the night together after their love-feasts. Yet one thing was the worst of all and decisive. In leaving the original discipline, the Catholic church did not take seriously any more the administration of the ministry of the keys. The last writing which we possess from Tertullian's pen was directed against this abuse. Its ostensible cause was a certain relaxation in the Catholic church of the penitential discipline for carnal sins. The details are disputed and are connected with the difficult problem of the development of penance in general. We are here only concerned with the fundamental attitude of Tertullian, who objected as a Montanist to the possibility of forgiveness of the gravest sins when committed by Christians. The most intimate understanding of Christianity and of the 'holiness' effected by Christ always comes to light in the way in which the question of actual forgiveness is treated.

'What else does God want but that we live according to his discipline?' (*de Orat.* 4, 2). For the sake of this goal of the *disciplina*, the church must, if necessary, be strict in refusing absolution. For 'where pardon begins, fear ceases' (*de Pudic.* 16, 14), and 'where there is no fear, there, likewise is no conversion' (*de Paen.* 2, 2; *ACW*, 28, 15). This logic was compulsive for Tertullian, but it is the opposite of Jesus Christ's treatment of publicans and sinners. But, answers Tertullian, were these people perchance already Christians? Had they already, like us, committed themselves to discipleship, and accepted in baptism the Holy Spirit as their mighty helper? And if one erroneously imagines that the apostles knew of a forgiveness for mortal sins, the answer to this is that they possessed an authority of a kind different from that of any

contemporary Christian. If appeal is made, however, to the
authority of the Holy Spirit, this Spirit Himself has taught us
in the new prophecy, that He never misuses this authority in
favour of the sinner, for He is holy. An official of the spirit-
forsaken Catholic church deciding otherwise is guilty of usur-
pation of office, and is meddling with the handiwork of God,
who has issued the strictest commandments. This exposé was
aimed in particular against a certain bishop whom Tertullian
mocks as 'the pagan parson' (*pontifex maximus*), as 'bishop of
bishops', and truly blessed father (*papa*) because of his frivolous
indulgence and presumption. He was not here aiming, as has
often been thought, at the far off 'pope' in Rome but at the
Catholic bishop of his own home town, Carthage. Against him,
Tertullian appeals to the freedom of the congregation; they,
and not a handful of bishops, constitute the church which lives
in the spirit and in obedience to God's word. In Tertullian we
come across for the first time an anticlerical polemic, which has
an almost Protestant sound, with its reference to the universal
priesthood, but is nevertheless not at all 'evangelical' in intention. What Tertullian wanted to achieve with his appeal to the
laity was just an unbreakable binding to the supposedly Biblical
'law'. To be sure, even Tertullian knew alongside God's
'justice', His mercy or 'grace'; once, at our entry into the
church, it had rescued us from the demonic sphere of influence
and had cancelled all previous sins. He also knew that because
of his weakness the Christian unfortunately cannot do without
the daily forgiveness of his venial sins. But first of all 'the whole
state of salvation rests nevertheless upon the solid rock of discipline' (*de Paen.* 9, 8). God's goodness shows itself primarily
in that He reveals His will, inspires us with His spirit, and calls
us to our personal responsibility. Man, as a Christian, lives less
from God's mercy and forgiveness, which has its limits, than
from God's commandment and man's obedience, which accepts
the discipline.

The end of Tertullian's life is lost in obscurity. It is mentioned
that he lived long and died very late, in 'feeble old age'. But

did he therefore find repose and tranquillity? It is hard to imagine. The vehemence and impatience of his will belonged to his nature and were not the transient expressions of a controllable passion. It seems that Tertullian finally broke with the Montanists, and founded his own sect. Augustine, at any rate, a century and a half later in Carthage came across an independent group of 'Tertullianists', whom he won for the Catholic church. Augustine's remarks about the 'heretic' Tertullian do not sound friendly, and Vincent of Lerins formulated a little later (434) the general verdict that Tertullian had been a serious tribulation to the church, and his later error had destroyed any confidence one might have had in the earlier, approved writings. Yet, Tertullian has remained the only non-Catholic theologian whose heritage was not lost, but has come down to us almost complete. This he certainly deserved. True, he remained a dissenter; nevertheless, the old Latin church had no more educated, more indefatigable, and—despite all exaggerations—more honest champion against her enemies than he. Nor did any by nature belong more to her. 'In him the Western spirit expresses itself clearly for the first time' (Holl). Tertullian has indeed also been called the last of the Greek apologists; but this is true only of his subject-matter and some traditional problems of his dogmatical and apologetical writing. In the powerful non-speculative and practical orientation of his theology, Tertullian appears beyond dispute as the first Latin father of the church. The same applies to the realistic, legalistic and psychological direction of his intellect, to his inclination towards social issues, and towards the congregation and church as a firm, political society, and also to his emphasis on will, standards, and discipline. He merits the title also by his affirmation of the authority of the Scripture and his love of the apostle Paul. Tertullian all his life 'loved righteousness and hated ungodliness'—more unselfishly and more purely than Gregory VII. Yet in all this he remains a Christian more of the Old Testament than of the New. Judged theologically, he is almost a Jew.

CHAPTER II

CYPRIAN

THROUGH Tertullian, Christian Africa had gained a voice. This area was now awakened to a new, vigorous life. The African church led the West intellectually for centuries; and only at her decline in the turmoils of the Arab conquest did she become silent forever. The generation which succeeded Tertullian brought forth another personality of extraordinary significance, whose influence went far beyond the African area, Caecilius Cyprianus. Cyprian was bishop of Carthage and never mentioned the dissident Tertullian by name; all the same, his inner relationship to him can be noticed throughout his writings. His secretary reported later that no day went by when Cyprian did not ask for the reading of his Tertullian; he called him simply 'the teacher'. The comparison of the two is instructive in many ways. The uneasiness, the radicalism, the unbalanced nonconformity of the writings of Tertullian were brought by Cyprian into balance and under ecclesiastical discipline. His world of thought has a quiet dignity, steadiness, and moderation which the former neither possessed nor desired. In the view of this leading ecclesiastic the same problems appear in a light different from the passionate partisanship of that individualistic, intolerant, and reckless man of letters. Also, the background has developed. The church has grown rapidly throughout Africa, her organizational structure has consolidated; she affirmed everywhere a distinct tradition which united and bound bishops and congregations. And to this difference in situation and personal position there corresponded, so far as Cyprian is concerned, also a character completely different in constitution and motives, which was in its own way no less definite and resolute, Roman and African.

We have no reliable information about Cyprian's development prior to his election as bishop. However, it is clear that in contrast to the gifted Tertullian, the soldier's child, he came from the circles of higher society, and was from the beginning accustomed to live in easy circumstances. Cyprian had personal connections with the authorities. We hear of his estates and gardens in the vicinity of Carthage. Furthermore, he himself was master of the conventions of high society with an easy self-assurance. Without doubt he had enjoyed a good and thorough education. His style indicates—without the originality and wilfulness shown by Tertullian—familiarity with all the requisites of the 'school'. His writings again remind one particularly of his African fellow-countryman Apuleius; yet Cyprian also knew the writings of Seneca and the traditional positions of Stoic philosophy. Yet he abstained from expressly attacking the pagan authors. 'There is a big difference between Christians and philosophers' (Ep. 16, 55). A new ecclesiastical pride considered it beneath its dignity to engage in a direct controversy such as that into which Tertullian had thrown himself with so much intellectual ardour. Besides Biblical quotations no wider 'literature' appears.

Although Jerome presumed that Cyprian had begun as a professor of rhetoric, we should perhaps suppose rather that he envisaged the career of a higher government official. He shows himself quite familiar with all constitutional laws and political ideas, and transferred them later quite naturally to the sphere of his ecclesiastical activity. With Cyprian began the line of 'curial' bishops who attempted to perform their ecclesiastical office in the magisterial style of the consuls and pro-consuls, with whom he did not shrink from being directly compared (Ep. 37, 2). Compared with the Greek East this was a novel and specifically Western type of Catholic priesthood. In any case, Cyprian cannot have gone very far in a secular career. His conversion put an end to all such efforts and directed his wishes and abilities completely into the new ecclesiastical path.

A presbyter named Caecilius (or Caecilianus) is supposed to have won Cyprian for the church; indeed, it was said that the latter had assumed the *cognomentum* Caecilius only because of this personal, spiritual relationship (while the derivation of his surname 'Thascius' remains completely obscure). If this was the case even his turning to Christianity indicated a close connection with leading ecclesiastical circles. Soon afterwards this newly converted member of the congregation published his first literary essay, addressed to a friend, Donatus, about whom we know nothing else. In a conventional, rhetorical manner, and with much artificial pomposity, he expounded the reasons for his conversion. The world torn to pieces by wars is in a frightful condition; the abominable gladiatorial fights, the immoral theatre, and the excesses in public and private life indicate clearly enough to him who can see, how things are. The rulers are unrestrained, even the administration of the law is corrupt; the whole social order is empty and undisciplined. There is only one port of peace, which is the life to come, and there is only one way leading to it, the God-revealed pure and simple virtue of the Christians. The man who is baptized is rescued at a stroke from all pagan abominations. He feels the stream of the influences of heavenly grace poured out upon him, and can, if he be willing to preserve and augment them, face the last judgement well-equipped. The material of these declamations, reminding one to some extent of Minucius Felix, consisted of the commonplaces of apologetics, although applied, one might say, individually and biographically. There can scarcely be deduced from this anything definite about Cyprian's inner experiences and intentions. It is nevertheless noteworthy how strongly the consideration of political and moral factors is placed in the foreground; theological questions, strictly speaking, are not introduced.

More significant theologically is another work which was probably written soon afterwards: the first two books to 'Quirinus', which were called later *Books of Testimonies (testi-*

monia). They contain a collection of Biblical quotations, an 'anthology' arranged topically under short sentence headings, and intended for practical use. We can see that for Cyprian theology consists basically in the exposition of Scripture. With this attitude no specific problems and difficulties occur to him. Later, for instance, he once just simply filled up the last page of a tract with Biblical texts. It suffices if God's word is always heard, learned, and known. Here, Cyprian saw himself already in the role of the superior teacher, who knew his Bible well, expressly trying to perform his task not only for himself but for others. In the first book there is a collection of material for the ever-present controversy with the Jews, and the second brought together texts Christologically significant. This kind of *pons asinorum* evidently met a widely felt need. Cyprian added later a third part to this compendium, concerning the practical ethics of the church, and after the outbreak of the persecutions he produced another Biblical manual. Similar to the others, it contained quotations regarding the vanity of idolatry, the necessity for making witness, and the promises for martyrs. From a post-Cyprianic time several other reference books of this kind have been handed down. Contemporary juristic literature seems to have known similar works. The beginnings of the ecclesiastical testimonies may go back as far as the second century; they continued the tradition of the oldest Christian apologetics against scholarly Rabbinic Judaism. But with Cyprian the old method now underwent an essential extension, and thus was introduced for the first time to the Christian public.

Although Cyprian, as he mentioned in his first preface, simply wished to facilitate the preaching and homiletical preparation of others, he had already certainly been ordained presbyter, if not bishop. It is said that he was still almost a neophyte when elected bishop; and even if this may be an exaggeration, nevertheless his rapid promotion as bishop of the leading and largest African congregation remains extremely unusual and surprising. Had Cyprian counted upon such a thing right from the beginning, on account of his position and intellectual superiority, and perhaps even aimed at this himself? We do not know; but it is certain that his election provoked misgivings among the older members of the clergy of Carthage over whom he had been promoted. And, unfortunately, the young ecclesiastic was not given much time to establish his position and prove himself peacefully. He had held the office for scarcely a year when the first extensively-organized persecution began and severely shattered the whole ecclesiastical order. Cyprian's authority had to undergo the test of fire before it had been really firmly established.

The persecution put into operation by the new emperor Decius in 249 at first appeared to be only a general festival in which prayers were said and sacrifices made for the benefit of the emperor and the empire, in which every subject had to participate. Anyone who refused was to be forced to comply in all circumstances by violent measures, degradation, confiscation, and tortures. When the offerings had been made, certificates to this effect were issued. Evidently this enactment was aimed against the Christians from the beginning. Decius hoped to bring about their apostasy and the destruction of the church. Two reasons chiefly prevented success. On the one hand the military and bureaucratic system of 'survey' was unavoidably defective, and since the persecution came to a halt one year later because of the emperor's death, it did not succeed in breaking up the congregations completely. On the other hand, the church in the critical moment revealed an elastic adaptability to the new situation which had not been calculated upon. The whole plan relied on the presumption that a Christian once brought to renouncing the church was lost to it once for all. In reality, however, those forced to sacrifice at once streamed back into their old congregations, and here means and ways to accept them were soon found, first as penitents, then even as members with full privileges. In retrospect, this development clearly appears comparatively simple and almost necessary. Only if one reads Cyprian's letters of this time is one aware of all the actual difficulties, the human dilemmas and embarrassments, and the apparently impenetrable darkness of the situation which those who lived through it had to face. In these crises and conflicts the young bishop and rhetorician finally matured into a man and became the leader of the church, superior and able to cope with all its miseries and sorrows.

After the sudden beginnings of the persecution the apostasy in Carthage was shockingly great, as everywhere else. 'At the first threatening words of the enemy, an all too large number of brethren betrayed their faith; they were not felled by the violence of the persecution, but fell of their own free will' (de Laps. 7; ACW, 25, 18). Others went straight to jail, while still others tried to escape to remote places. The presbyters still free had their hands full holding together their frightened lambs, pacifying and protecting them as far as possible. Cyprian was no longer in their midst. Obviously he had received notice of the dangerous events in time and retreated to the country with a few chosen companions. From here he attempted to retain the reins in his hand. While the people shouted, demanding 'Cyprian to the lions', the authorities had to be satisfied with an ineffective proscription of his person and initiated a confiscation of his property by public proclamation. He himself was in safety. This decision to evade the violent storm had serious results—most of the difficulties in Cyprian's remaining time in office were connected with this in one way or another. How has this step to be judged?

Without doubt, Cyprian was in more danger than others. Everywhere the police sought primarily to get hold of the bishops and make them recant; the congregations would be deprived of their leaders. In this way the bishops in Rome, Antioch, Jerusalem, and Caesarea were martyred in the very beginning of the persecution; only in Alexandria had Bishop Dionysius miraculously escaped arrest. Had Cyprian stayed in Carthage, the same fate would doubtless have overtaken him. But was it not all the same his duty to accept martyrdom? Escape in times of persecution was considered generally permissible, for the opposite and stricter standpoint of Tertullian

4

and the Montanists had not prevailed. Yet, could a pastor with the care of his congregation's souls leave his flock in the lurch? Had he not to stay with it, particularly in the time of trouble and, if he was of no other use to it, still by his death to leave behind an example of a confessor's spirit and faithfulness? This was evidently the opinion not only of some firebrands and personal opponents of Cyprian. We can see the embarrassment in a letter sent to Carthage by the Roman college of deacons after the death of their own bishop. Cyprian is not mentioned in the address. The letter remarks only in a preliminary statement that 'pope' Cyprian might as an official have had his reasons for his conduct; the Roman clergy, however, would feel themselves compelled to endure to the end according to Jesus' word and commandment (*Ep.* 8, 1). Therefore, they would be inclined to keep in suspense a judgement about someone else's bishop; yet we can detect that people had reservations and doubted the purity of his motives. Cyprian's reaction was no less plain. He acknowledged the receipt of the letter and congratulated the Romans 'with rejoicing' upon the splendid and glorious 'consummation' of their bishop, who had indeed all along lived and reigned flawlessly. But then he noted that the form and content of the Roman letter had made such a strange impression on him that he must question its authenticity and returned it to the senders for examination (*Ep.* 9, 2). Only later did there follow another letter in which he explained more in detail why he had considered it right to retreat, not for his own sake, but in the interest of public tranquillity and for the sake of the congregation. The Romans had obviously been informed (by a subdeacon of Carthage!) but not 'quite accurately and correctly' (*Ep.* 20, 1). Cyprian did not tolerate his authority being held in question even at a distance—already any explicit defence of his actions would have been a sign of uncertainty—and he categorically maintained that he was fully right. To this second letter is added as supporting evidence a bundle of thirteen letters of his correspondence with Carthage. It proved that Cyprian did not wish by his escape to save his own life, but was thereby enabled to perform the duties of his office 'being absent only in body but not in spirit'.

Indeed, everything now depended on the close ties with the distant congregation. We find the messengers perpetually travelling to and fro between Carthage and Cyprian's hiding-place. The letters they carried were on the part of Cyprian not limited to pious admonitions and abundantly flowing praise of the steadfast confessors; it was necessary also to make practical decisions and to take urgently necessary measures. Even prior to his departure Cyprian had provided money from his private fortune. Now he sent from the 'little' he had available considerable sums by which the congregation's faithful poor—and only they—were to be supported. They were not to sink into distress, lest that which could not be achieved by the frontal attack of the persecution might be brought about finally by hunger. The brethren in the jails were to be visited by the deacons regularly—but cautiously and in alternate turns in order not to attract attention. The released needed clothes, food, and work. The bodies of the martyrs were to be secured and all the execution-dates collected for future liturgical commemoration. It seems that the ecclesiastical machine at first functioned well and remained equal to the manifold problems. The actual difficulties began with the question of the attitude toward those members of the congregation who had yielded to terror and fear, and had obeyed the state order in one way or another. The earlier practice of the church had been in this respect, for the most part, very strict. But could the isolated, unthinking, and weak apostasy of former times possibly be compared with the temptations now being brought upon all Christians by cunning state action? As always the widespread nature of the lapse alleviated the feeling of its sinfulness, while the unlucky traitors themselves everywhere intensely desired forgiveness and re-admission to the congregation. The responsible clergy showed themselves uncertain, and the situation became even more confused by the role which soon began to be played by the steadfast confessors, who were generally considered as saints, enabled by the Holy Spirit himself to resist so gloriously. So their decisions were hailed as miraculous testimonies of the inspiration of the Spirit of God, and with them the penitents seeking help at first obtained a sympathetic hearing. As could be expected, things were handled frequently in an all too human manner. The new saints, who included some dubious figures, too readily welcomed the role offered to them of infallible judges, and the opportunity of making themselves popular by accommodating mildness without further investigation. True evangelical readiness to forgive was combined with a naïve, officious desire to dominate, with pious gullibility, and sometimes with worse things still. The 'letters of peace' for readmission into the congregation in the jails were obtained from one's friends and relatives, even in other congregations; appeal was made to the oral absolution of an already 'perfected' martyr and wholesale declarations issued for the sinners and their whole family were produced as well. All supervision and control were lost, and the situation threatened to become impossible.

Cyprian certainly realized the seriousness of the situation. He understood that a certain amount of accommodation was inevitable, yet, as things stood at the moment, it seemed to him impossible to commit himself definitely. He sought therefore to postpone the decision on the penitential problem to a later time, after the end of the persecution. He decreed that the lapsed should not be lost sight of, but for the time being they were to be treated as penitents and in no case to be readmitted. Similar provisions had been made in Rome, with whose clergy Cyprian was now again on the best of terms; and in order to fall into line with their order, he granted as an outward sign of accommodation the desired ecclesiastical readmission of penitent sinners on their death-bed. Above all, Cyprian tried to treat the holy confessors with indulgence so far as possible. He merely asked them to show a little more consideration and caution, and he accepted their decisions as in principle not readmissions, but only pious recommendations for a future readmission left to the responsible ecclesiastical leadership, i.e. to the bishop. It was certainly risky to have to make such decisions from afar and by letter. The longer the persecution lasted, the more difficult it must have become for Cyprian to keep in hand the reins of leadership. Nevertheless, it might have been possible to carry through his directions if he could have relied completely upon the loyalty of his clergy. Yet in this tense moment, the old irritations and rivalries also revived. A section of the clergy renounced obedience to him and made common cause with the confessors. The apostates themselves dared to send Cyprian in the name of the church a letter containing their demands, which he immediately repudiated sharply. The bishops, and they exclusively, he affirmed, are called according to the Lord's word to act in the name of the church. They, together with the clergy and the Christians who remained steadfast, represented the church. He was astonished at their overbearing insolence, whereas a humble, quiet, and ashamed attitude alone would have been appropriate (*Ep.* 26, 1). The situation became critical. Without himself surrendering Cyprian could not recognize a readmission carried out by them against his explicit order. An attempt was made to send two friendly bishops to Carthage, to intervene, to pacify, and in particular to arrange the distribution of the subsidies according to his wishes. The effect, however, was just the opposite. A certain Felicissimus, who had been ordained deacon against Cyprian's will, and had taken charge of the congregational purse, dared to take a stand against him publicly, and when Cyprian excommunicated him five other presbyters eventually joined the opposition. Cyprian had now to appoint new officials, and call upon the congregation to refuse obedience to their own rebellious ministers. In these circumstances he pointed time and again to the bishop's office as the one decisive ministry, which sustains the church. He who leaves the holy altar of the bishop and changes his allegiance to the wicked party of Felicissimus is lost to the people of Christ, and can never again join them. Yet the division of the congregation could no longer be avoided. The apostate group held its ground, and finally there was even a formal election of an anti-bishop. But this happened as a final, desperate step after the end of the persecution, and when after an absence of a year and three months Cyprian had returned and could begin to assemble and build the congregation anew.

Decisive for his victory was a synod of bishops which he called probably in the spring of 251. It not only supported him personally, but also established principles in the question of the lapsed which confirmed his previous attitude. Against open opposition from the 'left', which had granted admission to all the lapsed, and in spite of the misgivings from the 'right' originally shared by Cyprian, they agreed now on a central course. The aim was to graduate penitential punishments in accordance with the gravity of the lapse. The Christians who had not really sacrificed, but who had only obtained the necessary certificates by bribery were considered sufficiently cleansed by the penance already undergone, and were admitted again. Those, on the other hand, who had actually made sacrifices to demons should remain under penance; and the 'letters of peace' of the martyrs were no longer to be acknowledged. But to these penitents too absolution was to be administered when they were in danger of death and not taken away again if they recovered. The doctrinal aspect of these decisions remained essentially unclarified. The bishops obviously wished to retain a certain freedom of movement, and when a new persecution drew near two years later, they resolved offhand to accept into the community all penitents who had remained faithful. So they were able to face the threatening danger with a united front. Cyprian emphasized particularly that the penitents must not be deprived any longer of the Eucharist, and of the Spirit who lives in the church, if they were to withstand new afflictions. For additional security in the case of such decisions he referred to the heavenly signs or illuminations given to him, as he often did at other times.

The principal outcome of this turbulent time had been reconstructed by Cyprian earlier in two important writings: *Con-*

cerning the Lapsed and *The Unity of the Church*. The latter work
was perhaps begun while he was still in hiding, while the tract
on the lapsed must have been written immediately after his
return to Carthage. It represents a comprehensive justification
of the standpoint repeatedly advocated by Cyprian on this
question, now somewhat more distinctly and resolutely than
before. Cyprian was not among those of tender-hearted nature
who, from indulgence or uncertainty, are willing, once victory
and success begin, to leave behind and forget a painfully maintained position. But it must be a victory of the cause and not a
personal triumph. A true pastor 'weeps with the lamenting',
and feels himself affected and humbled by the defeat of his own
congregation. 'Believe me, my brothers, I share your distress,
and can find no comfort in my own escape and safety' (*de Laps.*
4; *ACW*, 25, 16). The glory of the steadfast members of the
congregation stands inviolable, and Cyprian did not neglect
once again to pay the respect and praise due to all confessors
and steadfast brethren; yet the attitude of a substantial section
had disappointed him bitterly. The worst part is, however, that
some had still not fully realized their guilt; indeed, that there
were tempters encouraging them therein and deceiving them
about their true salvation by false flattery and assurances. Only
immediate repentance and conversion could save these. The unruly presbyters and confessors signify 'to the lapsed that which
hail is to the crop, tempest to trees, to the flocks the catastrophic
pestilence, and to ships a violent storm' (*de Laps.* 16). Only
with the bishop is salvation, not with the unauthorized who
lightly assume the privilege, reserved by God to Himself, of
forgiving sins. Even little children trying to deceive their bishop
by coming to the Lord's Supper unreconciled, have been punished terribly by God. Others when they sought to receive the
eucharistic elements got instead only ashes in their hands (*de
Laps.* 26). Cyprian used all available means in order to paint as
black as possible the danger to the impenitent sinners, and to find
hearing and obedience to his appeal for spiritual responsibility
and submission. He was for the most part successful in this.

Even more significant historically is Cyprian's writing on the unity of the church, in which he brought to an end his controversy with the schismatics. Here no tactical considerations were necessary, no doubts and vagueness existed. The security of the institutional church meant for Cyprian the security of salvation, and of Christian faith itself, for which he suffered, lived, and fought. The church is the Bride of Christ, the 'mother church' for all faithful; 'you cannot have God for your father unless you have the church for your mother' (de Un. 6). Outside her there is no salvation. But there is only the one church founded by Christ and entrusted to the apostles as leaders. She remains one even after having spread throughout the world—'just as the sun's rays are many, yet the light is one, and a tree's branches are many, yet the strength deriving from its sturdy root is one. So too, many streams flow from a single spring' (de Un. 5; ACW, 25, 48). These are illustrations used already by Tertullian to render the mystery of the triune God intelligible. They were now transferred to the church, eternally one in its multiplicity, in order to demonstrate from this the impossibility of a schismatic 'church'. One cannot separate a ray from the light, a branch from the tree, a creek from the spring without its vanishing, withering, drying up. This unity of the church, however, exists because of the bishop's office. The church is in the bishop as the bishop is in the church (Ep. 66, 8). Woe to those who will not recognize this! They are become the company of Korah, and they tear apart the seamless robe of the Lord. Satan invents schisms, and the schismatics stand under his power. Cyprian did not hesitate at once to brand everybody leaving the 'Catholic' community as a morally depraved individual having to answer for countless sins. A Christian can only turn away from him with disgust.

The bishop's office, that which upholds unity, was for Cyprian no mere concept or religious idea. In the confused situation which now obtained in all the congregations after persecution and lapse from the church, it was vitally important that at least the bishops should stand together, remaining united with each other, and following the same practical principles. Cyprian assembled his colleagues at various synods and sent to them his messengers, letters, and encyclicals. He laboured for exchanges of opinion, for joint declarations, and for mutual confidence. It was not only his African colleagues who congregated round him, thus protecting each other mutually by their decisions; Cyprian likewise corresponded also with the newly elected bishop of Rome, Cornelius, who had to hold his ground against a rigorous opposition (from the 'right') led by an important theologian, the former presbyter Novatian. In the name of the priestly college, Novatian himself had earlier addressed letters to Cyprian and received answers in agreement with his views. Now, however, the situation had changed. Cyprian stood firmly by that bishop for whom the majority had decided, and sought to recommend him in all instances as the only valid bishop, the only one worthy to be regarded as holder of 'Peter's chair'. So the unity of the Catholic church became a tangible, firm, and canonical reality in church politics, which determined the order of the Western church as far as Spain and Gaul.

Cyprian's strength of will and drive were not exhausted by these problems of ecclesiastical government. In these years he turned again to literary work with increased success. He became a productive writer of devotional literature, the model of the episcopal teacher and preacher. The topics and even the thoughts of these writings were frequently derived from Tertullian. Yet the impatient fiery verve, the moral radicalism and the enthusiasm of the 'master' had disappeared, and issues of systematic or dogmatic significance no longer came to view. There remain a sturdy rationalism and moralism, and a practical reasonableness of argument, which were simple, easy to understand, and popular. The dominant tone is one of instructive persuasion, versatile admonition, and lively earnestness, full of impressiveness and dignity. Cyprian's style is never harsh and sarcastic, but solemn and grave; in the words of a later writer, it always flows smoothly like pleasant oil (Cassiodorus). He loves to describe the same thing two or three times

over in synonymous words, and repeats certain idioms, illustrations, and thoughts. In short, Cyprian speaks the language
of the experienced preacher, which is what he is. His rhetorical
passion does not sound, as in the case of Tertullian, artificial and
hollow. It had taken shape in the practical use of daily church
life, and had been united with the clear expression of the trained
official, and with the vivid plainness of the African Bible, into
a new Latin religious style, whose echo we hear again and again
from now on throughout the centuries.

Alongside the empirical ecclesiastical demands and decisions
which had to be expounded to the people of the church, Cyprian dealt by preference, in his pastoral letters and tracts, with
practical problems of life concerning religious education and
individual virtues. For this the Bible always served him as an
inexhaustible treasure of illustrations. He poses the problems
plainly and simply without any individualization and refinement. Cyprian pays special respect to the devotion to asceticism
of the consecrated virgins in the congregation, to the praise of
abstinence as such and the glorious example of the holy martyrs. Peaceableness, humility, and modesty are virtues especially
esteemed, for they uphold peace in the congregation. Also
'love' viewed in this way attains the character of a chief social
and ecclesiastical virtue, which is injured most severely by the
arrogance, quarrelsomeness, and insubordination of the schismatics. The benefit of good works is stressed everywhere with
startling naïvety. God has 'given man his freedom and made
him dependent on his own will; he himself has to strive either
for his death or his salvation' (Ep. 59, 7). For that purpose it is
necessary to perform with fasting and prayer 'righteous works',
which bring salvation from the punishments of hell. Alms in
particular extinguish the flames of the sins of the Christian, as
baptism has washed away the previous offences of a pagan life.
Such admonitions were heeded. When Numidia was devas-
tated by invasion, its bishops asked Cyprian to help their
congregations. He arranged a collection and received 100,000
sesterces to send for the ransom of prisoners. In times of hunger

and of great pestilence the congregation was ready to make sacrifices in the same wonderful manner. 'Practical Christianity' was certainly no meaningless phrase in Cyprian's church.

In these troubled times Cyprian also composed apologetical writings. The old accusations against the Christians were revived, and against this weaker Christians needed strengthening, instruction, and encouragement. 'We must, dear brethren, consider well and continually ponder the fact that we have already renounced this world and as foreigners and strangers have only to live in it for a short time. Let us welcome with joy the day which leads each one of us into his home, carries us away from these surroundings, releases us from the bonds of the world, and restores us to paradise and the kingdom of God. We see paradise as our homeland; even now we begin to have the patriarchs in some measure as our fathers. Why then do we not hasten and run, so that we can see our home-country and greet our fathers?' (de Mort. 26). The way this political and eschatological longing is put is truly Cyprianic. The old, early Christian expectation of the coming kingdom of God was combined with the consciousness that we face a lost and senile world which is beyond help. Nature has also grown old; rain and sunshine fail to come, the earth is exhausted, population has decreased, people die sooner, business and trade have become stagnant, the state and society, the arts and science are declining (ad Demetr. 3 f.). All these are signs of the divine anger towards the ungodly, while the Christians who are being accused because of these events are the least guilty. By them the time of trouble must be welcomed as a time of probation.

Cyprian's ecclesiastical position was strengthened further during these difficult years. He became an authority even far beyond the borders of the African church. Everywhere in the Latin West his letters and books were read; people from afar turned to him for information and advice. The answers he gave were always delivered in a friendly, polite, but firm tone, and it can be seen from them that Cyprian was by now used to his directions always being observed. It could not be long before the difference of ecclesiastical principles between the various provinces came up for discussion in such a correspondence. Cyprian avoided demanding impossibilities in such cases. He put his confidence in the 'cement of concord' which, despite all, united the bishops in the whole *Catholica*, and made them stand together against all external and internal foes of the church. With this we have the background of the serious ecclesiastical conflict which broke out once again and embittered the last years of Cyprian's life. His opponent was the only bishop of the West who, on account of the traditional significance and power of his see, could still dare to defy the 'pope' of Carthage, the newly elected Pope Stephen I of Rome.

Until this time the ecclesiastical leaders in Carthage and Rome had co-operated well, as we have seen. Cyprian could refer to a corresponding Roman procedure when regulating the problem of penance; moreover, Cornelius owed a good deal personally to Cyprian in his contested position, and seems to have acknowledged the intellectual superiority of his senior colleague without question. But Stephen, who had now taken over the helm of his church, was quite another man. He felt Cyprian's advice as an unwanted tutelage and evidently considered it time to make powerful and effective once again the independence and ancient superiority of the Roman church. There was, in addition, a definite difference of opinion of considerable importance. The efficacy of baptism administered outside the true church had occasionally been discussed in earlier times. The divisions and confusions brought about in the aftermath of persecution posed anew the problem of the proper attitude toward 'baptism by heretics'. For Cyprian the decision had already been quite clearly made in accordance with his whole conception of the church. All sacramental acts performed outside the one Catholic communion of salvation are in his opinion null and void. How could apostate persons, possessed by the devil, confer the gifts of the Holy Spirit which they themselves had lost? In this opinion, Cyprian was in agreement with the ancient tradition of his home-country. Tertullian had already demanded rebaptism of heretics. A generation earlier Cyprian's episcopal predecessor Agrippinus had decided likewise at a council in Carthage of seventy African bishops. On the other hand, in Rome they had earlier gone over to the other side and had affirmed in principle the validity of heretical baptism. Now, they declared themselves willing in addition even to recognize the 'Novatian' ordination in case of conversion. This had the great advantage of making considerably easier the return of the schismatic clergy. Stephen with great determination put his weight behind the Roman practice, which he quite calmly pronounced to be an 'old' custom (and this could at most mean 'customary at Rome'). 'No innovations—stick to tradition' was the effective battle-cry, which he sent down the ranks.

The alarming aspect of this issue for Cyprian was above all that it did not confine itself to Rome or Italy. There were bishops in Africa, too, who, under the pressure of necessity, were willing to conciliate the schismatics, or had already decided for this course. They were now backed up by Stephen, at least indirectly, against Cyprian. Yet he still hoped to come at least to a practical settlement, without giving up in the least his own definite opinion. He called his adherents together to a council in Carthage, which endorsed the accepted African practice, and addressed a letter to Stephen informing him as usual about the decisions. They expressed their expectation that Stephen, known as a pious and truthful man, would likewise agree to what had clearly shown itself as true and pious to the assembled bishops. Cyprian, however, who had naturally composed this letter, added at once that they knew well that some brethren in office found it very difficult to change a decision once made, and that in such cases they preferred to adhere to the existing order 'for the preservation as colleagues of the bond of peace and concord'. 'We on our part do not wish to put pressure on anybody or to give him directions. Every leader of a congregation has the right to decide for himself freely according to his own discretion; he will have to answer for his actions to the Lord alone' (*Ep.* 72, 3). Cyprian was thus aware from the beginning that he had neither the ability nor the right to carry his point of view to complete victory, and here, if you like, was a dogmatic weakness of his position. As a matter of fact, there was then really, as things stood, no other way to sustain the peace and unity of the church.

Stephen had a different opinion. It is open to doubt whether he had a clearer theological understanding of the whole bearing of the decisions than Cyprian. We get the impression rather that for his part he was more concerned to pick holes in the arguments of his colleague, and so he began with a frontal attack. Of course, we know his utterances only from the echo in Cyprian's correspondence; nevertheless, it is evident that amongst other 'presumptuous, irrelevant and contradictory matters' which he 'scribbled ignorantly and thoughtlessly' . . . (*Ep.* 74, 1) Stephen also demanded that in dealing with heretics in Africa there should be compliance with the 'traditional' Roman proceedings. And for proof Stephen referred to the 'primacy' (*primatus*) which was his to claim as the holder of Peter's throne. The other bishops were thereby placed expressly in a lower position, subordinate to the Roman bishop, and were to be obliged to pay allegiance to him.

This was a hitherto unheard of demand, and it is understandable that Cyprian was indignant at the 'insolent and arrogant' attitude of his younger colleague. He felt the impudent claim of 'tradition' in this case to be an impertinence. It will never do, he averred, with tacit reference to Tertullian, for directions to be issued at will, and with reference to a mere 'custom'. They have to be supported by reasonable arguments. Above all he was insulted by the improper reference to Peter, who neither had claimed 'primacy' nor demanded the obedience from his younger fellow-apostles who joined later (*Ep.* 71, 3). Cyprian, in common with the whole early church, regarded Peter as the first holder and representative of the episcopal office in general, in the authority of which all bishops, each in his own area, participate 'in solidarity' (*de Un.* 5). When the Lord at first founded the episcopal ministry solely on the one rock Peter, he only intended to emphasize symbolically the necessary unity and concord of the entire episcopate. But the other disciples were not therefore inferior to Peter, and they possessed the same authority and dignity as he (*de Un*. 4). The idea of a legal priority for Peter's local Roman 'successor' does not fit into this train of thought. If this nevertheless seems to be present today in a striking special edition of Cyprian's book on the *Unity of the Church*, this is hardly likely to be the text that Cyprian wrote, but is a tendentious emendation introduced later along Roman lines. However, we need not concern ourselves further with this very controversial special problem; for the picture of what Cyprian, on the whole, meant is clear in any case. In Stephen and Cyprian there are opposed for the first time two fundamentally different ideas about the nature of the Catholic hierarchy and church. Stephen with his 'monarchic' conception of the entire church is, so to speak, the first pope. On the other hand Cyprian, with his idea of a firm but free union in love of bishops having equal authority, is the classical representative of 'episcopalism'. We can see now how easily a unity of the organized church so conceived could actually be upset by conflicts between ecclesiastics. But the peculiar greatness of this concept should not be overlooked. The unity of the church was no simple, secure matter of fact to Cyprian, but appeared as the spiritual calling, and, at the same time, as the ethical task of her leaders. In any emergency they have to demonstrate and prove their faith in the church by their personal decision.

Cyprian proved to be equal to the serious situation. On September 1, 256, a new council gathered in Carthage at which he brought together no less than eighty-seven bishops. It developed into a protest on the grand scale against baptism by heretics. Nobody mentioned the Roman bishop; his declarations were treated as if they did not exist, and yet it is evident against whom this demonstration was politically directed. We still possess the minutes with the votes of the individual participants. After the decisive letters of Cyprian had been read, he, as the chairman, called upon those assembled to proceed to a final vote. Everybody should declare his conviction openly; nobody would be subjected to any unpleasantness in consequence. 'For no one of us has created himself bishop of bishops or tries violently to force his brethren in the ministry to an absolute obedience by despotic pressure. Every bishop possesses definitely the freedom and right to hold to his own opinion as he pleases and is to be condemned as little by another, as he himself can condemn. Rather we all together await the judgement of our Lord Jesus Christ, who alone has the power to raise us to be leaders of the church, and to pass judgement on what we do.' All assembled bishops then assented, with shorter or longer arguments, to Cyprian's standpoint, and—appealing to his earlier pronouncements—he cast his vote last.

The delegation which was to deliver the council's decision to Rome was not even received by Stephen, and was left without quarters. He considered that communion with the African churches was broken. Stephen did not shrink from abusing Cyprian personally as a false Christ, a false prophet, and a deceitful worker (II Cor. xi. 13). Cyprian now no longer remained on the defensive, but conducted a sharp and extensive propaganda campaign for his point of view, and against the unbrotherly attitude of his reckless Roman colleague. Even the Christian East was involved in this controversy, and since the Christians there also frequently repudiated baptism by heretics, and did not at all acknowledge ecclesiastical centralism in the Roman style, Cyprian found some support from them. Among his correspondence is found a letter, undoubtedly translated and circulated by Cyprian himself, from bishop Firmilian of Caesarea in Cappadocia which agrees completely with Cyprian in this matter, and further expresses in strong language indignation at the 'open and obvious foolishness' of Stephen who boasts about the privileges of his episcopal seat, and thinks he possesses the succession of Peter (Ep. 75, 17). Dionysius, the influential bishop of Alexandria, finally tried to mediate, and admonished Stephen to peace, but in vain. The controversy was ended by outside factors. In the summer of 257 persecution by the state set in anew. Stephen died as a martyr, and in the following year the same fate overtook his successor, Xystus. Cyprian too was no longer free by then. The deadly seriousness of the church's situation pushed aside the quarrel of the parties, and made it a matter of secondary importance. So, as it appears, the relation between Rome and Carthage was restored of its own account; the differences of baptismal practice were not further mentioned. This was in substance a complete victory for Cyprian, who had in truth never asked for anything else. Only much later, and in a time when circumstances had changed, did the Roman church succeed with governmental help in putting into effect as law even in Africa her principles regarding the baptism of heretics. Over this issue the church split once again. The issue in these later Donatist controversies was still Cyprian's heritage; but Cyprian himself and his general ecclesiastical authority were no longer affected by this.

By and large Cyprian had served as bishop for one decade at most—ten years full of cares, of almost uninterrupted conflict, and of difficulties from without and within. However, Cyprian was not one of those natures who wear out and exhaust themselves in such trials. On the contrary, he felt himself to be in the right place, and under the burden of overcoming all his difficulties became more and more fully his resolute true self. Cyprian knew that in his activities he was a fellow-worker with God, who sustains his church. The bishop did not doubt his rights and even in obscure situations always knew what it was all about and what had to be done. By this he remained master of the situation and held his ground. At the start he was a beginner sitting on a swiftly won episcopal throne, supported only half-heartedly and insufficiently by his assistants, in hiding from persecution in voluntary exile, while 'rebels' fought about the leadership in his congregation. Yet he emerged to be the spiritual head of the entire African church, enjoying the

5

confidence of distant colleagues, a teacher to the whole of the West and respected and honoured even in the East. A Numidian bishop wrote to Cyprian that through his letters the wicked were corrected and the pious strengthened. His writings built up the faith, converted infidels, and set the example of his own character before the reader's eye without his knowing it. 'For more than anybody else you are a great preacher and a master of speech, wise in counsel, and plain in your wisdom, generous in your works and holy in your abstinence, humble in obedience and unselfishly ready for any good deed' (*Ep.* 77, 1). Only one thing was lacking: the glory and crown of the highest perfection, which is what he himself considered martyrdom to be. This too was now to be his portion.

Cyprian was arrested on August 30, 257, but it was deemed sufficient to remove him from Carthage. He was therefore banished to Curubis, a small place not too far away. It seems as if he was able to make an appeal to the emperor for clemency some time later, and that this appeal succeeded. Through a personal letter Cyprian received permission to return to Carthage, and he was assigned as his lodging his own gardens, which he was not to leave! This mild arrest lasted a long time. Then the situation changed. A new edict of the emperor Valerian ordered stricter measures everywhere, and in particular that the lives of the clergy should no longer be spared. In the course of time Cyprian was informed of what was to be expected by messengers who had gone on his behalf to Rome, perhaps even before the newly appointed proconsul himself. He now saw the situation clearly, and made his last arrangements swiftly and quietly. Not only did his own clergy have to be notified, but also his episcopal colleagues 'in order that everywhere, by their exhortation, the brotherhood may be strengthened and prepared for the spiritual conflict, that every one of us may think less of death than of immortality; and, dedicated to the Lord, with full faith and entire courage, may rejoice rather than fear in this confession . . .' (*Ep.* 80, 2; *LPNF*, V, 408). There is no more talk of escape. Without doubt it would have been possible, but this time he could be sure of his congregation. He was resolved to give them an example of how one should suffer martyrdom as a Christian and as a bishop, and he trusted completely in the merciful support of his Lord. The new proconsul apparently wanted to avoid disturbance, and to have Cyprian transported to Utica for execution. When this was known Cyprian left his quarters secretly, to return later. 'For it is proper that a bishop make his confession to the Lord also in that place where he heads the Lord's church and that the whole congregation be glorified by their leader's confession in their midst.' The words expressed by the confessor-bishop in the moment of his testimony are spoken by God's inspiration 'in the name of all' and as if 'through the mouth of all'. As they had so often been directed, the clergy were instructed to observe that complete peace was to be kept 'and that none of the brethren was to incite a tumult or to surrender himself voluntarily to the heathens' (*Ep.* 81).

Cyprian was arrested in proper form and taken into custody by two high officials. The congregation followed him, and the house in which he was accommodated for the night was surrounded by a vast crowd which wanted to 'die with him'. The interrogation on the following day was formal and short: the sentence was to be carried out at once. Having arrived at the place of execution, Cyprian took off his robe and knelt on it for his last prayer. Then when he had undressed completely, he stood there in silence with his eyes turned toward heaven until the executioner was at his post. As a final lordly gesture of superiority, Cyprian ordered that he be paid five and twenty gold pieces for his pains, and then he was blindfolded by two of the clergy while the people spread linen cloths in order to catch the precious blood of the martyr. The body was at first buried at the place of execution 'to remove it from the curiosity of the pagans', but was the same night brought in by the people carrying torches and candles and solemnly buried, 'accompanied by the prayer and loud jubilation of many of the brethren'.

No Latin church father can compare with Cyprian in popularity until Augustine. The account of his death rapidly circulated in many different editions and copies. A panegyric of his life and death, supposedly written by his deacon Pontius, is the oldest Christian biography. His writings and letters are all preserved in various collections and arrangements—the Roman collections, of course, omit now and then the embarrassing sections dealing with the quarrel about baptism by heretics. An old record lists Cyprian's works immediately after the writings of the Scripture. Even more significant is the great number of books falsely attributed to his name, which often, however, breathe his spirit and clearly display his influence. The sober use of the Bible, and practical moralism combined with a strong churchmanship, which his writings display, evidently corresponded to what the Latin Christianity of the time accounted eminently Christian and edifying. In the integrity of his faith Cyprian appears as the embodiment of the ecclesiastical *disciplina*. In his fidelity and steadfastness as an ecclesiastic, he is the very model of an independent bishop of the old Catholic period. His dedication to the new reality of Christian life does not lack warmth. It is genuine and of a striking practical seriousness. It is, one could say, the single-mindedness of the Roman official, now become a Christian, who has affirmed and accepted the saving faith simply and without question in order henceforth to fulfil his duty as a man in the Christian community justly and without compromise. We are surprised what polished ecclesiastical Catholic thought confronts us in Cyprian at a time when in the older and more developed Oriental congregations so much was still unclear, disputed, and in flux. Yet it is precisely this well-rooted moderation which explains the rapid formation and compactness of this ecclesiastical world. Latin Christianity is indeed not represented by Cyprian in its maturity, but only at the beginning of its development, not yet having attained to its real, full possibilities.

CHAPTER III

LACTANTIUS

In the whole early church being a Christian and a Catholic meant belonging to the church, and to belong to the church usually meant to belong to a certain ecclesiastical province and congregation. In Latin Christianity there were missing the representatives of that class in the East which had always preserved a certain ecclesiastical independence and freedom to live where one liked on account of one's profession, the Christian 'philosophers' and scholars like Justin and Clement of Alexandria, or even Julius Africanus and Methodius. This was due to the slight moral significance which higher learning and philosophy as a whole possessed in the Latin world. In place of the philosophers there here appeared the public figures of writers and rhetoricians, who as a rule had only a very superficial knowledge of philosophy. When they became Christians, they retained no further respect for their former occupation. They entered the service of the church as instructors of catechumens or clergymen, and at least inwardly bound themselves, like Tertullian, completely to the new tasks imposed by the Christian community. On this the rigid simplicity of the Western theological tradition is based. From the pre-Constantinian period we know of but one single exception, Lactantius, and it is no accident that he is found at the transition to the new period. Like Tertullian and Cyprian, Lactantius was an African. While still a pagan he was driven to the East and witnessed there after his conversion the beginnings of the 'Constantinian' revolution. The new position of Christianity offered novel possibilities, especially to an apologist and rhetorician. So far as we know, Lactantius was the first theologian to make the most of this chance. Through Constantine he received an excellent and independent position, and a new field of action. Having become a Christian in the time of persecution, he enjoyed for the first time in old age, as an imperial favourite, the advantages of the new-found union of state and church just beginning, of Christianity and the dominant culture. Yet outwardly Lactantius remained what he had always been, a teacher or professor, an aesthete and Christian writer without ecclesiastical ties and office. This role in life gives his personality and development an interest for the history of the church, as well as of ideas; otherwise, despite his unusual literary talent and pure and estimable character, he cannot be placed among the great.

We are indebted for what little we know of the biographical facts of his life almost exclusively to a short account and occasional remarks by Jerome. From his name Lucius Caecilius Firmianus—Lactantius is his personal Christian name—little can be inferred. In Sicca Veneria, a large country town in the neighbourhood of Carthage, Lactantius received his rhetorical education from Arnobius, a renowned teacher of his time, who was also later converted to Christianity. He also had a good knowledge of the law, yet according to his own testimony never appeared publicly as a practising lawyer or speaker. Lactantius was interested in rhetorical training for its own sake, i.e. with the intention of becoming, so to speak, an academic teacher of rhetoric. He succeeded. Already by the end of the century, the emperor Diocletian had called him to his residence at Nicomedia, the imperial capital prior to Constantinople on the Sea of Marmara, in order to contribute to the glory of the new capital as *rhetor Latinus*. He was thus transferred into purely Greek surroundings. He was needed, however, because Latin was still the official language of the empire and its legislation. Anyone who wanted to have a public career had to learn it at least in some measure.

We can only guess how Lactantius then thought of religion. His early writings are lost, only the titles being handed down. The *Symposium* may have discussed some educational themes in the usual manner; a travel book *From Africa to Nicomedia* was composed in hexameters—for poetry was in those days appropriate to a representative of higher rhetorical education. Undoubtedly no Christian influence was yet to be noticed in these works. Nevertheless, it is possible, even likely, that Lactantius had already gained his first impressions of the church in Africa. For a long time the Christians there could not be overlooked; even pagan ridicule and polemic brought them to notice. Perhaps Lactantius never was in real opposition to them, for as a Christian he still held to the principles of his pagan religious world-view. He lived in the tradition of a Platonism understood more devotionally than philosophically, which attempted to base all truth on a higher revelation and illumination, and upheld the recognition and veneration of God as the true goal of human life. The supposedly very ancient writings of '*the divine Hermes*', translated from the Greek, are the most important testimony to this piety, which was already adopted to a certain extent by Apuleius, and then by Arnobius too. It is surely no accident that Arnobius, and then Lactantius, and after him Flavius, a grammarian, who like him was called to Nicomedia, all became Christians in turn. These men represented a religious and philosophically coloured education, and half-education, which was seeking a religious focus. Only in the church, with its clearly revealed doctrine and actual ethical community, which at once imposed obligations and helped in their fulfilment, could their religious longing, when taken seriously, be satisfied. This ideological derivation probably also explains the gradual and growing approach which we must presume to have led to Lactantius' conversion. In his own opinion, naturally, only the baptism which he must have received in Nicomedia counted as the decisive event of his life, which imparted salvation.

The promoted rhetorician may at first have felt lonely and isolated in Nicomedia. It seems as though Lactantius never really learned Greek. His studies were limited to 'our', i.e. the Latin authors, and so later when dealing with Christian literature he took notice only of the church fathers who wrote in Latin. Lactantius knew even classical philosophy only through the medium of Latin. He knew the 'shrewdest of all Stoics' (*Inst.* II, 8, 23) Seneca, and above all Cicero, 'the prince of Roman philosophy' (*Inst.* I, 17, 3), completely and thoroughly. He modelled himself primarily on Cicero so that his writings, according to Jerome, could be considered in form an 'abstract' of all the Ciceronian dialogues. In the matter of style also Cicero remained his ideal all his life. Most likely Cicero had been recommended to him as a pattern by Arnobius, but the latter's own undisciplined vehemence always remained foreign to Lactantius. He strove for a high-minded, lively, and at the same time, in the traditional sense, elevated style. He was a classicist and in this respect really no 'African'. He consciously repudiated the careless colloquialism and vigour of Tertullian, whose literary style appeared to him as difficult, obscure, and uncultivated. Yet he also criticized Cyprian's brilliant eloquence because in choosing his words he did not show enough consideration for non-Christian readers. Lactantius did not forget that an outstanding pagan rhetorician had once mocked this first teacher of the Christians, calling him a '*Coprianus*', i.e. dirty fellow (*Inst.* V, 1, 27). Of course, Lactantius also could not entirely evade barbarous loan-words and neologisms when he came to speak of Christian conceptions and things. But he employed them as little as possible, and if he realized their strangeness tried to paraphrase and explain them. Here the academic, and keen apologist, comes to light, openly deploring to his educated audience the low literary ability shown in Christian propaganda. It was, however, no mere artificial tactics, no forced new expression of his thoughts which he desired, for the cultivated and well-balanced manner of Lactantius' writing was natural to him. It corresponded to his genuine, unobtrusive, cool and restrained nature, and therefore in his writings appears appropriate and pleasant.

We have, however, been anticipating with these observations. In his own words, in Nicomedia Lactantius first trained

the young men, as he had done formerly in Africa, 'not to
virtue, but rather in cunning wickedness' (*Inst.* I, 1, 8); that is
to say, he imparted to them a pagan education, and the usual
devices and tricks of rhetorical presentation. This met his teaching obligation. The persecution now breaking out under Diocletian first brought a change. The very first edict against the
Christians, issued in February 303, denied them any public
office and dignity, and accordingly forced Lactantius to make
a decision. It became even more inescapable when the campaign of anti-Christian propaganda presently spread to his immediate vicinity. Not only Sossianus Hierocles, the governor of
Bithynia, but also an unnamed philosopher—as it appears a close
colleague of his—placed themselves at the disposal of the government in this attack, and supported it with pamphlets hastily
written against the sect of the Christians, who were henceforth publicly outlawed. In view of the brutal governmental
measures this was an attitude which was to some extent felt to
be ungracious even in pagan circles. In spite of this, Lactantius
may still have hesitated for a while; but then he drew his conclusions. A formal renunciation of his conviction would never
have entered his mind. But he also did not want to be regarded
directly as a 'slave of his time' (*Inst.* V, 2, 10) and therefore he
resigned his appointment as teacher. The general remark of
Jerome about the financial distress of Lactantius, and his lack of
tuition fees, apparently has to be related primarily to the years
that followed. Lactantius, he says, had always remained so poor
in his earthly life, despite his brilliant rhetorical talent, that he
often lacked the necessities of life. One might add to this his
own words which he had formulated on the dangers of wealth:
men who could pander to concupiscence, to ambition and to
avarice, and who had never run into need, would not enter the
way of truth. And 'so it happens that the poor and humble
more readily believe in God' (*Inst.* VII, 1, 19); for they need
not carry the luggage which burdens the rich and makes them
unfit to march. From such statements there perhaps speaks not
only the experience of the period of persecution, but also the

general conviction of one who is concerned more about moral than about material values, and who therefore has an ear for the Christian message. At any rate, readiness to help and to suffer remained a fundamental requirement of Christianity for Lactantius all his life. If we really want to do God's will, he says, we must 'despise money and "deposit" it in the heavenly treasures. There no thief digs it out, there no rust destroys it, and no tyrant steals it, but under God's protection it remains reserved for us as an eternal treasure' (*Epit.* 60, 9).

We must not imagine that Lactantius wanted to make a noisy demonstration as he left. Against this speaks the fact that he could still remain undisturbed in the capital, although he was known personally and was to some degree prominent. Lactantius affirmed explicitly the ecclesiastical rule according to which nobody was permitted to give himself up for arrest in time of persecution, and press for martyrdom. It was sufficient if he remain faithful to his belief and 'does not evade what he then has to suffer and bear' (*Inst.* IV, 18, 2). It would seem that he refers to himself when he speaks, in relation to that philosopher who is a slave to the state, and to avarice, of the Christians who, in view of the present circumstances, had contented themselves with inwardly 'mocking at him', that they therefore had not really and outwardly separated themselves from the world (*Inst.* V, 2, 9). Yet however that may be, Lactantius, now free of his teaching office, found all the more time for literary pursuits. Only now did his Christian literary work begin. The first treatise we possess by him deals with providence in God's work of creation, *On God's Workmanship*. It is dedicated to a pupil named Demetrianus. He may here discover the occupation in which his former teacher is now engaged in this time of trouble and so will not be entirely deprived of instruction. This instruction now covers 'a more precious subject matter' than before 'and in a better system' (*Opif.* 1, 1). Demetrianus had obviously also become a Christian; but in distinction from Lactantius, he continued his occupation. All the more urgently he is admonished not to succumb imperceptibly, for the sake of worldly goods, to the devices of temptation which the devil has put into operation everywhere.

In form this treatise appears to be a mere expansion of Cicero's writing on the state, and as to the subject-matter, it simply contains an extensive description of the human body and its relation to the immortal soul. The care and providence of God, although foolishly and blasphemously denied by the Epicureans, is evident, it is argued, from the glory of the creature. This is not original, for Lactantius most likely obtains the material for his statements from the current medical and philosophical textbooks, and one might almost think that he has no specifically Christian purpose in mind at all with this little study in anthropology. This, however, would be a misunderstanding. Providence remained for Lactantius at all times a central point in his Christian teaching, and is to this extent a theological conception. In reality, he wants to defend the Christian belief in creation, and to take under his protection the despised 'Philosopher of our school' (Christ) (*Opif.* 1, 2) against all others, including 'Marcus Tullius' (Cicero), whom he mentions, of course, only with the highest respect, for even Cicero 'had already been often vanquished' (*Opif.* 20, 5) by certain people void of learning and eloquence, who nevertheless knew how to fight for the truth, namely the Christians. As he himself admits, it is only in consideration of the perilous times that the author feels compelled at present to express many things more concisely and obscurely 'than is really proper' (*Opif.* 20, 1). Lactantius was certain that he had now found his calling and life's work. Eloquence mattered no more, but something more serious, namely truth and life itself. He would know that he had not lived and laboured in vain if he should succeed in 'freeing some men from errors and directing them to the way which leads to heaven' (*Opif.* 20, 9).

Meanwhile, the horror of persecution took its course. Lactantius also lived outside Nicomedia for a considerable time— where, we do not know; soon after 310 we find him again in 'Bithynia' as the witness of the last measures of oppression.

During these years he composed his principal book, which he had already envisaged in his first treatise. It looks as if it were put together by placing one after another a number of such thematically limited essays; yet in this way it finally became a well-arranged whole. The *Divinae Institutiones*, '*Seven Books of Divine Institutes*', are even in modern print an imposing volume of several hundred pages. It is the most comprehensive apology which Christianity created before the end of the time of persecution. As a manual of religion it is modelled even as to the title on the *Institutes* of Ulpian, or similar manuals of the lawyers. The subject-matter here too is 'justice' and Christian law. Educated pagans are envisaged as readers, the representatives of just those circles to which Lactantius had himself belonged, and who in their conceited superiority are pleased to regard Christianity as contemptible. To them the work is explicitly addressed. Lactantius knew that it was not easy to win a hearing in this society. He 'knows the obstinacy of the people' who would much rather prove themselves to be in the right than learn the truth, and who 'enjoy themselves with the flow of blood rather than the flow of words of the righteous' (*Inst.* V, 1, 18). Yet the truth is nevertheless stronger than all lies, and one must not faint-heartedly despair. At least some, at least the better, among his readers must allow themselves to be won. As always, however, the Christian apologist thinks also of his own fellow-believers who, hesitating and unstable, need spiritual help. When they begin to rise into educated circles, and when they have acquired a taste for the reading of the pagan philosophers, rhetoricians, and poets, just then are they especially exposed to danger. They should learn that true knowledge does not necessarily destroy a man like the former false instruction, but rather makes him wise and just. The idea is to combine the good old form with the new good content, to make men devout by understanding and learned by true piety.

Lactantius began as usual with the refutation of false pagan religion. Monotheism is to him the only true and reasonable form of belief in God; the general conception of perfection itself excludes of necessity the idea of several divine beings. On this account man possesses his reason and for this God has created him, in distinction from the animals, erect with a face turned toward heaven, that he might know his almighty Creator, pray to him alone, and follow and confide in his providence and guidance. Faith in providence is, as already observed, a basic truth to Lactantius, which only Epicurus and his school have dared to deny. Whenever he comes to speak of it—and for this the opportunity offers itself in the very beginning of the book—he separates himself with indignation from this religious 'arch-pirate and robber-chief' (*Inst.* III, 17, 41). Also monotheism should be a thing natural to man; Sibyls and prophets have again and again testified to it. Despite this, polytheism has become a common evil. In the manner of the enlightened criticism of Euhemeros (*c.* 300 B.C.), Lactantius explains it from the deification of deceased leaders and rulers, and then from the malice of wicked demons which reveal their nature sufficiently in the abominations of the ancient cults. Here he follows even to the details of his description the Christian apologetic tradition. In doing so, however, he endeavours, more than do his predecessors, to understand the power of evil as a unity, as a single great principle of perversion 'always hostile to the truth' and knowing but one goal, namely to darken the minds of men so that they do not come finally to 'look to heaven', and to desire to live according to their nature (*Inst.* II, 1, 13).

The third book on 'The False Wisdom' leads to the centre of the discussion: it contains the refutation of philosophy. Lactantius distinguishes between serious philosophical research and mere rhetoric. The latter is designed for external beauty and earthly success, and therefore is not an adversary worth fighting. Yet philosophy also does not contain what it promises. Even in the Bible its ideas were already rightly rejected as folly. The eagerness with which some philosophers strive for truth deserves no blame at all, to be sure, and it must also be conceded

that some of them have made real sacrifices for virtue, by renouncing lust and wealth. But, nevertheless, they did not find
the truth, but at best fragments of the truth, which without a
trustworthy criterion can never be joined together into a unity
(*Inst.* VII, 7, 4 f.). This was further prevented by the perpetual
quarrel between the philosophical schools. The reason for the
failure is simple: human endeavours could not succeed from the
outset, for 'the truth, the mystery of the highest God who has
created all things, cannot be comprehended by one's own mind
and reason' (*Inst.* I, 1, 5). Hence, the philosophers 'could as
learned men make clever speeches, but not true ones, for they
had not learned the truth from him who is alone the master of
it' (*Inst.* III, 1, 14). This answer is firmly adhered to and constantly repeated anew. Lactantius is a theologian of revelation.
Even when he refers to the nature and reason of man, it is
always God who must make accessible the way to real cognition. Man is a religious being, who finds truth only in finding
and venerating God. Without God self-knowledge too is impossible, and 'the ignorance of oneself' remains the source of
all evil (*Inst.* I, 1, 25). This inclination toward revealed truth
was prefigured by his pagan understanding of religion, as we
have seen. Yet now he knows only the one Christian answer.
All philosophers have erred because they remained attached to
the earth with their inquiries, teaching, and volition. Even
Plato occasionally appears as a sheer atheist (*Inst.* II, 4, 26), and
Socrates, admittedly the wisest of all, ended notwithstanding
with the 'desperate' confession that he had come to know
nothing else than his own ignorance (*Inst.* III, 28, 17). Christianity is no more understood—as it could appear to be in the
early work—as a new or more perfect philosophy. It is commissioned to outdistance all philosophies, and to replace them
as the truth itself.

God did not leave mankind to its self-earned misery. He
showed it the way of life, and in such a way that it is really
open now to everybody, without distinction of age, education,
or sex. 'There is only one hope of life for men, one harbour of

salvation, one castle of freedom.' One must open one's eyes and look at God 'who is the only home of truth'; one must despise the earthly and regard philosophy as nothing—in this way one attains wisdom and by wisdom, i.e. by piety, immortality itself (*Epit.* 47, 1). Immortality is seen everywhere in Lactantius as the real meaning of salvation, or philosophically speaking, as the highest good (*summum bonum; Inst.* III, 12, 18), given by God to the pious as a reward and fulfilment of their life. At the same time, immortality is also an attribute of every created soul, imperishable by virtue of its spiritual nature. As so often, Lactantius did not succeed at this point in fully reconciling these two types of ideas, the Biblical-Christian and the philosophical-religious tradition.

The following book, *The True Wisdom and Piety* (they belong inseparably together!), reveals even more strangely the combination of the academic philosophical debate in its tradiditional form, with a completely heterogeneous, and in part fantastically enlarged, Christian soteriology and mythology. The difference is concealed and brought into a seeming harmony by the constantly streaming flow of a Ciceronian eloquence, always correct. The heavenly origin and redeeming work of Christ are described, and pagan objections against the meaning and possibility of the incarnation, and especially of the crucifixion, are rebutted in many ways. Generally speaking, in Lactantius Christ appears as above all the teacher of the true religion and virtue. One can trust him all the more safely, because he convinces us at the same time by his pattern and example. The fifth and sixth books deal with Christian 'righteousness' and the true worship. The golden age described by the poets existed as long as people still venerated the one God. With polytheism righteousness departed and the only righteous ones, the Christians, are persecuted with incredible fanaticism. Yet the Christians disprove all accusations by their heroic patience. With the Stoic emotionalism of a Seneca, Lactantius talks about the martyrdoms but emphasizes at the same time that only with God's assistance is it possible to prevail over such agonies. The action of the persecutors is in any event just the opposite of all true veneration of God. God desires brotherly love and humanity among men, a pious thought, and moral conduct of life. In the religious field this corresponds to the renunciation of every act of worship performed reluctantly, and thus to a practical attitude of tolerance. Lactantius finds once more an opportunity of attacking the merely external cult of the pagans, the foolishness of idolatry and sacrifice with which God is supposed to be receiving a favour of extraordinary value, when the altars drip with blood. True service 'does not come from the purse, but from the heart; it is not offered by hands, but by the spirit, and the truly agreeable victim is to be found whenever the soul sacrifices it from its own property' (*Epit.* 53, 3). This is the worship known to the Christians. Lactantius practically never mentions the social and sacramental side of the church's life.

The last book deals with the 'Happy Life' and once again enters systematically into the problem of immortality. At the end, the Christian teaching of the 'Last Things' is expounded. The astonished reader realizes with what enthusiasm our seemingly enlightened author clings to the particulars of the cosmic eschatological drama. He is far from interpreting spiritually the statements of John's apocalypse, and even adds further apocalyptical material. In two hundred years at the latest the millennium will begin. Christ will descend from heaven with His angels and will establish His throne in the middle of the earth. He will furnish the just who have risen with new bodies and will put the anti-Christ in chains. But toward the end of the seventh millennium anti-Christ will regain his freedom, and over the city of God a terrible fight will take place, until the 'last wrath' of God breaks out and brings all things to an end. Heaven will be rolled up, the earth changed, and the unjust will be condemned to eternal torment, while the just now attain the nature of angels 'dazzling as the snow' (*Inst.* VII, 26, 5). 'Therefore let us strive after justice; for it alone, as a faithful companion, will lead us to God. Let us, "while a spirit rules these limbs" (*Aeneid*, IV, 336), render untiring military service to God. Let us stand guard and watch, and boldly take up the fight against our familiar foe, in order that as victors and heroes we may then obtain from the Lord the reward of virtue promised us by God Himself' (*Inst*. VII, 27, 16).

When we look at the whole, we see clearly what sort of man has composed this comprehensive work. He is an old experienced scholar, thoroughly at home in Latin literature, who now places all the resources of his long-standing rhetorical experience at the service of the Christian 'truth' (*Inst*. I, 1, 10). God's spirit, says Lactantius, assists me, for without it the truth could neither be comprehended at all nor described (*Inst*. VI, 1, 1). The material he is working with, however, is, for the most part, not of Christian but of pagan origin. With his proof from prophecy, to which he attaches great importance, this is particularly evident. It is almost exclusively built upon actual or supposed pagan testimonies, above all on the (Jewish or Christian interpolated) Sibyllines, on the revelation of 'Hermes' and passages from oracles and poets of any provenance. Later, Lactantius considered Virgil also to be a prophet, for he had already foreseen and prophesied the last persecutions of the Christians. Lactantius stands here at the beginning of the Christian interpretation of Virgil. Only where it was wholly indispensable, in the Christological passages of the fourth book, does he quote to any considerable extent the Old Testament, and here he follows mostly Cyprian's collection of testimonies. But one must not without further ado conclude from this that he had a correspondingly superficial knowledge of the Scripture. A man who acknowledges the divine authority of the Holy Scriptures as decisively as Lactantius does, has certainly read and come to know them. But Lactantius is now writing in order to win a pagan audience. He realizes what aversion the 'vulgar and common' language of the Bible causes, especially 'with wise, educated, and authoritative personalities', and therefore tries to refer to known and accepted texts. They are indeed in accordance with the Bible and therefore equally true. The truth is

6

finally able 'to illuminate by virtue of its own light even where it cannot be verified by divine testimonies' (*Inst.* VIII, 7, 5).

What Lactantius accomplishes in this way is more than a mere apology. His work, as he himself emphasizes, is not intended merely to refute, but also to instruct (*Inst.* V, 4, 3). For this, it is necessary to present the entire content of the Christian faith and life; it was likewise necessary to deal with 'hope, life, salvation, immortality, and God' (*Inst.* I, 1, 12). The church had not until then possessed such an over-all study in Latin, and furthermore the systematic work of the Greek church most comparable to the *Institutes*, that written by Origen in his early years, was differently oriented, and remained 'Dogmatic' in a much stricter philosophical and esoteric sense. One might think of Clement of Alexandria, who had attempted but not completed something similar in his great trilogy. A comparison with him is instructive in other respects too, for Lactantius reveals the completely different nature of the Latin theological attitude—even when both are connected by similar Gnostic-Platonic traditions. It is significant that Clement recognizes his pagan predecessors as such, loves, and to some extent approves of them. On the other hand Lactantius contents himself with stressing time and again the frustration and final failure of all philosophers. The tone in which he speaks of them is seldom respectful, never friendly, and almost everywhere decidedly hostile, at any rate in substance. Different likewise are the ways by which both seek to win men for the Christian teaching. Clement dares to approach the mysterious reality of God only hesitatingly, if at all, and this he does in various ways by a certain diffident dialectic. He stresses that an inner maturity and a special understanding is needed really to comprehend it. Such difficulties and detours are completely unfamiliar to Lactantius' thoroughly realistic and rational understanding of revelation. Christianity is the truth; i.e. it should really be intelligible immediately to every unbiased person. God has given it; one need only learn it, and one can then also defend it by means of reason. The decisive proof lies in the moral effects it accomplishes. On

the other hand what is the use of a philosophy if, as the lives of
the philosophers show, it does nothing to make men better?
(*Inst.* IV, 3, 2). This is the point at which the alleged wisdom of
the world must undergo its trial, and here Christianity finally
shows its superiority. This is a thought not unfamiliar to
Clement also, and known more or less to every Christian
apologist. But with Lactantius, it is the crown of his theological
endeavours. Clement understands the free, glorifying 'Gnosis',
the association with God which enables one to love and to
see him as transcending and perfecting all human knowledge,
whereas Lactantius points to the clear demand of the 'righteousness' which surely is 'the highest virtue, or the fountain of
virtue itself' (*Inst.* V, 5, 1). This righteousness is a markedly
moral and social conception. The religious ideals of late Platonism are thus interwoven with the practical emotion of the Stoic
and in particular the Roman-Stoic tradition. The old demands
of ecclesiastical Christian ethics can then be easily attached to it.
The five chief commandments of true humanity now read:
hospitality, redemption of prisoners, care for widows and
orphans, nursing of the sick, and burial of the poor and strangers.
The virtue of justice includes above all 'humanity'. Indeed,
with Lactantius it is sometimes almost identical with 'mercy'.
Christianity was evidently adjusting itself to the sad changes of
the enfeebled and impoverished ancient society in its decline.
It is no accident that the new teaching on virtues is rooted in the
religious sphere; 'almost all the ties of humanity' which bind
us together, says Lactantius, really arise from 'fear and the
consciousness of our own frailty' (*Opif.* 4, 18).

If, on the other hand, we inquire concerning his theological
views in the narrower sense, the result is disappointing. Everything Tertullian and Novatian had achieved for a systematic
teaching on the Trinity is forgotten by Lactantius. What he has
to offer instead is a massive mythological genealogy of divinities. We hear that God—even before he created the multiplicity
of angels—had brought forth as the 'Second' a dearly beloved
Son. That means that Christians worship 'two Gods'; but this

need not disturb anybody, because a 'Father' and a 'Son' always belong together in their nature, and a complete harmony exists always between these two. Even Plato, taught by Hermes, speaks almost 'like a prophet' of a first and a 'second God' (*Epit.* 37, 4). God created, however, yet a third spirit, in whom the 'nature of his divine genus' failed continuously to prevail (*Inst.* II, 8, 4). Followed by a part of the angels, He rebelled out of jealousy against the second and therefore became a wicked anti-God, the '*antitheus*' (*Inst.* II, 9, 13). This quarrel within the divine family is interpreted by Lactantius in terms of the philosophy of religion with the help of Stoic teaching on the elements. The condemnation of the devil is no mere fate which he has brought on himself, but was foreseen and planned by God from the very beginning. As God wanted to create and effect all good things through His Son, so He destined from the very beginning the third as His opponent. 'The one spirit is his right, the other is his left hand' (*Inst.* II, 8, 6; *LA*, 2). For no life exists without opposition: two principles govern the world, and the good has evil as its indispensable presupposition. There is no warmth without cold, no light without darkness, and also in the ethical life no victory without an adversary and a preceding fight. How foolish are the people who accuse the divine world order of defect and injustice! So long as he lives, man is confronted with the necessity for decision and for good reasons. His body is earthly, and in it dwells evil. His soul is heavenly and must prove itself in its freedom. Evil does indeed cause many to fall, but on the other hand, it is also defeated by many, and thrown to the ground (*Opif.* 19, 8; *LA*, 5). Truly, the whole world, a thing in essence disunited in itself, was created only for the sake of man, in order that man, who is not to remain a child for ever, might learn virtue by struggle and 'that his virtue might reward him with immortality' (*Inst.* VII, 5, 27; *LA*, 17). As we can see, Lactantius, the student of the Roman Stoa, feels no difficulty in combining in this way his monistic theology with a sharply dualistic ethic, and this theodicy now serves as justification for a traditional speculation more Jewish than

Christian, about the struggle and fall of the angels! He may perhaps have later had theological misgivings about these bold statements, for without change in the over-all conception, the most daring passages of this kind are now deleted in the majority of the manuscripts.

In his writings Lactantius fails to mention the Holy Spirit as such. The 'third' was indeed the devil! In a letter Lactantius is even supposed to have later denied expressly the 'substance' of the Spirit, and to have treated him as referring simply to the person of the Father or that of the Son, whose 'sanctity' was sometimes designated by this 'name' (Jerome, *Ep.* 84, 7). Such slips by Lactantius were of course taken amiss in later times. An index of the early sixth century lists his books explicitly among the 'apocryphal', i.e. among the more or less disreputable literature not ecclesiastically approved. Yet this is in fact only the weakness of a self-taught man, who collects his theological ideas from wherever it suits him, or creates them himself without, as a moralist and practical apologist, being really much concerned about the details of his 'system'. Far from his home country, and all the more isolated in his Greek surroundings, Lactantius personally at all events feels himself to be completely orthodox. He is offended as a good Catholic that the 'unity of the holy body' (of the church) is torn apart by sects, reckless, ambitious, or simply foolish and lacking in judgement. At times he planned to write a book of his own to refute them (*Inst.* IV, 30, 14). Fortunately for his later reputation, this was not written! Even Jerome, who is well disposed toward him, cannot suppress a sigh that such a successful fighter against pagan error had shown so little skill in describing his own belief (*Ep.* 58, 10). His theology, superficial, and more rhetorical than philosophical, would definitely not have been equal to such a delicate task.

In spite of this, one must not underestimate the Christian content of his convictions. Occasionally there are interesting transitions between the ancient and the Christian elements of his thinking. A small monograph on the *Anger of God*, written

after the *Institutions*, show this particularly clearly. It again deals
with an apologetical problem. The passionate, personal, temperamental action of God, as it is described particularly by
the Old Testament, was in ecclesiastical preaching always ob-
noxious to feeling determined by Greek thought. Is it not just
the nature of the deity, not to have any 'emotions' like man?
Tertullian had in opposition to this rightly emphasized God's
purpose of salvation, and hence a compulsive attention to the
world and its 'afflictions'. Wrath meant to Tertullian, as it
were, only the reverse side of the divine mercy. Lactantius
knew the explanations of Tertullian, yet approached the problem in a characteristically different way. He sees in God's anger
above all the expression of the penal justice, of the '*iustitia*'
emphasized so strongly in all his works. In his opinion, therefore, God is the 'Father', just because He is simultaneously
'*dominus*', the Lord, and as such exercises the '*imperium*'. His
merciful and just government has to inflict evil also where
necessary and let His sovereign wrath rule. This is an interpretation of the Biblical idea of God which precisely corresponded
to Roman feeling. Indeed, it might be expressed even more
strongly; here we come across an extensive, true 'commensura-
bility' of Biblical and Roman thought (Kraft). The Roman
understanding of legal lordship and governorship, also characteristic of the '*pater familias*', is completely thought through to
the end when it is applied to the sovereign God of Christianity.
The Bible on which Lactantius here rests is still primarily the
Old Testament, and indeed the Old Testament narrowed down
to its most moralistic.

The negotiations, favourable to the Christians, of the emperors Constantine and Licinius, and the decline of Maximin,
the last persecutor, ended oppression in 313. Lactantius must by
then have been elderly, perhaps, as Jerome thinks, a very old
man. Like all Christians, he welcomed Constantine's victory
and rise with rejoicing. In him—at first in common with Licinius—he saw the divinely elected saviour of order and justice,
the protector and liberator of the Christians, who had been

unjustly oppressed for such a long time, and presently praised him personally as the worshipper of the true God. He was most likely acquainted with him already from earlier times. Before the outbreak of the great persecution, Constantine certainly stayed for some time at the palace of Diocletian in Nicomedia as a kind of hostage for his father. It is a likely guess that the young foreign prince had at least already met the equally foreign rhetorician of distinction. Now he appointed him tutor to his oldest son Crispus, and Lactantius gladly accepted this honourable summons which brought him again to the Latin West, to Gaul. The writer, for years proscribed and without financial support, now suddenly again held a position, and a more splendid one for a man of his standing could not be imagined. Constantine felt it to be a matter of importance that he be taken as a patron of the Christians and a promoter of religious education and culture. One may imagine how Lactantius was received as a celebrity in the palace of Trèves, or how he lectured to his imperial pupil in one of the beautiful villas of the Moselle valley. Trèves may have been his usual place of residence, but it is not impossible that he occasionally accompanied Constantine himself on his journeys. We cannot give details of this, because it is not the way of Lactantius to write about himself in his books, and other data are not available.

In his new position Lactantius had also enough time for his literary work. Perhaps it was only now that he finished his *Institutes* or edited them anew with an enthusiastic dedication to the emperor. Later, as a work written in his old age, an abbreviated version of this book in one volume was published. This '*extract*' (*epitome*), the condensation of his main thoughts, eliminating all meandering details and repetitions, is an especially successful achievement which reveals Lactantius' undoubted talent and his calm nature in a particularly pleasant light. The little work is dedicated to 'brother Pentadius', who set great importance upon being named by the famous man in this way. Also a part of the literary work of Lactantius the rhetorician, which is, so to speak, professional and not actually

Christian, is undoubtedly a product of this period. Lactantius is the first Christian letter-writer, who published a number of collections of letters, certainly not only for the sake of their content, but also as a pattern of a good epistolary style. Jerome still had those collections available, as well as a *Grammaticus* and the earlier writings already mentioned. In these letters, to be sure, theological problems were also discussed, yet only 'seldom', and mingled with a broad variety of items of general interest, in the manner approved by ancient culture. At any rate Pope Damasus, who borrowed the collection from Jerome, considered them verbose and boring, and at best interesting to schoolmasters, with their anecdotes about philosophers, and their information about metre and geography. Lactantius tried once more to write poetry, by dealing in his own way with the traditional material about the phoenix. This was most likely intended by him as a Christian allegory, but would be scarcely understandable to an outsider in this connection. Incidentally, a conjecture in Virgil handed down under the name 'Firmianus' seems to go back likewise to our Firmianus Lactantius.

Lactantius' further activity, however, was not exhausted in the fostering of old interests in this new environment, now favourable to Christians and completely peaceful. As a matter of fact, his horizon had widened in this new situation and surroundings. The Christian and the theologian began to be interested in the fate of the empire. The old learned apologist still showed surprising open-mindedness and inner versatility. In a certain way, Lactantius always had been a conscious, practical Roman. When in his main work he censures the past of Rome, and when he prohibits the Christian from military and judicial service (*Inst.* VI, 20, 16), he has traditional and specifically theological reasons. It is not an expression of any particular attitude of hostility to the state, and of renunciation of the world. Lactantius likewise shows an interest in social and political problems and regards it as quite right that Cicero 'gives preference, above teachers of philosophy, to men employed in public life' (*Inst.* III, 16, 2; *ANF*, VII, 85). He distrusts the superficial and

gossiping manner of philosophizing Greeks who have always
'esteemed the most trifling things as of great consequence'
(*Inst.* I, 18, 7; *ANF*, VII, 31) and insists upon order and justice.
It is hardly accidental if this side of his nature seems to be intensified in the later 'extract' of his handbook. Full justice is
now done to the courage which protects the homeland (*Epit.*
58, 4), and the teachings of many a philosopher are also criticized politically. 'How could states exist', it is asked, if for
instance the principles of the Cynics were to find general
acceptance? (*Epit.* 34, 5). Lactantius now lived at the court of
an emperor friendly to Christians. Political tasks now automatically appeared in a new light, and the matter did not rest
with such theoretical discussion.

With his essay on *The Death of the Persecutors* (*de Mortibus
Persecutorum*) Lactantius takes for the first time a step into contemporary political literature. As long as Christians were still
excluded from public life this sort of study did not come under
consideration. To be sure, Lactantius even now wrote as a
theologian—if you like, as the first representative of a Latin
Christian theology of history. As to the content, his book presents a piece of 'contemporary history'. After a short introduction concerning the older persecutors, he describes the
measures of all emperors since Diocletian against the Christians,
and portrays the horrible punishments which the persecutors
thereby without exception brought upon themselves. Fortune
regularly deserted the rulers whenever they allowed themselves
to be carried away into the 'defiling of their hands with the
blood of the righteous' (9, 11). Even their wives and daughters
were stricken by ruin, and only the pious rulers inspired by
God could hold their ground, or can now enjoy undisturbed
peace and glittering fortune. The lesson resulting from this
is obvious, and it is emphasized. It is the special duty of the
historian to hand over the truth to posterity, so that future
generations may be warned. God protects justice and leads all
ungodly men and persecutors without fail to their deserved
punishment. This is just as much a theological as a political

truth. Lactantius had dedicated his book to a surviving confessor whom he knew personally, but it is evident that he
envisages not Christian readers alone. He is thinking not least
of the emperor Licinius himself, who was then beginning to
turn again toward the party hostile to Christianity. Unfortunately, we cannot date this writing accurately. At any rate, it
belongs to the years of the beginning of alienation between
Constantine and Licinius, who is portrayed with noticeable
criticism, i.e. the time of the beginning of the 'cold war' between the Western and Eastern halves of the Empire, which
turned some years later into a hot war and ended in 324 with
Constantine's undivided sovereignty. We may assume that
Lactantius published this book with the approval of Constantine, or at least after indirect contact with him. Seen in this way,
the apologetical tract attains almost the character of a religious
and political pamphlet with a particular aim.

On the whole, the historical statements of this small volume
are entirely reliable. Lactantius is, of course, writing a polemical
and partisan work, as is usual in such cases, but he guards against
consciously distorting the truth anywhere. As to form, the essay
is a complete success. The strong personal involvement in the
events makes the rigid, academic style unusually lively. Sometimes the description becomes almost dramatic. Nevertheless,
in places it is almost intolerable to the modern reader. The
glorification of the bloody martyrdoms has a repulsive effect,
and the merciless triumph over the cruelly overthrown enemies
of Christianity is rather offensive; it reminds us of Nietzsche's
interpretation of the Christian 'inferiority complex'. In former
times the attempt was frequently made to deny completely
Lactantius' authorship of this book, in order to attribute it to
some unknown 'pupil' of his, in accordance with the familiar
means of escape of the philologist from embarrassment. The
'fanaticism' and hostile tone did not seem to match the noble
humanity, culture, and love of one's enemies which Lactantius
at other times displays. But Lactantius is not the last Christian
humanist to change his view and lose his vision in this way

when passing over to the ground of politics and of real controversy. With his natural, logical morality, and its corresponding
political theology, he stands unconsciously at the threshold of
a new period with a 'dominant' church, to which the demands
of tolerance and intellectual respect for the enemy will have
hardly any practical weight.

His book is most interesting if understood as a document of
the growing political consciousness of a church destined to
govern. The basic idea has already been prepared to some degree in the older apologetics: 'He who persecutes justice can
only be a blackguard' (de Mort. 4, 1). Tertullian's thesis, that
the tolerant emperors had always reigned happily, while all persecutors have been accursed both as men and sovereigns, is taken
up by Lactantius, and for the first time based upon a corresponding historical narration. Out of a tactically and polemi-
cally adduced argument of apologetic conflict has now arisen
a principle of the theology of history, to which the Christians
will henceforth refer, and upon which they will rely for edification! It is indeed they who represent justice on this earth, and
he who attacks them takes God himself as his enemy and must
bear the consequences. In this temporal framework the Christian idea of judgement, however, now also links up with the
older Roman political ideology. According to this, the victories
of Rome from time immemorial had been the result of Roman
virtue and justice. Now, however, it is the one, true God of the
Christians who takes under his protection this justice, moral,
religious, and political in the person of the pious emperor.
God's hand shelters Constantine (de Mort. 24, 5) while the
wicked, persecuting emperors appear throughout as incom-
petent 'tyrants' suppressing simultaneously with Christianity
justice also, and introducing 'barbaric' morals. They are evil
'beasts', which can tolerate the truth of God as little as the old
Roman freedom, virtue, and discipline. Such exaggerating
statements must not be condemned as adulation or hypocrisy;
they are understandable enough in the mouth of a Christian
who experienced the change under Constantine. Lactantius,

however, stands here at the same time under the shadow of a primitive pagan tradition, against which his Christianity has not really any counter-weight to offer. Scarcely had the revolution been completed, when the old church ideology of martyrdom and persecution vanished, and changed almost to its opposite. The Christians are no longer strangers in this world, and do not suffer through holding to a truth essentially different from that demanded and known by the world. The only connection with the past which, one would like to hope, will never come back, is the glorifying remembrance of the old fighters and their sufferings. One must not overlook the positive elements in this point of view, for combined with the over-hasty optimism and moralism of this outlook there is an unquestioning readiness for political co-operation and an affirmation of public life within the framework of a very definitely understood new 'justice'.

All this is just beginning to be delineated in this last work which we possess from Lactantius. The menace of, and triumph over, the 'persecutors' is still more strongly present than the promise and praise of the pious emperor who respects the Christians, and the traditional Roman political feeling is more evident than a Christian ideal of the empire. All the same, the new line of political thinking is announced. The common denominator for state and church seems to be found in the idea of 'justice' as Lactantius had developed it already in his *Institutes*. Constantine had an ear open to such statements. Furthermore, Lactantius' fundamental theological ideas in the strict sense agreed largely with his own politico-religious ideas. The stress upon the monotheistic belief in providence and upon ethical culture, the demand for religious tolerance and a better morality, and the emphasis on the old Roman greatness and tradition fitted well into his policy of renewal for the empire, which intended to extend patronage to the Christian and yet not give offence to the pagan majority. Constantine's decrees and speeches are in such close agreement with Lactantius' conceptions in principle, and sometimes even in formulation also, that this can hardly be an accident. To all appearance, he had

occasionally called upon his son's tutor for his own instruction.
If the missionary preaching of Lactantius in Constantine's version occasionally sounds somewhat more neutral, vague, and
general, this is understandable in the circumstances and must
not be seen as a lack of inner agreement. Perhaps Constantine
was more of a theologian in his political ideas than Lactantius
had become a politician.

We should probably know more about these things if development had not led so rapidly from these Western beginnings to a new politics, though not yet in the later sense the
politics of a state church. Lactantius did not follow the emperor
to the East. With new ecclesiastical and theological problems,
new advisors soon took his place here. The detailed theology of
the Christian empire was created only by Eusebius, who has
therefore in this area almost completely overshadowed his older
predecessor in the eyes of posterity. We do not know how
Lactantius would have reacted to the Arian controversies, and
to the resulting ecclesiastico-political decisions. He certainly
would not have become an Athanasius. He did not have the
theological requisites for this. But he might perhaps not have
yielded so thoughtlessly to the 'opportune' necessities as did
Eusebius, whom he otherwise closely resembles in his basic
political and apologetic attitude. The whole nature of Lactantius was not that of a church politician, and he belonged to the
older generation. Moreover, we do not know the exact date
and detailed circumstances of his death. He probably did not
witness the terrible end of his pupil, who was sentenced to death
by his own father (326). Otherwise one could bring the dele-
tion of the enthusiastic addresses to Constantine into relation
with this incident; it is closely parallel to the dogmatic elimina-
tions already mentioned. Yet these are vague assumptions
which we must leave at rest. There was certainly no public
break with Constantine. Lactantius was no courtier and no
careerist; but, always cautious rather than bold, calm, and con-
siderate in his attitude, he probably preferred to conclude his
days in quiet retirement.

His immediate effect was at first small. Only Jerome, as we have seen, occasionally mentions him sympathetically; Augustine also must have known him well and has made use of his writings. The great enthusiasm for Lactantius began only with the Humanism of the fifteenth century. The Salerno *editio princeps* of his works in 1465 was the first book printed in Italy, and in the same century there followed a good dozen further editions. Pico praised the perfect literary form of the 'Christian Cicero'; Erasmus and Zwingli esteemed him because they saw the ideal union between Christianity and ancient culture accomplished in his writings. Right up till the Enlightenment Lactantius remained a frequently read author. The attempt to become free from the burden of theological traditions by appeal to the ancient humanities today is certainly a very different thing from the attempt of Lactantius to accommodate himself to the ancient society, to which he himself belonged, in order to convert it to the new 'Christian Way'. Lactantius indeed had hardly an idea of the difficulty of such an undertaking. He did not take seriously the intellectual power of philosophy, and he thought that he could control the historical revolution of which he had become a witness theologically with a general teaching of retribution. He therefore reflects only the first naïve reactions with which educated Christian circles met the new era at the time. They were as superficial and unreflective as they were honest and serious in intention. It took almost two generations' time, with new experiences, and a theology more profound than that of Lactantius to do justice to the new situation.

CHAPTER IV

AMBROSE

WITH Constantine in sole power (324), and with the foundation of Constantinople, the weight of ecclesiastical decision shifted again entirely to the East. Here the alliance between empire and church was firmly established in the next years; here began the Arian controversy with its violent commotions; but here also began a general rise of ecclesiastical and theological life. The West did not participate herein and created nothing comparable. Always 'behind the times' compared with the East and intellectually backward, the development of the Latin church seemed to stagnate for almost a generation after the death of Lactantius. Only after the middle of the century did it begin slowly to wake up. The impulse was given by external ecclesiastical circumstances which brought the West once more into connection with the Greek church.

After the death of Constantine the Great (337), the administration of the empire was divided among his sons. The relative political independence of the West intensified its intellectual isolation from events in the East. They would, to be sure, have decided in favour of Athanasius; but even decades later educated Christians had not heard anything about Nicea (325) and its creed. This situation changed only when Constantius, the emperor of the East, was able to take control of the West also in 353, and at once tried to establish here too his ecclesiastical government which was directed against Athanasius and the Nicene Creed. He succeeded superficially; only a few firm confessors had to be deported into exile. Yet the majority of the Latin church nevertheless wanted to remain 'orthodox'. The pressure which she had to suffer here and there at the hands of the new imperial bishops determined her further development. The Arian controversy—nobody really had much idea of its theological presuppositions—appeared to the West from the beginning as a dispute concerning the independence of the church, and its freedom of decision in creedal matters. Under Julian the Apostate (361–363) all schools of opinion were tolerated, and the Nicene party rapidly gained the upper hand. In spite of this, his successor Valentinian I, who was orthodox in his personal beliefs, was not yet successful in restoring full unity. The Arian bishops of Constantius remained in office and the synodal decisions which were made against them were not executed. The government was weary of the ecclesiastical quarrels, and it seemed simplest just to ignore them and 'put them on ice'.

This confusion of ecclesiastical relations was accompanied by the continuing obscurity of the intellectual situation. The Arian controversy was based on the data of Greek theology, particularly as created by Origen one hundred years earlier. The problem was to combine the idea of Christ's divinity with monotheism, and to fit it rationally into the setting of a metaphysical view of the world. This was a systematic task in which the West had until then barely taken any part. Even now there remained a widespread inclination here to be satisfied with a plain acknowledgement of the unity of nature of the Father and Son, and to cut short all the further questions that were sure to arise by simply referring to the Nicene Creed. The renunciation of a theologically responsible solution of the problems threatened to separate the West from the like-minded 'Nicene' circles of the East, which were still involved in fierce fights and controversies with the dominant Arian parties. Old differences, bygone misunderstandings, and countless practical and theological difficulties everywhere stood in the way of a general 'Catholic' termination of the church struggle and blocked the way to the desired peace. Only this much was clear: a final settlement had to be accomplished on a firm dogmatic basis, and could not possibly succeed without a positive relation to the political power, or without a re-ordering of the state establishment of the church.

Ambrose was the man who accomplished this task intellectually and politically. Prior to him, there can be named only one who at least understood and aimed at the same goal in a similar way: Bishop Hilary of Poitiers. In many respects he was a forerunner whose work was now completed by Ambrose. Hilary belonged to the inflexible Niceans who had been banished by Constantius to the East. Here, outside the circle of all Western prejudice, the full implications and theological complexity of the quarrel became gradually clear to him, and from then on he tried to enlighten his Western colleagues by continually writing new treatises, 'white papers', and pamphlets about the existing ecclesiastical and theological connections, and to mediate between them and the 'new-Nicene' leaders of the East. Having returned home, he began to establish a practical union in ecclesiastical affairs and forced the remaining Arians more and more on to the defensive. Nevertheless, even Hilary finally failed because of the resistance and indifference of the governmental agencies. His attempt to overthrow the influential bishop Auxentius of Milan ended with his expulsion from Italy, and soon afterwards he died. The new organization of the state-church on a Nicene basis was first accomplished by Ambrose. He brought to an end the intellectual controversy with the Arians. Yet he too could obtain his goal only gradually, and then only with the assistance of the state, and had to maintain it in ever-renewed and wearing contests until at last the new order was firmly established for all time.

Ambrose was the first Latin church father to be born, reared, and educated not as a pagan, but as a Christian. He was likewise the first descendant of the Roman high aristocracy to stand up publicly for the church, and to have found in it his life-work. Both elements were important for his historical significance and decisive for his activity itself. In Ambrose there was an inner confidence and imperturbability of nature which appeared only the more clearly during the crises and storms of his outer life.

7

Of superior intelligence, energetic, a born diplomat and where necessary an extremely adroit tactician, he seems never to have faltered in his real purpose and in his religious and ethical convictions. He was thoroughly genuine in what he demanded, and for all the hardness of his conduct was never rigid, inhuman, or unscrupulous. Detest as we may the aims and method of his actions, the man himself continues to command respect, just as even his adversaries could not withhold respect and recognition in his lifetime. The same clarity and integrity distinguished Ambrose as a theological teacher. His numerous writings, practical, devotional, and dogmatic, are neither particularly original nor especially brilliant, but they display in their objectivity and straightforwardness something earnest and trustworthy which carries conviction. Like all fathers of the Latin church, Ambrose was well trained in rhetoric. Wherever it seemed appropriate, he did not hesitate to use the appropriate devices of passionate overstatement, emotion on display, and highly coloured language and imagery. Yet none is basically less of a rhetorician than he. One realizes that Ambrose stood under the double responsibility as preacher and political leader of his congregation. His speech is always aimed at the essential and the decisive for practice. It is uncomplicated, realistic rather than studied, yet it keeps the entire man in view. Its earnestness moves the conscience, and reveals not the slightest vanity or desire for applause, despite a well-founded self-assurance, which grew over the years.

Ambrose was born in 339 in Trèves. His father, Aurelius Ambrosius, who had risen to the high rank of the prefect of Gaul, resided here. An early death terminated his career, and his widow moved back to Rome with the three children. Even in later years, Ambrose had friends and relatives among the first families here, and perhaps he really did belong, as his family name may indicate, to the famous line of the Aurelians. In these circles of the Roman aristocracy education and culture, which had become rare elsewhere in the West, were still alive. This explains how Ambrose came to learn the Greek language thoroughly and not merely as a school subject—an advantage which proved very useful to him in his later life. As was natural for a man of his ancestry, he at first entered on a career in the Civil Service. Toward the end of the sixties we find him working together with his brother Satyrus as *advocatus* at the central court in Sirmium, then the most important metropolis of the Balkans. Around 370, when he was approximately 30 years of age, he was already appointed governor of the upper Italian provinces, Liguria and Emilia. His residence was Milan, the capital of upper Italy, which had already repeatedly served as residence for the emperors of the West.

Ecclesiastically, Milan was still governed by Bishop Auxentius, a Cappadocian by birth, who had been brought into this office by Constantius after the dismissal of his orthodox predecessor Dionysius. Auxentius, of course, like his whole party, strongly repudiated the name of 'Arian', but he refused to acknowledge the Nicene Creed, and would not promote those who accepted it in Milan. Otherwise he tried to evade any dogmatic controversy and so to maintain his ecclesiastical power; but his opponents already considered him a back number. We do not know what Ambrose's attitude toward him was. The position of Ambrose as a civil official prohibited him from recklessly revealing his personal conviction. On the other hand, his strongly Nicene orthodoxy certainly could not have remained completely unknown during his years in Milan. With Auxentius dying in 374, the Niceans believed their hour to have come; now at last the heresy was to vanish for ever. Against them the adherents of Auxentius fought no less enthusiastically for their ecclesiastical existence. The election campaign threatened to degenerate into a tumult, and Ambrose hastened to the church to establish the necessary order. There—it is related—a child raised his voice to the complete surprise of all, and called 'Bishop Ambrose' into the room, and thereupon as by a miracle those present agreed spontaneously and unanimously to his candidature (*Vita*, 60). The prophetic voice of the child may be a legendary addition; otherwise it appears to be quite conceivable that the quarrelling parties realized it to be the best solution at this critical moment to create as bishop a Nicean, to be sure, yet to a certain extent 'neutral' personality, who was not prejudiced by the previous controversies. Ambrose assures us that he was completely surprised, and sought at first to avoid election. From his career up to then he could certainly not be regarded as prepared for this high ecclesiastical office—he was not even at that time baptized—and without imperial consent he could not possibly accept the appointment. He asked for his ordination at least to be postponed; but when the unconditional consent of Valentinian I arrived from Trèves, he no longer resisted. Before the end of the year 374, the 35-year-old government official was consecrated bishop of Milan.

If government and people had expected from him above all the preservation of the peace of the church, Ambrose did not disappoint them. He naturally insisted upon receiving first baptism and then ordination from a Nicean, and one of his first official acts was the solemn return and burial of the bones of his predecessor, bishop Dionysius, who had died in exile. The change in favour of the Nicene Creed was thus publicly demonstrated. On the other hand, Ambrose showed himself willing to take over into his service the entire staff of Auxentius' clergy. He thus avoided engendering conflict and carrying differences too far. The period which followed justified his generous procedure, for from now on the Milan clergy firmly and faithfully gave their support to their episcopal lord in all disputes.

The abrupt change 'from the platforms of this vain world and the clamour of public acclamation to the chants of the psalmist' (de Paen. II, 8, 72) is somewhat reminiscent of the similar rapid rise of Cyprian; but times had changed since then. This change in the now Christian Roman empire meant much less to Ambrose than to Cyprian any denial of his former interests. The office of bishop of Milan was certainly not inferior to that of the governor of the province in public influence, authority, and responsibility. Indeed, in the precincts of the church he could now find a new, and yet entirely appropriate, sphere of activity for his aristocratic Roman traditions. On the other hand, it is not to be doubted that Ambrose was a convinced and determined Christian already prior to his election. Orthodoxy belonged to the tradition of his family. There was a martyr among his ancestresses, and prior to his elevation to the episcopate his only sister, Marcellina, had vowed life-long virginity. It is hardly accidental that he himself and his brother were still unmarried. Celibacy was esteemed by Ambrose at all times as a higher form of life, particularly appropriate to the Christian ideal, and its maintenance had never, it seems, caused any difficulties to him. If Ambrose was still unbaptized this was nothing unusual, and speaks for rather than against the seriousness of his conviction. An official had at times to decree enactments involving bloodshed and also tolerate opinions and customs in his environment which seemed to be irreconcilable with the idea of a perfect Christian life. Ambrose had possibly already occupied his mind with theological, or at least semi-theological, matters before his change of office. There is something to be said for the view that he was the author of an edition of Josephus' *Jewish War*, and of a paraphrase of the Biblical books of Kings mentioned there but no longer extant. These would then belong in his early years. The choice of a politico-historical subject would fit Ambrose well, and an early literary activity would explain at the same time how the young bishop succeeded in becoming a significant writer so shortly after his election.

To Ambrose, the most essential task of a bishop was at all times Biblical instruction and preaching. However many duties his office imposed upon him in the course of the years, duties of administration and pastoral care, the education of his clergy, and ecclesiastical and civil politics, Ambrose never neglected or failed in his obligations as a preacher. In this, above all, he saw the meaning of his spiritual calling. Although he had a soft voice, he was yet esteemed everywhere as an outstanding preacher and was therefore, as we know from Augustine, heard with pleasure not only by the faithful members of his congregation, but also by outsiders. This admiration applied also to the matter of his sermons. Modern readers may be surprised at this, but the allegorical interpretation used by Ambrose with a credulous and unsuspecting neglect of any literal meaning, was then something new in the West. There were any number who breathed freely when all at once they saw the Old Testament in particular liberated from all apparently meaningless externals, such as painful human weaknesses otherwise beyond comprehension, and many conceptions of God and of the divine nature which to the educated way of thinking appeared unworthy. Instead they found everywhere unsuspected spiritual mysteries and wonderfully profound revelations. Ambrose did not himself invent this method of spiritualizing reinterpretation, but adopted it in essence from his Greek models and particularly from the Alexandrian theologians. Their writings were continuously drawn upon for his sermons, and for the writings resulting from them. Ambrose had no ambition to appear original, and he took the material which he needed from wherever he found it. Entire Biblical books were explained as a whole or in selections by means of the Greek commentaries. Ambrose preferred series of sermons. He began, as it appears, with the first book of the Bible, for which he had an especial liking all his life, and later published tracts on Paradise, on Cain and Abel, on Noah and the ark, etc. Besides Origen, his main source was the Jewish theologian Philo, although recent Greeks as well were called upon. The later exposition of the *Work of the Six Days*, popular and voluminous, was chiefly compiled on the lines of Basil. His one-sided inclination toward spiritualization is here kept in check by a strong affirmation of God's creation and its visible beauty. Older Stoic and other classical traditions have obviously contributed. All the same, the adoption of the material was never carried out uncritically; in the course of time Ambrose revealed an increasing independence also of his Greek theological models. The practical and ethical admonition of the congregation occupied increasing space, and in the beautiful expositions of the Psalms and Luke's gospel,

which date from the last ten years of his life, teaching on redemption and the devotional proclamation of Christ in particular appeared in a new, vividly personal form. However,
Ambrose retained all his life a certain inclination toward speculative explanation and mysterious discoveries on the basis of the
divine word. Allegory seemed to him the higher and proper
theological form of Scripture exegesis, and he took its conclusions especially seriously. In this there is revealed perhaps a
sort of need of his otherwise very practical and realistic nature,
with its inclination to plain faith and morals, for spiritual
expansion.

With these remarks about Ambrose the preacher we have
already anticipated further developments, and must turn back
to the beginning. The first writings which the young bishop
published were two memorial addresses for his brother Satyrus.
Satyrus had also left the public service after Ambrose's election,
and had taken over for Ambrose the administration of his household, but he had died a few months later. The elaborate description of his virtues and career, and of the inseparable love
of the brothers, his grief over the loss, and the exultation at the
thought of his abiding memory of the deceased, all these followed the primitive Roman aristocratic tradition. Only everything has now become at the same time a sermon, being
set in a light of religious edification, and connected with a
corresponding instructional purpose. The orthodox zeal of the
deceased is emphasized, and the whole meditation ends in a
proclamation of the certainty of resurrection, by which it lifts
itself beyond the purely personal. The traditional grounds of
solace thereby attain a far more earnest background. Both
speeches were actually delivered before publication, and are of
interest as to the form of contemporary Christian memorials of
the dead. Soon afterwards, Ambrose took the liberty of paying
a similar spiritual tribute to his sister. He concluded his work on
virgins with the speech which Pope Liberius is supposed to have
delivered at her initiation as a nun.

In the same way, Ambrose had already expressed himself

repeatedly on the topic of virgins and virginity orally as well as in writing during the first years. This was an aspect of the practical life of the congregation which he took especially to heart. His ascetic recommendations are directed almost exclusively to the female sex, to the virgins and 'widows' consecrated to God, who were then not yet grouped together in convents, but had their own status in the church. Ambrose shows himself still untouched by the new impulses which monasticism had brought to the old ideal. In its content his ascetic preaching barely went beyond what was already taught by Cyprian in this respect. There are basically three stages of chastity in the church: marriage, as far as possible only once, widowhood, and the holy virginity of the 'brides of Christ'. Voluntary virginity is a virtue first brought into the world by Christianity; its value and special merit are considered as unquestionable. However, Ambrose was no friend to exaggerated competition or asceticism. The virgin should lead a quiet, secluded life, and within her family dedicate herself above all to prayer, fasting, and sanctification; the inner disposition of humility and dedication is the decisive thing. Nevertheless his ascetic preaching aroused a stir and some anxiety. Women came to Milan from afar in order to receive the veil from his hands. On the other hand, he also met resistance, especially within his own congregation. Many parents preferred to see their daughters well settled as wives, and sought therefore to dissuade them from their ascetic enthusiasm. Yet these were wishes of which Ambrose had not the slightest understanding. In such cases he firmly took the more pious children under his protection against their parents. In all this, he is the authoritative representative of a fourth-century tendency which was growing in other ways also. Ambrose is a typical defender of the contemporary Christian and late classical ideal of life, which recognizes spiritual seriousness and ethical discipline in matters of sex almost solely in the form of renunciation.

In the long run, the new bishop could not content himself with practical theological tasks. The dogmatic situation in

upper Italy and the areas adjacent urgently required, as we have
seen, a settlement, and Ambrose was not the man to withdraw
for long from the expectations fixed on him by the Niceans
from all sides. Their position was far from being firmly established, especially in the neighbouring Illyrian provinces. Their
adversaries were frequently predominant, and spread their influence from there to Italy too. As a first victory, Ambrose and
his fellow-believers were successful in promoting the election of
an orthodox bishop in Sirmium. In addition, the validity of the
Nicene faith was solemnly endorsed anew at a Council held
there. In these controversies which were to accomplish the final
victory of the Nicene party, it would be wrong to regard
Ambrose only as a church politician. Faith and church policy
completely coincided in him. Acknowledgement of the unqualified and consubstantial divinity of Christ was in accordance with the nature of his personal soteriology. It was therefore
for him also the only possible foundation for a truly Christian church. The earnestness of this claim made of him a dogmatic theologian in the years that followed. Ambrose did not
rest until he had worked through the whole range of the Trinitarian problem, section by section, and had established it anew
in public. Going beyond Hilary he followed here the modern
Neo-Nicene theology of the East, yet did not renounce the older
traditions of his Latin homeland. Independently and preg-
nantly they were united with the results of the more advanced
Greek theology into a new system. By this means Ambrose
brought the Arian controversy to an end in the West intellectually also.

The study of the most important writings did not cause him
any difficulties, owing, as we know, to his knowledge of Greek,
and he undertook it with zeal and earnestness. Moreover, he
also got personally in touch with Basil the Great. The old
Western distrust of 'academic' theology was out of the question to a man of his type; the frequent suspicion of the Greeks
that the Westerners were incapable of differentiating at all
between Father and Son would have been entirely unfounded

in his case. The distinction between the one inseparable 'substance' of God, in which alone rests the divine unity, and the three 'persons' of the deity, not to be confused one with another, was a matter of course to Ambrose, and from the outset made any confusion impossible. All this had long ago been formulated into concepts by Tertullian. The problem now was to vindicate against the Arians also the equality of the Persons, and to exclude finally that subordinationist doctrine of the emanation of the Son from the Father, and of the Spirit from the Son, which lessened their rank. All three are equally eternal, equally original, in their respective special natures indissolubly united one with another. From this point of view, the adoption of essentially Athanasian and 'Neo-Nicene' ideas caused no further difficulty. Ambrose unfolded his teaching on the Trinity—always in the medium of sermons—first in a voluminous work *On Faith* published in two parts. There followed a three-volume treatise *On the Holy Spirit*, the position of the third Person having been until then only inadequately dealt with in this connection. The circle closed finally with Ambrose's great examination of *The Mystery of the Lord's Incarnation* in which the consequences of the Trinitarian theology are drawn in respect to the Person of the God-man. In this important book Ambrose went most decisively further than his Eastern predecessors, and began to examine new problems.

The determination and confidence with which Ambrose dealt with this complex of problems within a few years (378–382) is astounding. It would be incomprehensible if in respect of philosophy his mind had been a *tabula rasa*, as was the case with most of the Latin theologians of the time. From the outset of his ecclesiastical career at the latest, Ambrose must have come in contact with that Platonic and Neo-Platonic philosophy which, for a deeper systematic understanding of the doctrine of the Trinity, could hardly be neglected. The priest Simplician, who instructed Ambrose as a catechumen, lived in these traditions. If he nevertheless condemns the philosophers in the usual way, he is thinking of the Epicureans and Stoics, and above all of Aristotle. The Platonists are tacitly excepted; at any rate they are nowhere explicitly attacked, and of Plato it is said once again that he derived his theological knowledge from the Old Testament. This concept of philosophy would have been nothing new in the East. In the West, however, it signified a change, which was to prove decisive in Augustine's conversion, and pointed to the future. As to Ambrose himself, this statement needs yet again a proviso. Indeed, it is just the limitation of his philosophical interests, and of his philosophical ability, which makes the speed and general success of his dogmatic work understandable, although he hardly could have accomplished it without philosophical education. Ambrose was willing to learn from the Neo-Platonists. He adopted, for instance, their conception of substance; yet what he was looking for was not a new metaphysic. Problems of this kind he did not pursue. All that mattered to him was to define the revealed Christian truth in an intellectually neat and consistent form and thus make it unassailable. His knowledge of God as such is not a conclusion of his systematic thinking, but is based on the Holy Scripture. Proof from the Scripture is with Ambrose not something adventitious, but an absolute necessity. It receives the most attention in his dogmatic writings. Inasmuch as it deals with God, all theology is for Ambrose exclusively a theology of revelation, and must not seek to be anything else but this. The radical and, if you like, Neo-Platonic emphasis on the distance separating the divine from every created being, has the purpose of making impossible any analogical, speculative bridge built from the side of the creature. Only God's own work and word can span this gap. This ontological dualism is also the presupposition for the essential understanding of Christ's divinity, and for the corresponding extremely 'dyophysite' construction of his doctrine of the Person of the God-man, which sharply separates the two 'natures' of the Saviour. There is no emanationist and gradual combination of divinity and humanity, or of the supernatural and natural worlds.

This once established, it is comparatively easy for faith to be

satisfied with a few concise formulae. It will show how much
it is in earnest from the religious point of view by the very fact
that it prefers to fear rather than comprehend the depths of the
Godhead (*de Fid*. V, 18, 221). In this renunciation of all speculative reason, and this stress on faith, and the obedience of faith,
as the essential element of religion, Ambrose is a true Westerner.
In this his thoughts remind one of Tertullian's religious position. Also reminiscent of Tertullian is the close relationship
between revelational theology and a determined, almost massive rationalism. Nobody has expressed so inflexibly, so forth-
rightly, and so powerfully the logical force and form of
Trinitarian thought as Ambrose himself. There is therefore
something to be said for the view that he was also the author
of the so-called 'Athanasian Creed', the typical Western profession of faith in the Holy Trinity which endeavours to close
once for all with its forty stereotyped and rhythmically formulated clauses any conceivable gap in the construction of the
doctrine. This also is characteristic, that Ambrose after having
once developed his doctrine of God in the controversial years
of his youth, never later returned to this area of dogmatic
theology. The truth is considered as already found and finally
established. The only concern henceforth was to preserve it
immovably and to defend it and, furthermore, to deal forth-
rightly with the manifold spiritual and practical problems of the
church's daily life and to solve them.

As has already been said, Ambrose's attitude to church politics was in complete accord with his theological convictions.
His goal was the public recognition of the one, true Catholic
church, standing on the immovable foundation of the one
orthodox, and therefore also only legitimate, creed. This ideal
marked an innovation in so far as the imperial church as such
had scarcely been a real 'Confessional Church' until then.
Indeed, in the course of the Arian controversy different creeds,
among them also the Nicene, had been formulated and proclaimed; but the church policy of the state had for tactical
reasons again and again put them aside, changed them, and

finally endeavoured to save the unity of the church by eliminating all question of a creed. Now a new period began. As the
outcome of the Arian controversy the Nicene Creed was
understood as the dogmatic and 'confessional' solution of the
problem of the state-church, and no weakening or exception
was any longer tolerated.

We misjudge the religious meaning of the contemporary
Catholic ideal of the imperial church if we place it, in this form,
in direct opposition to the idea of freedom of conscience, and
try to understand it merely as a result of priestly love of power
and intolerance. The decisive thing is the underlying faith in the
clear objectivity and general accessibility of the dogmatically
formulated truth, which must therefore remain in force 'ecu-
menically' for the whole world. Ambrose himself indeed was
a convinced exponent of freedom of faith and gave it unrestricted scope in practice in the personal relations of individuals.
If he unconditionally defended the Nicene foundation of the
Catholic church, he did not have in mind the individual believer. His concern here was to protect the independence of the
church as a whole against the illicit interference of the political
powers, whose lack of dogmatic scruple had been sufficiently
experienced in the early disputes under Constantine. In view
of the despotism and caprice of the imperial religious policy,
this was a very understandable concern, with the West having
an absolute Nicene majority. Everything taken into consideration, the conflicts in which Ambrose carried his demands clearly
prove his moral superiority too. Yet the contest for the 'freedom' and 'rights' of his church, which he undertook in the
name of 'faith', was of course always simultaneously a fight for
ecclesiastical supremacy, i.e. it was a power struggle which, as
such, he attempted to win by co-operation with the state, and
with use of governmental measures against all 'heretics' who
thought differently. Ambrose did not sense the contradiction
arising at this point. He still held to the old ideals of the period
of persecution, and liked to stress that faith must remain independent, and can be accepted only in freedom. He abhorred

external pressure. For instance, he indignantly broke fellowship with the Gallican bishops, because they had for the first
time, with the help of the state courts, had ecclesiastical opponents executed. Nevertheless, Ambrose the church politician
sought to secure as far as possible the predominance of his
church. In his actions even Ambrose could not always escape
the ambiguity of all ecclesiastical power policy.

We will not pursue in detail the complicated incidents of the
church politics of those significant years, in part so difficult to
grasp. They were in their perpetual ebb and flow determined
in no small degree by the over-all political situation. In 378 the
Goths had decisively defeated the Roman army, and overflowed
almost the whole Balkans. Only with much trouble were they
gradually calmed and settled in the newly conquered terri-
tories. For the most part the Goths were still pagans; however,
in so far as they had been converted—by Ulfilas—they had not
become orthodox, but (in the opinion of the Niceans) 'Arian'
Christians. Wherever they came, Arianism raised its head again.
Ambrose recognized the gravity of the danger to the church
and was, not without reason, convinced that the political
fidelity of the Roman heretics too, now allied religiously with
the Goths, could not be trusted. From this standpoint he tried
to warn the rulers and arouse them to ecclesiastico-political
resistance. He observes that the Goths are the people Gog, of
whom Ezekiel had prophesied (Ezek. xxxviii f.). He who
wants to fight them has to stand fast in the true faith and can
then be certain of the victory. On the other hand, 'belief in the
Roman Empire was first overthrown, where faith in God gave
way' (de Fid. II, 16, 139; ANF, 10, 241). With disgust Ambrose
describes an Arian bishop who dared to appear 'in front of the
Roman army, defiled with Gothic ungodliness, and dressed like
a heathen with collar and bracelets'. Such conduct, he thinks,
is not only sacrilegious for a priest, but must be regarded as
altogether unchristian, for it is 'contrary to Roman custom'
(Ep. 10, 9). Even as a bishop, Ambrose remained wholly a
Roman; 'Germanic' and 'Arian', 'Roman' and 'Catholic-

Christian' become almost synonymous expressions. Fidelity to the empire is a Christian obligation. Ambrose commends it not only to the Roman citizens but also to the barbarians living outside the empire (*Vita*, 36).

Nevertheless, under pressure of emergency the government felt at times urged to compromise ecclesiastically with the Balkan Goths and those who shared their views. Ambrose had to tolerate the requisition of a church even in Milan, evidently in order that it might be offered to the Arians if necessary. But the political stabilization also restored the old ecclesiastical order. The young emperor Gratian, to whom Ambrose had dedicated his book on faith, took up his residence in Milan, and willingly allowed himself to be advised in questions of religion and church politics. His more important co-ruler, the Spanish general Theodosius, at the same time brought the Nicene Creed to recognition in the Orient also. The conclusion of these uneasy years came in 381, in the East at the great Council of Constantinople, and in the West at the Council of Aquileia, which stood completely under the leadership of Ambrose. Here, the last adherents of the older system of the state-church, who did not want to acknowledge the Nicene Creed, were arraigned in due form, and then dismissed from their episcopal sees by the agencies of the government. The minutes of the sessions are preserved. It is obvious that the proceedings at this religious convention were quite stormy. The condemned bishops, who came from Illyrium, had been deceived about the true purpose and character of the synod. Instead of the promised general and free discussion there awaited them a one-sided interrogation by their declared enemies who recklessly, and at last even violently, brought the transactions to an end without heeding their protests. In his official report to the government Ambrose set the proceedings in a considerably milder light. At all events the victory was won, and orthodoxy had officially attained exclusive control in the whole of Italy and also in Illyria.

In the following years Ambrose became a leading personality in the Privy Council of the Milan court and we find him repeatedly entrusted with political tasks. When Gratian was defeated in 383 by a co-emperor from Gaul, and then murdered, Ambrose together with the leading army officers took over the protection of his 12-year-old brother, Valentinian II. The bishop was twice sent to Trèves for diplomatic negotiations where he succeeded in saving Italy at least for the young emperor. The usurper later saw in Ambrose his real opponent, who had halted the eagles of his legions at the borders of the Alps (*Ep.* 24, 7). It was then still most unusual for the clergy to undertake political missions. Ambrose was no medieval hierarch. He would rather have understood his political services from the viewpoint of the bishop's traditional privilege to intercede for the weak (*Ep.* 24, 5). The emperor's mother, leading young Valentinian by the hand, had personally implored for his assistance (*Obit. Val.* 28). How could he then have refused? He wanted to act only in the framework of the duties of his office (*Ep.* 57, 12), for the protection of the faith and of his church. Ambrose tried to keep to this line also in his later years. He liked to emphasize that it was not his task to intervene in matters of state. But on account of his position and abilities political decisions came to him almost automatically, and the more his reputation grew with the years, the less could Ambrose withdraw from responsibility when things became serious (*Obit. Val.* 24). In his opinion, where peace, humanity, and justice are at stake, in the last resort even a bishop must not remain neutral. The line between spiritual and political competence naturally could not be drawn easily. It required a great deal of human tact, and of political acumen and responsibility, and all the cleverness and prudence of an Ambrose to give the right ecclesiastical verdict at the critical moment; that is to say, to make it not only morally convincing, but also politically effective. At any rate such action has nothing to do with opportunism in the usual sense. Ambrose never forgot whom and what he had to represent as bishop, and that is why he acquired the greatness and dignity of a churchman who really possesses authority.

It is not possible here to discuss all the political and ecclesi-astico-political happenings in which Ambrose came forward in this manner, and occasionally almost seemed to play the role of a 'Chancellor' or clerical Minister of State. We restrict our-selves to the most famous examples. The insecure political situation in which the Milanese government found itself after the fall of Gratian soon showed its religio-political implications. One after another, paganism first, and then Arianism too, sought to improve their situation, and to win back positions already abandoned. To be sure, the old Roman religion was neither forbidden nor had it disappeared under the Christian emperors, yet it was nevertheless more and more driven on to the defensive. Perhaps on Theodosius' instigation Gratian was, just shortly before his death, about to strike a new blow. The pagan Roman priests were deprived of their government sub-sidies and privileges, the altar and statue of Victory were re-moved from the Senate house, and from among the imperial titles there vanished the traditional designation of *Pontifex Maximus*, the highest pagan sacerdotal office. These decrees were of a far-reaching symbolical significance, for the new imperial régime, confessionally committed, now relinquished once and for all its still to some extent 'impartial' attitude to the old religion, and people had simply to accept this. True, the senate, in which the Christians did not yet have a majority, wanted immediately to protest against these enactments which especially affected Rome; but its delegation had not even been received in Milan. Now, after the change in government, an opportune moment seemed to have come to venture a new attempt.

The leader of the rejected delegation, Quintus Aurelius Symmachus, had in 384 just become the holder of the prefec-ture, i.e. the highest imperial office in the city of Rome, and was authorized to write the petition. He was the most famous writer and rhetorician Rome then had, educated in Neo-Platonic philosophy, himself a senator of a very old aristocratic family, and, in addition, a relative of Ambrose. We cannot read his

8

petition even today without being moved: it was the swan-song
of the proud, Roman religion. Symmachus defends the memories and institutions under which the venerable Rome had once
become great. He emphasizes that Victory had earlier been
protected even under Christian emperors, and had been of
service to their rule. He speaks of the unselfish service to the
general public of the priests, and particularly of the chaste
vestal virgins, and thinks that the revenues for this have long
ago changed from a free demonstration of favour to a historical
legal claim. He even dares to recall at last the famines, and the
terrible end of Gratian, who probably had not known at all of
the fateful order issued in his name. Not a single disrespectful
word occurs. Symmachus strains every nerve in order to make
retreat as easy as possible for the emperor, but basically he himself feels that he is fighting for an order whose historical day
has passed. He contents himself with begging for nothing more
than tolerance for the ancestral religion, and as a philosopher
refers to the heritage common to all religion: 'What difference
does it make, by what pains each seeks the truth? We cannot
attain to so great a secret by one road; but this discussion is
rather for persons at ease, we offer now prayers, not conflict'
(*Rel. Symm.* 10; *ANF*, 10, 415).

As a matter of fact, the advance seemed to have succeeded.
Pagan and Christian members of the Privy Council alike voted
in favour of this application, by which they hoped to put the
leading circles of the eternal city in their debt. At this moment,
however, Ambrose learned about the negotiations, and his
intervention forced a decision the other way. In such a case, he
declared, the bishop is directly responsible, for this is a matter
of God's business, and a question of religion. Without going
through the 'official channels' or waiting for special authoriza-
tion, he wrote a letter to the emperor as his spiritual adviser:
'All people who live under the Roman government serve you,
you Emperors and Princes of the world. You yourself, however, serve the almighty God and the holy faith' (*Ep.* 17, 1).
There was no more to be said. 'I am surprised how it came into

the mind of certain people to think you were obliged to renew
the altars of the pagan gods' (*Ep.* 17, 3). The emperor is a
Christian and has as such—no matter what his political advisers
might wish—to represent the cause of the faith in the empire
too. In such matters he must at least never seek to retract a step
he has once taken. After Ambrose had received a copy of the
petition on his request, he answered it in detail once more in a
second writing directed to the wider public. In this he takes up
to a certain extent the neutral position of his adversaries—
although there can of course be no question in principle of an
equality of religious rights. But this is precisely how he makes
it possible for himself to repudiate most effectively the complaints of the pagans. The church does not have to fear a comparison of her rights with those of her opponents. When they
complain about the removal of the altar—what shall the Christian senators say when they are again forced to participate in
an idolatrous sacrifice? When they lament the lack of subsidies
for their few priests and vestals—what about the countless
Christian nuns and clergy who receive not one penny from the
public funds and cannot even accept legacies? As a matter of
fact, the church, having become great under persecution, was
at the time still living essentially from her own strength, while
the ancient cult, having been connected with the body politic
from the outset, would because of its very nature go to pieces
without public support. Ambrose naturally also protested
against the superstitious conjuring up of an alleged anger of the
gods and declares, contrary to his usual manner, that political
successes or disasters are completely independent of the question
of religion. In an interesting historico-theological excursus, he
describes progress as the actual power that moves nature and
history, and he mocks the nostalgic complaints of the Roman
senate. Rome is in reality not senile and is by no means ashamed
to make a change for the better. 'Only this I had formerly in
common with the Barbarians: that I had not yet come to know
God' (*Ep.* 18, 7).

Ambrose had composed a refutation which was also a

masterpiece, more popular and robust, less considered and polished as to detail than the refined work of art of his opponent, whose nobly suppressed emotion is of a peculiar charm. But he is more powerful and fresh in what has to be said and is said, supported by the force of conviction of a determined faith, which is fully sure both of itself and of the victorious power of its reasons. Ambrose later represented it as though purely spiritual reasons had decided the issue of this matter. The young emperor had risen 'like a Daniel' against his advisers, and made the decision in the power of the Holy Spirit (*Obit. Val.* 19). Yet this has undoubtedly to be regarded as an idealization. In reality, the men of the Privy Council must have decided to yield. There was no ignoring the emphasis with which Ambrose referred among other things also to the older co-emperor Theodosius, whose hostile attitude to the pagans was sufficiently known (*Ep.* 17, 12). Indeed, he went even further: 'At any rate', he says, in his first letter to Valentinian, 'if a different decision should be made, we bishops cannot by any means accept it calmly or ignore it. You may come to a church—but you will not find a priest there, or if you find one, he will resist you' (*Ep.* 17, 13). 'We are not in a position to share in the errors of others' (*Ep.* 17, 14). This was an open threat of excommunication, and the government could at this time risk a church struggle even less than a humiliation of the pagans. Ambrose had prevailed, but the disposition of the authorities to him certainly had not become friendlier. In the following year, this became evident.

The last reaction with which Ambrose had to cope of the Arianism which had infiltrated with the Goths, was virtually insignificant with respect to the whole ecclesiastical development. It was not supported by any strong religious movement, and did not possess any popular power. The foreign adherents of the defeated Illyrian heresy who had gathered in the shadow of the small Milanese court did not as formerly seek leadership in the church. They wanted merely to obtain the right to exist of their ecclesiastical separatist group, and relied in this entirely on the assistance of the secular power. But just for this reason this conflict becomes important from another aspect. The church struggle of the year 385–386 was the crucial test of the stability and the duration of the new system which no longer tolerated any loosening or breaking of its dogmatic order. Here, therefore, also the secular power met a limit which it had indeed once drawn by its own authority, but could no longer itself overstep. Ambrose was the embodiment of this new order. He defended it against the crown, and reduced the quarrel immediately to ultimate principles, theological and canonical. Therein lies its permanent importance.

Without doubt, the beginnings of the conflict did not originate in a general framework of church politics, but solely in the personal desire of a single personality, temperamental and accustomed to domination, namely the emperor's mother Justina. Theologically and politically, the wife of Valentinian I still lived with the viewpoint of an earlier period. Gratian, under whom the change had taken place, intentionally kept his mother away from governmental affairs. On the occasion of the bishop's election in Sirmium, there had already arisen a conflict and on that occasion Ambrose had remained victorious. In the early part of the reign of Valentinian II she had of necessity restrained herself, for it was none other than Ambrose himself whom she had to beg for support in a humiliating scene. Now finally, Justina felt herself again free to foster, at least in the environment of her own palace, those ecclesiastical ideas which appeared correct to her. Her Illyrian court chaplain Mercurinus was chosen as the anti-Nicene bishop of Milan, and he assumed thereupon the significant name 'Auxentius'. The emperor was a child and submitted to her desires, and the court was so indignant at the dictatorial bearing of Ambrose that it wanted him to be humiliated. The demand directed at first to him in the spring of 385 could be considered as moderate: it was desired that a small church only, situated outside the city wall, should be placed at the disposal of Auxentius. We remember that Ambrose had to tolerate a similar action of the emperor

Gratian only a few years earlier. However, times had changed since then, and so he bluntly refused the request. Ambrose knew that public opinion, i.e. the whole Catholic population of Milan, shared his convictions and stood firmly behind him. How, he asks, could he as a priest of God deliver up the temple of God to the heretical wolves? He himself has described to us the dramatic scene in which the controversy took place. He had been ordered personally to the Privy Council to negotiate the conveyance. There, face to face with the authorities, he was, however, not at all abashed, and insisted on the right of his case 'with the steadfastness of a priest'. Suddenly there was a tumult outside. The people, who had been informed about the proceedings, broke into the palace, and the guards were unable to stop them! All were ready 'to let themselves be killed for the faith of Christ'. Frightened, the emperor waived his demand. Ambrose himself had to be asked to calm the crowd, which he succeeded in doing immediately. So the matter seemed to be happily settled. But, as Ambrose complains, disfavour was now aroused against him more than ever (*Serm. Aux.* 29). Neither the empress nor the government was willing to accept such a defeat. The court absented itself from Milan for a long time. The main object was to prepare the attack better and to furnish it above all with a formal legal basis.

In January 386 there was issued a regular imperial edict which granted the right of public assembly to all adherents of the faith, as formerly decreed 'under Constantius of blessed memory', i.e. of the anti-Nicene, so called 'homoean' theology of Auxentius. Those, however, who presumed upon 'having the exclusive power of such assembly' were at the same time threatened with death as instigators of revolt, as breakers of the church's peace, and insulting the emperor's majesty (*Cod. Theod.* XVI, 1, 4). According to this, the government seemed to be willing to renounce the unity of the state-church, yet combined this completely new regulation with sanctions the severity of which were entirely unheard of, compared with anything previously in force. Significantly, the responsible official had declined to draw up the law, and had therefore lost his position. However, this strange decree should not be taken at its face value. In reality, it was only issued to secure the desired public recognition for Mercurinus-Auxentius, and the exaggerated threats of the second portion were also aimed at one man only, namely, Ambrose, who was intended to be intimidated by this. Yet nobody could then know how far such an attack so menacingly opened would actually lead. Ambrose realized that only courage and inflexible consistency could save him and his cause in this situation, and made his preparations accordingly.

In order not to have to weather the storm upon his own responsibility only, he hastily gathered a handful of bishops from the surrounding area, who stood by him with admirable courage, and on their part unanimously encouraged him to persevere. When the imperial delegate then again demanded, not long before Easter, the surrender no longer of the outlying church, but of the larger new basilica, Ambrose had it occupied by the faithful populace, while he himself retreated to the church outside the wall. The congregation was inspired and held by sermons, addresses, and hymns. Ambrose had distributed gold-pieces among the crowd adhering to him, and after —very much against his directions and desire—an Arian presbyter had been thrashed soundly in the open street, very soon no partisan of Auxentius dared any more appear in public. The whole city, even to the street-gangs of youths, sided with Ambrose. In spite of the soldiers on guard the people streamed in masses into the church. These were days of enthusiastic exultation and of a general readiness to fight and suffer which, the young Augustine also, among others, lived through, and which remained unforgettable to all those participating in it. These were events simply unheard of in the declining years of ancient society. How far off were those times when the population of a city could yet be summoned to act upon its own political responsibility!

The soul and centre of the resistance was naturally Ambrose

himself. He restrained himself from public action and instead made 'the congregation' act—as though spontaneously. He declared, 'I have not stirred up the people. It is God's business and not mine, to calm them down, if he wishes' (*Ep.* 20, 10). Nobody wished to resist government measures if enforced; but still less could the possibility of yielding, or of approval of the injustice, be considered. Ambrose assured them time and again of his readiness for any kind of martyrdom: Christ desires the suffering of His disciples, and 'I know that whatever I must suffer, I shall suffer for Christ's sake' (*Serm. Aux.* 8). The emperor may do 'whatever royal power is customarily used for; I am willing to accept that which has been all along the fate of priests' (*Serm. Aux.* 1). Ambrose clearly understood that in his situation everything depended on keeping the fight on this spiritual level, for a violent riot would have had disastrous effects. On the contrary, the general readiness to suffer was his real weapon. They reproach us, he says, with a 'tyrannical' attitude: well then, 'we have our despotism; the tyranny of the priest is his weakness; "when I am weak", says the apostle (II Cor. xii. 10), "then I am strong"' (*Ep.* 20, 23). Ambrose had here made a discovery which he, of course wrongly, refers to Paul. Passive resistance, here for the first time exercised in the grand style, will remain henceforth the most important weapon of the church in all controversies with the secular power. It is in fact a weapon which Ambrose handled with calculation, and which opened to him possibilities of public propaganda even in the sphere of developed late Roman despotism. But this weapon demanded from the congregation which was to use it a high degree of readiness to make sacrifices and of moral energy, and from him who wished to manipulate it an extraordinary courage and cold-blooded determination. Moreover, Ambrose did not hesitate to make strong attacks against the heretics 'who make common cause with the imperial power' (*Exp. Luc.* VIII, 17). Auxentius appears as a bloodthirsty 'Scythian' barbarian wanting to move the church around as if it were a gipsy caravan (*Ep.* 20, 12); and that raging woman, the empress, takes the part of a tempting Eve, an Herodias or a Jezebel.

A direct assault upon the churches occupied by the people was in these circumstances impracticable for the government, so they tried another way. Shortly before Palm Sunday, the imperial tribune Dalmatius came to Ambrose and at first expressed his surprise still to find him about, for they had wanted for a long time to banish him. He then invited him in the name of the emperor to negotiations at the palace. The conflict with the anti-bishop had now to be brought to an end. Auxentius had already chosen his judges (evidently leading personalities of the court, among them even some heathens) and Ambrose had the same right. If he would, however, rather avoid such a court of arbitration, then he would be allowed to quit the field of his own accord. The carriage was ready, he could travel under safe conduct, and not a hair of his head would be touched. The government now obviously renounced half-measures and went all out. So much was clear: Ambrose could not agree to the offer of a court of arbitration at the palace without giving up as a lost cause what had been his case from the very beginning. The very alternative proposal of a voluntary retreat made this clear. But how could he now avoid the air of intransigence and open disobedience if he did not agree to a settlement which seemed such a fair compromise? Ambrose once more took up his pen and answered with one of his great political letters, addressed directly to the person of the 'most gracious Emperor and most blessed Augustus Valentinian'. First, the situation and legal order until then existing are depicted in a few concise lines. For this, Ambrose skilfully refers simply to Valentinian I. This emperor, he says, had always refused to transgress the limits of his political commission. 'In matters of faith, and in any problems of the ecclesiastical constitution, the judgement can be passed only by a person who is appointed to this on account of his office, and who is legally in the same position, i.e. bishops can be tried only by bishops' (Ep. 21, 2). Nobody is forcing the people to stand by Ambrose—they themselves have decided for him as their legitimate bishop, and for the cause of the faith (*Ep.* 21, 6 ff.). Ambrose, however, could not possibly appear before an alien political court of arbitration. Under the shadow of the new anti-Nicene law, this would in any case at the moment be a farce. Auxentius may act as a bishop in a city where he is considered to be one. Besides, were the emperor not so young, he himself would realize 'what kind of a bishop he could possibly be, who leaves to laymen the decision about his legitimacy as priest' (*Ep.* 21, 5). All this is said with the highest reverence and due respect for the imperial majesty. 'I have not learned', the letter ends, with a side-glance at his former activity as ambassador, 'to represent in the Privy Council anything other than your interest. I am no courtier and cannot participate in political intrigues at the court' (*Ep.* 21, 20).

As we see, the dogmatic inviolability of the church is now completed and supplemented by this further claim of the indispensable independence of her clergy, deduced from her legal structure. This is an essential product of the struggle which at first had begun as a conflict about the property of a single church building. The principle was not directed against the congregation as such, for as things stood its consent on the contrary could be presupposed without much ado. Hence, it needed for proof not a special divine law, and particularly no reference to the Old Testament. The bishop simply counts as the competent, elected, and authoritative representative of his church. If his right and independence in case of emergency were not to be respected, then the 'freedom' of the church was a deceitful word and an illusion. Seen in this light, the clerical claim against the secular power was simply necessary and consistent. Yet this implies that the imperial authority also was restricted by the right of the church. This is the second consequence of the controversy, drawn with full vigour by Ambrose. To the emperor, he says, naturally belong the palaces, but not the churches (*Ep.* 20, 19). As a Christian, he stands within the church and not above her. In the church the bishops are accustomed to rule over the emperor and not the emperor over the bishops (*Ep.* 21, 4). If therefore the emperor is designated a 'son of the church'—here Ambrose coins a new expression which will never again be lost sight of—this is no insult, but an honour (*Serm. Aux.* 36). Thus prior to all the popes, Ambrose already taught and defended a sharp, 'Western' distinction of the 'powers', and he did it with full awareness of its fundamental importance.

For him these ideas were set against a still broader background. Ambrose was not satisfied with securing the independence of the church. He claimed rather a quite general moral and legal control of all, even the imperial power. To be sure, he is told 'that everything is allowed to the emperor and everything stands at his disposal' (*Ep.* 20, 19), yet this insidious claim is false. In his own person, even the emperor is obliged to keep the law; even the emperor must never illegally bring under his power even the smallest hut. Yet the people, if necessary, must bear injustice in such instances, although they cannot approve of it (*Serm. Aux.* 33), while the rights of God remain completely unassailable, and the obedience of faith has absolute validity. Ambrose basically still thought in a republican way. As he understood and defended his own position and responsibility in the church in the spirit of the old Roman official, so he conceives of the authority of the monarchy—the mere existence of which is already to some degree a sign of political decadence (*Exam.* V, 52)—as by no means despotic or 'Byzantine'; it would otherwise become a 'tyranny'. Of course, one may say that we encounter elsewhere in the rhetorical tradition similar points of view and classical reminiscences. They are natural to Ambrose from the first, in consequence of his aristocratic Roman education and descent. But the decisive factor in the seriousness of his claim is that it is now brought forward in the name of God and backed by his commandments. Not in vain does the story of Naboth's vineyard (I Kings xxi) stand in the Bible. For the churchman God's word converts the ideal which cannot bind into a real obligation. 'God's law has taught us what we ought to do; human laws cannot teach this. They compel timid souls to change their mind by force; but to inspire faith, this they cannot do' (*Ep.* 21, 10). 'Trusting in God, I do not shrink from telling you emperors what in my opinion is right' (*Ep.* 57, 1). And behind such statements stands not merely an individual, private conviction, but the living social reality of the church.

On Maundy Thursday in the year 386, the government decided to break off the hopeless quarrel. Quietly and without bloodshed, the imperial colours were removed from the vainly besieged basilica, the punishments already decreed were annulled, and the prisoners released. There was no other way out. In the end even the soldiers to whom Ambrose had directly appealed in his speeches had left their posts and taken the part of the faithful people. This looked like the end of the exciting contest, when some weeks later on the occasion of the dedication of a newly built church the relics of two 'martyrs' were found, decapitated giants, 'such as the old days produced' (*Ep.* 22, 2). Saints 'Gervasius and Protasius' were transported triumphantly to the basilica, soon to be generally called 'Ambrosian', and here solemnly buried. There followed the expected miracles and healings. Ambrose conducted the service, and his sermon for the occasion directed the common enthusiasm into the desired direction: 'Now you all see; these are the comrades whom I choose. . . . Such men have I won for you, my holy people, as your helpers, men who are profitable to all, and harmful to none! . . . Lord Jesus, thanks to thee, that thou hast raised up again at such a time the strong spirit of the holy martyrs; for more than ever thy church needs thy protection today' (*Ep.* 22, 10). The tense situation was not to last much longer. A civil war between the Western rulers, which Ambrose tried in vain to prevent, drove Valentinian II to flight. After the overthrow of the usurper, the victor Theodosius took over the control of the whole empire practically alone. In strained co-operation with him, the life-work of Ambrose came to an end during the years that followed.

Theodosius 'the Great' was not only an excellent general, but also as sovereign an independent and by no means insignificant personality. He was the first emperor to adopt for himself the ideal of a dogmatically fixed state-church, which he had realized already in the East. This policy was at the same time in conformity with his personal, strongly Catholic piety. Yet the changing necessities of the day forced him also to proceed flexibly, and where necessary to show consideration for opposing groups. Personally, Ambrose had a proper understanding of such difficulties. Despite this, however, it was inevitable that the political interests of the emperor and the ecclesiastical interests represented by Ambrose should occasionally come into tension one with the other, and then their good relations were disturbed. Ambrose, like all his contemporaries, did not recognize any separation between the political responsibility and the personal religious duties of the ruler, and he considered the protection and advancement of the church in all circumstances an obligation of faith. In the years 388–391 Theodosius resided principally in Milan. It is fascinating to follow in detail the ebb and flow of the relationship between the two men during these years. We restrict ourselves, however, to the best known and most important incidents.

Theodosius also, as the new lord of Rome, was soon confronted with the question whether he should again grant to the city the cancelled religious revenues, for the senate had again forwarded the old petition. 'I did not hesitate', said Ambrose, 'to put my point of view publicly and immediately before the most gracious Emperor' (Ep. 57, 4). On account of its long history, the matter had grown into a question of ecclesiastical prestige, in which compliance had become impossible. Ambrose gave the emperor to understand that if necessary he was resolved to go to the utmost lengths, and he ostentatiously stayed away from the palace for some days until the problem was settled in his way. Even more dramatic was the course taken by another conflict. In the Far East of the empire, the bishop of Callinicum had instigated a tumult, and had allowed gangs of monks to set on fire the synagogue of that place. In great anger Theodosius vowed duly to punish this breach of public peace, and decreed rebuilding at the cost of the guilty persons. Yet again Ambrose raised a protest. It was, he declared, virtually blasphemous to permit such a triumph to the God-forsaken Jews. 'Which is more important, the idea of law and order or the cause of religion?' The penal law must take second place to the commandment of faith (*Ep.* 40, 11; *LCC*, V, 233). When Theodosius still hesitated, he was addressed by Ambrose during the worship before the assembled congregation. The bishop refused to offer mass until the emperor had expressly promised the revocation of his order. Thoroughly angry, Theodosius arranged henceforth to leave Ambrose uninformed about transactions in the Privy Council (*Ep.* 51, 2).

Yet Ambrose did not always appear in such a questionable role. There were also cases where he exercised his ministry less as a church politician than as a real pastor, and called the emperor to order as a 'son of the church'. The famous 'penance of Theodosius' belongs in this connection. In order to avenge a bloody riot in the Macedonian city of Thessalonica, Theodosius had had several thousand unsuspecting inhabitants enticed into the theatre, and one and all massacred by the soldiers (390). Even in a period accustomed to barbaric punishments, this butchery provoked general horror. Too late Theodosius himself had regretted his order, and vainly tried to revoke it. Now, the act was done. Theodosius belonged to Ambrose's congregation—what should his attitude be to this matter? Ambrose was well known for observing very strictly the obligation to require penitence after a crime. Was a horrible mass murder pardonable, because it was committed in the exercise of imperial power? Penance was at that time invariably a public act, and was, in case of murder, usually life-long, or at least a matter of years. At first Ambrose let some days go by, during which he left Milan and assured himself of the consent of his colleagues in the area. He then wrote a letter to Theodosius, with his own hand, as he emphasizes, in order that no third person would

have to read it. As always, this piece of writing is composed
with thorough consideration, carefully aimed at the person
addressed, and it is, if you like, a 'political' document. Yet
dominating everything is the intention to exhibit the religious
meaning of the penitential order as such, and to make the in-
escapability of the divine commandment theologically plain.
With deep earnestness the rigour of the 'law' and the consolation of the 'gospel' are brought into their correct relationship.
God is merciful and does not give up even the sinner; but He
forgives his sins only when he really regrets them, and is willing
to bear the consequences. 'Sin is taken from us in no other way
than by tears and repentance' (*Ep.* 51, 11). Nothing can be
changed in this divine order. It is not a matter of what Ambrose
wants, or does not want. 'I would of course like to enjoy the
imperial favour, and to act according to your wishes; but the
matter does not permit it' (*Ep.* 51, 15). 'If the priest does not
tell the truth to him who is going astray, he will die in his sin,
and the priest will be guilty of his punishment, because he did
not admonish him who erred' (Ezek. iii. 18) (*Ep.* 51, 3). There
is no question of destroying the imperial reputation. The emperor also is a man, and may fall into temptation. He must now
do nothing else but what had been done long before by king
David, or by the pious and mighty Job. If he does this, he then
rises to the same level as the great saints of old, just as Ambrose
stands with the old prophets (*Ep.* 51, 16). 'He who accuses himself when he has sinned is just, not he who seeks to praise himself.' If the emperor is a Christian, he will not make the vain
attempt to excuse his sin (*Ep.* 51, 15). He must decide himself
what profits him. However, if he refuses, Ambrose will here-
after never be able to offer for him a sacrifice in the church. 'If
you believe, follow me! I say, If you believe, acknowledge thus
what I say! If you do not believe, pardon me for what I do—I
must give the honour to God!' (*Ep.* 51, 17).
  The words Ambrose used were perfectly clear. He was
threatening the emperor with excommunication, but he did it
in a way which did not violate the obedience of the subject, and

which made it as easy as possible for the emperor to take the bitter step. Theodosius found himself in a desperate situation and capitulated. But it seems that he did not act solely under compulsion, but that he also gave inward assent to the penance and willingly took it upon himself in true contrition. It is certain that at least once he appeared without the imperial regalia as a penitent in the church, and there, as custom required, confessed his sin in front of the assembled congregation. One can see in this a first 'Canossa'; yet contemporaries saw in this event something other than the later medieval legend, which distorted the outward events to suit its purpose. They saw no bending of the secular power, nor triumph of the sacerdotal government, but a spiritual incident and a decision of conscience on the part of the emperor, who honoured himself by acknowledging the inviolability of God's commandments. Seen thus, the ecclesiastical penance of Theodosius is the final stage in the process of the Christianization of the imperial power, which had begun with Constantine the Great. Now the church had ceased to be merely the instrument or beneficiary of the governing power. She had also taken possession of it inwardly, and now tolerated public disrespect of her ethical principles as little as denial of her dogmatic commands.

This ecclesiastical penance had also brought Theodosius and Ambrose together again personally. When the emperor again moved to the East in 391, he left Ambrose behind in Italy as his most trusted supporter. Ambrose did not disappoint him. Soon afterwards, there arose in Gaul a usurper, not acknowledged by Theodosius. He sought immediately to establish contact with Ambrose and to win him over to himself. It is amusing to observe how calmly and inconspicuously Ambrose was able to evade all attempts at approach, and only came forward with an open rejection when he was able to support it ecclesiastically. Later on he withdrew to Florence to elude a personal encounter with the usurper, who had marched against Theodosius, and for a full year he did not see his Milan congregation again. A happier man, he hastened to meet Theodosius after his victory, and by his supplication procured clemency for the defeated. The emperor, moreover, declared publicly that he had been saved 'by the merits and prayers' of this bishop (*Vita*, 31). When he died soon afterwards, Ambrose delivered the funeral oration. Here he once more celebrated the dead ruler as the model of a truly great and pious prince, and did not miss the opportunity on this occasion to bind the soldiers' loyalty to his sons. A few weeks later an edict was issued, in which the new regents gave the explicit assurance that they were determined to take away from the church none of her rights, but for the future rather to augment their respect to her to the best of their ability.

Ambrose could thus finally feel himself at the goal toward which as a church politician he had striven during the whole course of his life. From now on we find him indefatigably active as preacher and teacher, as a theological writer and as the conscientious counsellor of all who turned to him, often from afar. His secretary Paulinus, who later, urged by Augustine, wrote his biography, assures us that five bishops would not have been enough to conduct the baptismal instruction given in his lifetime by Ambrose alone. On the return home from the consecration of a bishop abroad, he contracted a fatal disease. He was asked to pray for his recovery, but Ambrose refused: 'I have not lived among you in such a way, that I would have to be ashamed to live longer; but I am also not afraid of death, for we have a good Lord' (*Vita*, 45). In a barely audible voice he made his last arrangements. The 'good old man' Simplician, who had instructed him prior to his baptism, should also become his successor. Ambrose spent his last hours in silent prayer with his arms extended to form a cross. Immediately after he had received the Lord's Body for the last time, he passed away on the 4th of April, 397. He was buried in the Ambrosian basilica. The powerful Stilicho is supposed to have said at the time that the death of this great man would start the decline of Italy. Ambrose was spared from experiencing the collapse of the empire which from an early age had been his world, and which as a bishop he had served in his own way. Only the church of the

9

empire, as he had designed and built it, was still to remain even in a changed world.

Anyone who wishes to understand and judge Ambrose must not overlook the basic practical and political bent of his nature. Ambrose knew himself to be called by God to look after the rights and interests of his church, and this obligation he fulfilled as a matter of course, just as any statesman or official would do for the state. So far there was no problem for him at all. All the same, it would be utterly wrong to consider Ambrose a politician who was, as sometimes happens, accidentally driven from state to church politics. The goals Ambrose truly wanted to serve, and which inwardly determined him, did not lie in the realm of this world. They were given to him morally and spiritually. Whenever he extols the glory of the church—and this happens quite frequently—Ambrose is not thinking of her visible structure and constitution, but is thinking rather of her mysterious spiritual nature. The church is the bride of Christ, the holy city of God. She is the store-house of the peoples and lives at the same time in every individual pious soul. Her organization is never compared to the state. The people of the church are not a nation in the sense of Egyptians, Jews, and Arabs. Her nature is best seen in her worship. The Milanese church gained under Ambrose an ever richer liturgical life. In his sermons and writings he delighted to explain the meaning of the different customs. Ambrose was a productive theologian of the sacraments and sacramentals, the first definite upholder of a mysterious teaching regarding transubstantiation in the Holy Communion, which, however, he never developed before profane ears.

Yet, the church does not exist merely for the sake of the 'mysteries'. She should above all proclaim 'faith' and teach the people to know God's holy will. God has redeemed us in Christ and forgives us our sins. He demands that we now likewise forgive, and as Christians conduct a life of rigid discipline and sanctification. The church and the Christian have also a social task. They must help all the world's oppressed to obtain their rights, and seek to relieve the distress of the poor to the best of their ability. The rich are continually admonished to charity, and Ambrose himself sets a good example. In the troubled times of the Gothic invasion he unhesitantly had the precious church vessels melted down, and is not concerned about bitter criticism (*de Off.* II, 28, 136). The poor are the real treasure of the church; it is unnecessary that she be also rich herself. According to Jesus' words the first task of the Christian is the support of one's own parents; the next in order are the poor. Only then, after that, in the third place, the priest also might receive his share. Mercy is demanded, and not sacrifice (*Exp. Luc.* VIII, 79).

As to the canon law, Ambrose is an episcopalist, like all the ancient Latin fathers; i.e. the bishop elected by the people is the supreme pastor of his congregation. As such he co-operates well with the bishops of his own area, and acknowledges the common decisions at synods without question; but in principle he has no metropolitan or patriarch as lord above him. Even Ambrose, as bishop of the first city in Upper Italy, exercised only moral authority over other bishops. He conferred with the Pope on completely equal terms. The Roman church is certainly the focal centre of ecclesiastical unity and communion for the whole world, but this does not imply a legal primacy. 'I wish', says Ambrose with reference to the ceremony of foot-washing, usual in Milan, 'to follow the Roman church on every point. Yet, we too have our sound common sense, and what other places have done well to retain, we too do well to maintain' (*de Sacr.* III, 1, 5). In the last analysis, Peter only made the first confession to Christ (Matt. xvi. 16), and on the strength of that did not claim any supremacy: 'He exercised the primacy of faith and not a primacy of legal order' (*de Incarn.* 4, 32).

The classical document of Ambrose's conception of the ministry is his work *On the Duties of the Church's Servants*, or simply *On Duties*. It grew out of addresses to his spiritual 'sons', the clergy of Milan, and is most closely linked in construction and train of thought to the work of Cicero with the same name, from which he copies extracts almost verbally for pages at a

time. As Cicero's philosophical ethics were designed for the
Roman citizen and statesman, so also the first Christian 'ethics',
represented by this book, is intended to serve in a similar way
as vocational ethics, instruction in virtue, and as a handbook to
the clerical office. A churchman also must do in all respects what
is decorous, useful, and just, and show a dignified, serious
appearance. The man of God must not have a 'popular' de-
meanour; 'for how can he maintain respect from the people,
if he possesses nothing that distinguishes him from the crowd'
(*Ep.* 28, 2)? The ancient historical examples are so far as possible replaced by Christian and Biblical ones, especially from
the Old Testament. But it still remains astonishing how naïvely
the book is now presented as 'Christian' in distinction from its
philosophical model. Ambrose was so deeply involved in the
classical tradition that he did not yet realize his own relationship
to it. In spite of this, we can sense in the slight variations and
additions here and there the rising of a new spirit, which
changes the heritage from within. The Highest Good is no
longer considered as virtue, but as eternal blessedness, which
lies in the future, and in communion with God. Its promises
stand at the beginning of the teaching on duty, as the Beatitudes
introduce the commandments of the Sermon on the Mount.
The soul, which is the seat of the man's real life, is more and
more distinguished from the body, and from the world of visible things. A special excursus, going beyond Cicero, is concerned with the value of silence. Ambrose was, so far as we
know, the first figure in antiquity no longer to read books
aloud but only silently and in meditation. To be sure, he
had a weak voice which he protected by this practice; yet
beneath this new exercise which he inaugurated is hidden a
deeper change of literary apprehension and general intellectual
enjoyment.

These 'unclassical' changes of consciousness and intellectual
style, which point to the Middle Ages, must not be explained
at once as 'Christian'. They are a general symptom of the time,
and with Ambrose most likely due to Neo-Platonic influences.

But religious thinking is not satisfied with a general 'spiritual-ization' of life and the world. The force of a longing for per-sonal salvation transcends the philosophical level of conscious-ness, and seizes upon the historic Biblical statements on Christ as the actual living reality which redeems and saves man. It is precisely the traditional questioning of the old Latin theology, psychological and anthropological, which here rises above its hard moralism and legalism. Ambrose catches something of what is really meant by the freedom of the spirit, faith, grace and the dwelling of Christ in the faithful. Christ's coming into the world remains useless if He does not also come into the heart, 'and live in me, and speak in me' (*Exp. Luc.* X, 7). Christ must dwell in the human senses if not only sin is to disappear from them, but also the desire to sin (*Exp. Ps.* cxviii, IV, 26). God makes the will receptive and ready for the good (*Exp. Luc.* I, 10). Therefore 'I will not glory that I am righteous, but I will glory that I am saved. I will not glory that I am free from sins, but that my sins are forgiven.' Christ who died for me has also become my intercessor. 'Guilt has brought more blessing than innocence; innocence had made me proud; but guilt has sub-jected me anew' (*Jac.* vi. 21). One only needs to compare such words with any of the statements of Cyprian to feel immedi-ately what spiritual discoveries have been made since his time, and what new, mighty developments have been put into motion. Ambrose has really read Paul, and we already stand quite near to Augustine. Certainly we have here only isolated utterances. The new view does not present a theological pro-gramme in Ambrose; it announces itself only involuntarily, and allows all the traditional conceptions to coexist with it. Yet by this very means we perceive that it is a matter of genuine ex-perience, whose power dwells within the soul to touch and change the real religious life.

Even today we come closest to Ambrose through his hymns. Although their original melody can hardly be reconstructed, these verses still speak distinctly of the nature and piety of this man. For Ambrose was a poet. He was certainly not a poet in the modern more subjective meaning of the word. Nor did he write poetry in the sense of the formal art of his time. Yet he was a genuine poet of almost classical originality in the way he harmonizes task and accomplishment, the form and content of his message. The hymns are the songs of the congregation. Here for the first time the spiritual feeling of the old Latin church achieved an adequate expression, great and strong. From now on 'Ambrosian' meant a whole new kind of poetical style which inaugurated the ecclesiastical hymnology of the Middle Ages. The first hymns are supposed to have originated in the days of oppression during the church struggle of 386, when the task was to gather the people in the besieged churches, and strengthen them spiritually by these 'magic melodies'. The model of this innovation was most likely the congregational singing of the Syrian Greek church, which had already existed for a long time. Ambrose, however, succeeded in what Hilary, himself a man of a remarkable poetic talent, had attempted in vain before him. He rendered into the ethos and spirit of the Latin ecclesiastical language both the genuine and simple thought of the people, and the completely different genius of the East. As to form, the hymns consist of faultless classical verses ('acatalectic iambic dimeters'), now arranged in stanzas of four lines, but they avoid any complication, and thus the natural stress of the word regularly coincides with the accent of the verse. Like the pillars of a sunny, spacious basilica, the plain stanzas join in a steady rhythm, and express what the Catholic congregation believed and felt. Acknowledgement of the Triune God is combined with different Biblical themes, and harmonized with the experience of the time of day and its changing light. A wonderful simplicity and strength lives in these hymns. No less a man than Augustine has described to us how these plain verses alone were able after his baptism to infuse a new, sweet happiness into his uneasy heart (*Conf.* IX, 6), and after the death of his mother the frantic pain found release in liberating tears with the harmonies of the Ambrosian evening hymn:

Maker of all things, God most high,
Great ruler of the starry sky,
Who, robing day with beauteous light,
Hast clothed in soft repose the night.

That sleep may wearied limbs restore,
And fit for toil and use once more,
May gently soothe the careworn breast,
And lull our anxious griefs to rest.

We thank Thee for the day that's gone;
We pray Thee now the night come on;
O help us sinners as we raise
To Thee our votive hymn of praise.

To Thee our hearts their music bring;
Thee our united praises sing;
To Thee our rapt affections soar,
And Thee our chastened souls adore.

So when the parting beams of day
In evening's shadows fade away,
Let faith no wildering darkness know,
But night with faith effulgent glow.

O sleepless ever keep the mind,
But guilt in lasting slumber bind!
Let faith our purity renew
And temper sleep's lethargic dew.

From every carnal passion free
O may our hearts repose in Thee!
Nor envious fiend, with harmful snare,
Our rest with sinful terrors share.

Christ with the Father ever one,
Spirit! the Father and the Son,
God over all, the mighty sway,
Shield us, great Trinity, we pray.

(tr. John David Chambers, 1854)

Incidentally, Ambrose is the only church father of whom we still possess a portrait today. It is extremely expressive, by no means idealized, and can claim with good reason to be regarded as 'authentic'. It is a mosaic with his name in the chapel of the Ambrosian basilica dedicated to his brother Satyrus, and was made at the beginning of the fifth century, and therefore only a few years after the death of its subject. Before us stands a lean, slender figure in a long tunic, and the simple but elegant cloak of a man of distinction (there was as yet no special 'clerical' dress). The face, slightly tilted, long, and not entirely symmetrical (an examination of the relics has confirmed the slight dislocation of the left eye) is framed by short-cut hair, while above the puffy lips and the almost invisible chin a small moustache is visible. The characteristically distant and almost melancholy expression of his face is fully apparent in the wide open eyes. They seem to look penetratingly upon the assembled congregation, yet the deeply earnest, calm gaze looks right through it and beyond it into infinity. Naturally we cannot now make out how much of the inner life of this picture really goes back to genuine, historical recollection, and how much is perhaps based on a later artistic interpretation. But at any rate this picture portrays Ambrose more nearly as he really was than do the countless sensational pictures from later times, which glorify the proud Milanese prince of the church or the learned bishop.

CHAPTER V

JEROME

EVERYONE knows Dürer's engraving 'Jerome in His Study': a comfortable, well-furnished scholar's chamber in which a silent old man, completely absorbed, writes in a book by the light of his halo, undisturbed by the panting of the little dog and the purring of his lion, with the warm sun shining through the roundel windows on to his fur. The whole is a symbol of inner and outer peace, of perfect harmony between scholarly work and true spiritual composure. This is not a picture of the historical Jerome. He was indeed a scholar and a theologian, but the wildly, agitated, baroque portrayals of the 'penitent' old man in front of the rock-cave give in this case a far better idea of the real temper of the man, although the external setting here is also not quite typical for him. Only for a short time during his youth did Jerome make the attempt to live as a hermit, and he did not persevere with it. Despite his ascetic zeal and his scholarly interests, he was never really able to turn his back upon the world around him. Passionate and craving for recognition, he sought its appreciation, applause, and response, even when he thought he despised it, and poured upon it his reproaches. Jerome was always occupied with himself; he knew no inner peace, and made enemies for himself everywhere, whom he then pursued with fervent indignation and personal hatred. Alongside his brilliant qualities, the weaknesses of his character were always manifest. This was already seen by his contemporaries, and to this day his biographers have not found it easy to narrate his life without polemic or apologetic prejudice. If we want to understand the interest and historical importance of this man and his influence we must suspend moral and theological judgement.

129

Jerome was a child of his country and of his time. In the second half of the fourth century a new intellectual life began to stir in all northern Italy. It was not only on account of the influence of Ambrose that, in areas where Christianity had until then been without any intellectual significance, and had probably been quite weak outwardly as well, preachers, theologians, and writers now everywhere took up their pens. We can sense the altered situation after the conversion of Constantine, the new ecclesiastical and cultural possibilities within a Christian order now favoured by the state. Jerome was born around 347 in the otherwise unknown little town of Strido(n), in the remote corner of Italy which bordered Dalmatia, or, on another view, still further to the south-east, in Dalmatia itself. The population of this place hardly recognized any intellectual, let alone spiritual, interests. As Jerome puts it himself, 'their gods is their belly'; anyone who was rich was also counted as pious, and the bishop was the lid you would expect on this pot (*Ep.* 7, 5). Jerome's parents belonged to this world, and, according to all appearance, were in no way exceptional. They were well-to-do, good Catholic people, but did not provide for their son any serious stimulus. After he had learned reading, writing, and arithmetic, they decided to send him to Rome to acquire higher education there, and make a career in one or other of the secular occupations. Jerome was apparently in full agreement with this. Together with a school companion from home, he received the usual education in Rome. Even as a grown man his student days came to him in nightmares, and he had to stand in his toga before his teacher, and as part of his rhetorical exercises make a speech. He heard the great grammarian Donatus, but also listened as a student to the lawyers in the public courts, and light-heartedly participated in students' jests and amusements. Even at that time he began to lay the foundations of his dearly-prized library of classical Latin authors. Jerome was, we may suppose, from an early age a diligent, untiring reader. He possessed an astonishing memory and even in old age could quote without effort from Virgil, Horace, and many other poets. He also read Quintilian, Seneca, and various writers of history; but for him, as for Lactantius, the real teacher and model of good style was the incomparable Cicero.

Jerome occasionally lamented in his later years the way in which he frequently slid on the slippery paths of vain and sinful youth. This does not surprise us from an ascetic convert! Jerome was open-minded, eager to get the most out of life, and receptive. That he was well acquainted with the temptations of the sensual side of life, his later writings sufficiently indicate. Yet there is no real reason to take his retrospective and quite general statements too seriously. At the same time, the ecclesiastical life of Rome had also impressed him vividly. The rich congregation no longer occupied a position of obscurity; imposing church buildings and palaces testified to the beginnings of a Christian Rome. Jerome participated with pleasure in the magnificent, well-attended services, and also visited the catacombs outside the city gates, rich in memories and at that time not well cared for. As it seems, all the friends with whom he associated, Pammachius, Rufinus, and others, appear later to have turned to a markedly Christian, ascetic life. At the end of his studies, when he was approximately 19 years of age, Jerome decided to receive baptism together with his school friend Bonosus, whom we have already mentioned. This was, as we have seen in the case of Ambrose, not then usual for a young man with ambitions in public life. In 367 the twenty-year-old student set off on a long trip to Gaul. He presumably meant to apply for a well-paid position in Trèves, the imperial capital. However, he was now interested in ecclesiastical and theological as well as classical literature. In Trèves he experienced his first conversion. Jerome renounced a secular career and decided instead to dedicate himself completely to pious meditation and to spiritual work. He also induced the faithful Bonosus to consecrate himself in the same way to the service of Christ. It would be a mistake, however, to see in such a decision the monastic ideal in the later meaning of the word; an inner crisis must not be presumed. Jerome was committing himself as a Christian to a new form of life, intellectual, and to a certain extent also spiritual. This meant, however, neither 'poverty' nor strict subordination and 'obedience'. It would just provide him rather with quiet, and with personal independence for his studies and intellectual hobbies, in addition to the enjoyment of friendship, and exchange of common interests. At any rate, that is how it appears in the light of the way in which it worked out. It is a typical change of career, frequently to be observed in other cases in these decades. For an intellectually active man political life had become uninteresting. The normal activity in schools and academies likewise appeared as formal and empty, showing no sign of any stirring and vital new ideals. It was different in the realm of the church and her religion. Having suddenly attained recognition and influence, she needed every- where men who would take up the new tasks imposed on her, preserve her inner resources, and carry on and fill with new life the spiritual traditions she possessed. Some, like Ambrose, must pass directly into the service of ecclesiastical government and administration. To others new 'inner' tasks and possibilities re- vealed themselves, which had only to be grasped in order to lead to a higher life of freedom, meaningful before God and men. The injuries, upsets, and contempt which earlier menaced the Christians had now gone forever. The Christian writer, saint, and scholar, needed to be neither lonely nor unproduc- tive, and could count on general recognition and admiration if he now proudly claimed that henceforward he served Christ alone, and wished to take his truth seriously. In doing this he even became a helper and example to the church and the world.

After a stay, probably only short, in his home-town, Jerome found in Aquileia the surroundings and society he sought. Here in the house of the priest Chromatius he again met his old friend Rufinus, and a large number of clergy interested in asceticism, with whom he was soon at one in lively spiritual friendship. Years later he casually erected a memorial for his friends in his chronicle, by making a note under the year 373, that the clergy of Aquileia resembled a choir of angels. He also established relations with the neighbouring town of Concordia, and with a community of devout ascetic women in Laibach. Unfortunately, we do not know anything in detail of these years; but we may suppose that in those days all the elements had already come together which we find again in Jerome's later life: the common cultivation of ascetic and theological interests, the human exchange with like-minded friends and the pious admiration of spiritually inclined women—all perhaps still somewhat more primitive, provincial, and youthfully immature than later. And this phase of his life ended for Jerome, as so often in the time that followed, not peacefully, but with personal disputes and quarrels. We do not know whence the 'sudden whirlwind' came, which tore apart almost the whole circle of friends; it may be that self-conscious ascetic zeal had upset the people of a church not yet used to it, and perhaps also the higher clerics. Jerome was not the only one to be affected; but he felt himself even more disgracefully defamed than others. Even in Laibach the devout would have nothing to do with him, and the good relationship with his parents and relatives, who were probably not impressed by their offspring's change of career, was now completely destroyed. The fact that Jerome succeeded in arousing in his younger sister an enthusiasm for asceticism, and bringing her under the influence of a deacon who was a friend of his, may have been a contributory factor. We still possess a letter crammed with quotations from the Bible, with which he tried to reconcile an angry aunt—evidently in vain. After this Jerome never mentioned his parents, and he never saw them again.

The young ascetic genius, for whom his native soil had become too hot, now decided to travel to the East (373-374). Jerusalem and the Holy Land were already by then the goal of countless pilgrimages, and anyone who wanted to distinguish himself in practical holiness could find in the deserts of Syria or Egypt patterns of the monastic life, which was known in the West only from hearsay. Moreover, the Greek Orient was still the land of education and higher theological learning. Jerome thought of himself as a pilgrim and future hermit, but there can be no doubt that the intellectual treasures and stimulus which he could expect there also attracted him. Having arrived in Antioch on the Orontes, he did not think of proceeding at once into the desert. He felt himself ill and overworked—a complaint which appears time and again in his letters both now and later. His 'poor body', which in reality was to remain unusually tough throughout his long life, feels itself to be suffering 'even when it is in health' (*Ep.* 3, 1). Jerome already believed that he was near death (*Ep.* 6, 2). He met with a hospitable reception in the city, and on the estate of his friend Evagrius, and soon revelled in all the excitements offered him by the intellectual life of the metropolis. Jerome now tried hard to learn Greek thoroughly; he went to lectures, and plunged into all available theological literature. His studies of the Aristotelian dialectic also probably belong to this period. It was not long before his own first literary attempts appeared. At the request of his friend Innocent who was at his side, he described a striking criminal case of the recent past: a young wife, falsely accused of adultery and sentenced to death, was wonderfully preserved alive, and finally saved by Evagrius' intercession. The little narrative, arranged like an account of martyrdom, concludes with an encomium of his host at Antioch. It is no masterpiece—in spite of, or rather because of, the rhetorical splendour and bombast which Jerome bestowed upon it. Much the same seems to be true of an exposition of the prophet Obadiah, which has not been preserved. After twenty years Jerome recounts, when commenting on the same text, how embarrassing it was to him afterwards when immature readers tried to praise to its author's face the supposed profundity of this elaborate piece of work. He saw in this little writing a youthful folly which he simply could not acknowledge any longer.

The earliest letter preserved gives direct, and still more indirect, information about the state of mind in which he found himself at that time. It is addressed to the head of a community of hermits with whom he had stayed during his travels, pre-

sumably a letter of thanks after safe arrival, which takes the
form, however, rather of a letter of confession and a cry for
saving intercession. The pathos with which Jerome contrasts
his woeful state in the wicked world with the happy solitude
of the holy recipient produces a thoroughly artificial effect.
Jerome 'does not want to retreat and cannot advance'. There
has obviously been a discussion about his ascetic plans during
his visit, and he therefore 'incessantly' assures his correspondent
that now as ever his heart possesses the burning desire to pursue
the prescribed way. Yet he still lacks the strength to decide, and
only the intercession of the hermit can ensure that perhaps one
day his aspiration will be followed by fulfilment (*Ep.* 2). The
young rhetorician wanted to be a Christian saint, and the decision once made was not abandoned; yet he had still not found
the way by which he was able to find a place for his ambitious
dreams and his literary inclinations and abilities within the
framework of a monastic way of life. He hesitated, and he suffered from his own hesitance, while at the same time he let the
bright, rich life, the friends, and the unexpected possibilities of
work and study in Antioch have their effect upon him.

Meanwhile the conflict lay not only in externals: Jerome felt
it also in the intellectual field of his actual work and interests.
His heart still clung to his old loves, and was by no means
inclined to tie itself exclusively to the Holy Scripture and theological research to which his life was now to be solely dedicated.
The uneasiness torturing him is reflected in the famous dream
which probably took place at about this time. To be sure, it
was only recorded ten years later. The account is found in a
letter of ascetic instruction, and it is obvious that Jerome had
written it up in a stylized form to fit the purpose of this tract.
The miraculous conclusion, also, is to be evaluated in this way,
and not, of course, to be taken seriously in a literal sense, although that is what Jerome intended. All the same, there is no
conclusive reason to deny the reality of the dream altogether.
Jerome writes (*Ep.* 22, 30): 'Many years ago I renounced home,
parents, my sister and my relatives and, what is much more

difficult, the familiar good kitchen too' (this, coming right at the start, is a surprising confession, yet characteristic of Jerome!); 'for I had made myself a eunuch for the sake of the kingdom of heaven (Matt. xix. 12), and I wanted to move to Jerusalem to perform the military service of the spirit. Yet I could not part from my library, which I had brought together in Rome with so much labour and diligence. So miserable was I: I fasted —to read Cicero afterwards! I lay awake many nights, I wept with all my heart thinking about my former sins—and then I took Plautus in my hands. I then repented and began to read a prophet; but I found the uncultured language detestable and, because I could not see the light with my blind eyes, I thought the sun was to blame and not my eyes. As the old serpent thus played his tricks on me, a consuming and ceaseless fever came over my exhausted body during the fast, which so wasted my unfortunate limbs, that I finally—it sounds almost incredible— really consisted only of bones. They were already making arrangements for my burial; my body was quite cold, and only in my frozen breast was there fluttering a little spark of the natural warmth of life. I was then all of a sudden seized and in the spirit dragged before a tribunal. An awful light shone upon me, and from those standing around it there went out a flashing brightness—I threw myself to the ground, and did not dare look up. Then I was asked about my calling and answered, I am a Christian. You are lying! said the One on the throne. You are a Ciceronian, and not a Christian! (*Ciceronianus es, non Christianus*): Where your treasure is, there is your heart also (Matt. vi. 21).' Jerome described furthermore how under the terrible blows raining upon him, he kept begging for grace. The bystanders also interceded in his favour, that a lenient view be taken of the lapses of his youth, and opportunity be given him for improvement. He vowed never again to wish to possess secular books: if he read them once more, this might be considered denial. So he was released, and returned to life, to the surprise of everyone. These were, Jerome assures us, no mere dreams. When he awakened he still felt the blows, and his shoulders had blue marks. From this time on, he turned to the divine writings with a zeal which he had never known yet for the 'mortal' authors.

Cicero—in this name Jerome included the whole 'classical' cultural heritage. He did not, like Lactantius, think of Cicero primarily as a philosopher. Jerome never had any interest in philosophy itself, and he did not find it hard simply to thrust aside its representatives as ignoramuses and babblers. Jerome thought of Cicero the orator, the master of cultivated language and of a noble style, Cicero the teacher of general education and culture, Cicero who belongs in the succession of Plautus, Virgil, Horace, Seneca, and the historians. The school education of late antiquity, of which Jerome is thinking, had a strong bias to the study of language. It was the advantages of its formal expression which—besides his lively need for conversation—above all made him enthusiastic for the ancients. There is no need to think of deeper, human, and aesthetic values: despite all the sensitivity and versatility of his temper, Jerome had basically a prosaic or, at any rate, a totally unpoetic nature. That is why the external advantages of a perfected cultural language played such a paramount role, while in contrast the Bible appeared to him raw, tasteless, and almost unbearable. But Jerome knew now that with this attitude he was on the wrong path, and he was determined to change direction. From now on his literary work and his whole will concentrated exclusively upon the Bible, exposition of the Bible, and theological studies pertaining to it.

Is this claim correct? Later, when their friendship had broken up and had turned into bitter hostility, no other than his intimate friend Rufinus openly raised the accusation that Jerome had in reality been disloyal to his vow made in the dream, and had constantly broken the oath not to read the profane authors. He collected the evidence: he referred not only to the innumerable quotations, but also to copies of such proscribed books, which Jerome as an enthusiastic collector of books had again and again ordered and paid for at great expense. The petty and insincere manner in which Jerome defended himself against

10

these reproaches did not improve his position. In the long run the 'vow' was obviously not kept in a literal sense. Nevertheless Rufinus did Jerome an injustice; for in intention and conscious purpose Jerome never returned to profane studies in the old sense. He used the pagan authors henceforward only as a help to Biblical exegesis. He no longer read them for their own sake, for mere pleasure. Even pagan historians he quoted 'not from caprice, but only because of cogent necessity'—namely in order to demonstrate that the Biblical prophecies are true and have really been fulfilled (*Comm. Dan.* prol.). That did not mean, of course, that Jerome hid his rich knowledge under the bushel, or meant to renounce the rhetorical elegance of his style. On the contrary, he was just as fond as ever of showing it off: occasional phrases assuring the contrary are simply part of a rhetorical convention, and are not to be taken seriously. It was his secret ambition to vie with his pagan models, and wherever possible to outdo them, but this was done now only in the interest of God, and of higher, holy culture. According to the precepts of the Bible (Deut. xxi. 11), the hair and nails of the unclean slave girl are to be cut first, and her whole body must be washed and cleansed from idolatry and sensuality before she can find admission to Israel (*Ep.* 70, 2); i.e. the good things of pagan culture are not accepted directly, but are assimilated into a new context. 'What has Horace to do with the psalter, Maro with the gospels, or Cicero with the Apostle? . . . Certainly "to the pure everything is pure!" (Tit. i. 15), and nothing is objectionable that is enjoyed with thanksgiving (I Tim. iv. 4). Nevertheless, we shall not "at the same time drink the chalice of Christ and the cup of the demons" (I Cor. x. 21)' (*Ep.* 22, 29). Jerome preferred to depict the situation as though Christian culture was already perfect in itself, and had no need at all of such borrowing. 'Our Simonides, Pindar, and Alcaios, or Flaccus, Catullus, and Serenus' is king David (*Ep.* 53, 8). A man like Theophilus, Bishop of Alexandria, unites in himself the talents of a Plato and a Demosthenes (*Ep.* 99, 2). Our Athens, that is to say, the university of Christian learning, is Jerusalem (*Ep.* 46, 9).

The brief outline of the history of literature written by Jerome after the model of Suetonius, on *The Illustrious Men*, i.e. the writers of the church, serves the sole purpose of setting forth the rank and significance of the intellectual giants of Christianity, so that the pagan libel-mongers may be put to shame, and instead of asserting the philistinism of the Christians may realize their own ignorance (*Vir. Ill.*, prol.). Yet, of course, Jerome is quite aware that this proud attitude is premature, that Christians cannot possibly dispense with pagan education, and so, in defence of his borrowing, he refers again to the men of the Bible who from Moses to Paul were supposed to have acted in this same way (*Ep.* 70, 2). This is precisely his task, and that of all Christians with the same intention, to make up at last for the church's backwardness, and to justify the public glory she has attained, by corresponding intellectual achievements.

Tertullian and Clement of Alexandria had previously been concerned with the problem of ancient culture, namely, whether or no the indispensable pagan education was allowable to Christians. It was no accident that the problem now in the fourth century assumed an increased importance. Jerome is unique only in the intensity with which he experienced this conflict as his personal fate. His dream was hence of deep symbolical importance. The solution he found was comparatively external and unrefined just because he only saw the advantages of the ancient culture quite externally, in the richness of its knowledge, and above all in the beauty of its language. His decision to forgo its enjoyment was forced; it was typically ascetic and led to a purely external and thematic limitation of his work and reading, measured according to the Christian or pagan content. Not without pain, yet with a bitterness all the stronger, and almost scornful, the converted Christian repudiated the pagan authors, just because he still loved them, and could never really dispense with them. On every possible occasion, and often enough more passionately than truthfully, he assured others that he had studied them all and knew them well —and just for that reason he did not need them any more, and professed himself interested only in God's word. But in the service of the truth of this he hoped now the more to be a Christian Cicero, an equally comprehensive teacher of Christian culture, and in addition to be a monk and a saint. The inconsistency of this ideal reached to the roots of his being, and had a decisive influence on Jerome as long as he lived. It drove him to restless work, and to his, on the whole, astonishing achievements. It explains at the same time his human weaknesses, his inordinate vanity, and his frequent failure in the realm of ethical and personal relations. There was no real theology behind this ascetic cultural ideal, for which he fought with such conviction. He remained attached to the traditions which he endeavoured to suppress and conquer. Jerome was as much a monk as a humanist. Projected on world history, this has determined the whole cultural tradition of the Western Middle Ages proceeding from him—in so far as it did not draw from other sources, or obtain by Augustine's mediation a deeper understanding of what Christian humility, spiritual life, and Biblical truth and culture really mean.

After about a year and a half Jerome had come to the point at which he could say good-bye to his host, and actually go into the desert as a hermit. He chose an area not too far off, the desert of Chalcis, situated south-east of Antioch and outside the gates of Chalcis on Belus, the last important town of the Syrian fertile zone. For a long time, the rock-caves of the deserted valleys had been inhabited by hermits living apart from each other, among whom the newcomer at first attracted no further attention. Jerome most likely moved into a vacant cave. It must have been quite spacious, and for the desert 'comfortable'; for he could provide a place for his whole library here, he could copy books and occasionally receive visitors. The hermits were not totally secluded from each other and from the outside world: Jerome regularly received and dispatched his letters. From this time, a number of early letters are preserved which were sent to his friends all over the world, and almost every letter contains the earnest admonition to write to him and write again, no matter what they wrote—they must write! Jerome praises the stillness and saintly life he had found—but the silence did not make him silent. Of a thoroughly sociable nature, he welcomed solitude only to organize his thoughts and to set them in the right form. This accomplished, he was the more consumed with impatience to communicate them to others, to have intellectual exchange, and to maintain at least a correspondence with like-minded persons.

Jerome undoubtedly took upon himself the ascetic exercises belonging to the life of a true hermit, but one does not get the impression that he was particularly happy in them. Jerome was not a man to whom renunciation could be an enjoyment and the opening of new emotions. Even in later years we hear scarcely anything of the exaltations, illuminations or ecstasies of his inner life. The hard bodily achievement as such is what stands out. Asceticism was to him a means of discipline and of sanctification, in this respect meritorious and indispensable, yet also always a strain, wearisome and unpleasant. So he himself described in thoroughly realistic terms the beginning of his monastic strife, laying the colour on thick in his usual way: 'Ah, how often I took myself to Rome in my thought, to all the splendours I had once enjoyed—in those days in the desolate, lonely desert which, parched by the glowing sun, furnished a frightful home for the monks! There I sat alone, my heart full of bitter despair, my limbs stuck into an ugly sackcloth, my skin like that of a negro, dark from the dirt. Day after day I had to cry and sigh, and once, falling asleep against my will, my fleshless bones lay nakedly on the bare soil. I do not want to talk about eating and drinking! Even sick anchorites drink only cold water, and a cooked meal is regarded as an excess. And he, who in fear of hell had banished himself to this imprisonment, and had company only with scorpions and wild beasts—he notwithstanding this found himself time and again in company with dancing girls! My face grew pale with hunger, yet in my cold body the passions of my inner consciousness continued to glow. This human being was less alive than dead; only his burning concupiscence still continued to boil' (*Ep.* 22, 7).

The hidden instincts of the ambitious zealot did not change direction. Jerome continued to work indefatigably. He had new books sent to him, and soon he also won friends to copy them. He was proud not only to augment his library by this 'manual work', but also to be able to make his living himself like a real monk. At this time, Jerome began to learn Hebrew from a Jewish convert. Otherwise, he testified, he could not keep a tight rein on his thoughts. He had to combine bodily fasting with intellectual toil. 'I knew the brilliant style of Quintilian, the eloquence of Cicero, the dignified loftiness of Fronto, and the soft charm of Pliny, and now I learned the ABC again, and memorized the hissing, jarring words. What a labour! What difficulties! How often I was about to despair, and then began anew from the start, driven by the ambition of learning! I have gone through all this, and can testify to it from experience; and those who then shared life with me know it too' (*Ep.* 125, 12).

However, one must not only consider those complaints. Jerome also realized the advantages of this life. He could place it in an ideal light, and then like an outsider rhapsodize over the poetry and calm perfection of the monastic solitude. The most charming fruit of such moods is the small volume on *The Life of Saint Paul, The First Hermit*, which was written in those years. Until then, the anchorite's calling had been intimately known to the general public only through the famous biography of Anthony written by Saint Athanasius. Evagrius, Jerome's friend, had translated this into Latin for Western readers: an earnest book, reporting the demonic temptations and heroic purification and trial of the wonderful saint, who was supposed to have founded the new monastic way of life. In his book Jerome competed to a certain extent with this model. His Saint Paul, it is explicitly maintained, is older and more perfect than Anthony, who had hitherto been unjustly counted as the beginning. Apart from this, however, the little book is quite different. Its aim is primarily to entertain and recount the story

in an edifying way. To achieve this, it restricts itself to the first
and last days of the hero's stay in the desert, which lasted one
hundred and thirteen years. We hear how, persecuted and forsaken by the world, he finds an enchanting solitary refuge in the
wilderness. A palm-tree grants him food and clothing; a raven
brings him daily the necessary portion of bread. The whole is
an idyll, nor does Jerome avoid the usual classical convention-
alities: a friendly centaur and a Christian-minded satyr show the
way to Anthony, who has been ordered in a dream to go to
Paul. Both men then humbly converse at a bubbling spring
under the palm-tree. Finally the deceased Paul is covered with
a coat once given to Anthony by Athanasius. The burial is performed by two pious lions, who beg and receive from Anthony
his Christian blessing for this task. The religious content of this
little romance is modest, but nobody can fail to recognize its
charm. Jerome proves himself to be a brilliant popular story-
teller who, according to the occasion and need, knows how to
tell his story in an edifying, exciting, humorous, and even quite
piquant manner, without transgressing the limits of good taste.
It is idle to inquire for the 'historical' core of this story; it is
probably at best no more than the name of the hero. Later
Jerome composed biographies of two other monks, which are
somewhat more trustworthy with regard to their content.
After all, he drew here from partly recognizable sources, and
one of the saints he even knew personally. In spite of this, the
harmless sketch of the *Vita Pauli* yet remains his most perfect
writing from a literary point of view. Jerome became in the
course of time more scholarly and impressive, probably more
theologically serious, and in his way, more important. His
talent as a writer, however, was finally developed when he was
thirty years of age, and he never reached again the gentle charm
of this little work of his youth.

The little book closes, quite like the monastic literature of the
Middle Ages, with the supplication to the reader to be mindful
of 'the poor sinner Jerome', and with the assurance that Paul's
tunic would be much more precious to him than all that royal

purple which provokes divine punishment. In reality, his own life as a monk was, as we have seen, by no means an undisturbed idyll, and with time the dissensions began to increase. The dogmatic controversies, which even in the quiet colony of monks he could not evade for long, caused him particular trouble. The whole Orient, then in the last stages of the Arian controversy, was split into different parties attacking each other. All intellectually important personalities of the Greek church, and also Westerners like Ambrose, were involved in these quarrels, and were passionately interested in their outcome. Jerome, however, considered them only an annoying disturbance of his personal peace, and found that the whole quarrel of the Greeks was fundamentally of no concern to him as a Roman. He was indignant at their tactlessness in refusing to leave him in peace, and in expecting his theological judgement and support. What possible concern could he have with the new sophistries regarding one or three hypostases? Jerome was not interested at all in questions of speculative theology and metaphysics; if necessary, he was willing to accept any solution which did not directly contradict the decisions already made. When he saw no escape, he resolved upon an unusual step: he wrote a letter to the new Roman Pope Damasus, who was completely unknown to him personally, and asked for brief information as to what faith he had to confess, which formula he now had to affirm, and which of the opposed bishops of Antioch he had to follow. He stressed that he was a 'Roman' by virtue of baptism by Damasus' predecessor, and he wanted to remain such. The Pope shall therefore make the decision for him—however Arian it might sound, Jerome will nevertheless accept it as his orthodox instructions. Now the sun of righteousness no more rises in the East, but in the West. 'For the moment, I only exclaim: "He who is installed in Peter's chair, he is my man"' (*Ep.* 16, 2). When he received no answer, he wrote a second letter imploring the great shepherd with most flattering phrases not to leave his 'black sheep' in the lurch. But Damasus had no intention whatever of committing himself in such a naïve manner in the difficult ecclesiastico-political situation then existing—least of all to an uninfluential and virtually unknown writer and hermit.

A little later, Jerome left Chalcis forever. It was probably hardly two and a half years altogether that he endured monastic life in his cave. He himself tried to give the impression that the dogmatic quarrelsomeness and obtrusiveness of his companions had spoiled his further stay in the desert, and even made it impossible. But this is not a very convincing excuse. Jerome had had quite enough of this form of striving for sanctification. Otherwise nothing could have hindered him from seeking out another, quieter refuge, in any other place East or West. In reality, he longed again for the world, for people, for communication, and for intellectual stimulus. In a deeper sense, Jerome was probably right in breaking off his monk's career, which at first sight appears somewhat embarrassing. His development was not yet concluded, and the scholarly possibilities for which, without admitting it, he longed could not be offered by the wilderness. Only many years later did he succeed in finding the appropriate combination of intellectual work, asceticism, and community, to which he then remained faithful. Now, the great cities of Antioch and Constantinople were the goal of his wishes.

In Antioch Jerome finally had to choose his ecclesiastical party. He joined the side of the extreme 'orthodox' theologians, represented by the old-Nicene, Western-looking Paulinus, whom Evagrius also followed. Jerome considered it all his life safest and most convenient to follow the most definite-sounding theological slogans—just because they did represent nothing else but slogans of ecclesiastical orthodoxy. For his scholarly interests, however, he resorted to any book, however much under suspicion, and where he could learn or experience something concrete, he did not shrink in certain cases even from dubious acquaintances. Thus in Antioch, for instance, he heard the exegetical lectures of Apollinaris, bishop of Laodicea, whose Christological teachings were condemned as heresy despite his being acknowledged as a Nicean. Yet Jerome shielded himself against suspicion by also signing if necessary, i.e. as soon as anyone wished it, any dogmatic sentence of anathema. He let nobody excel him in orthodoxy and ecclesiastical devotion. It was during this period that Jerome was ordained priest by Paulinus, in gratitude for his support. Jerome felt himself now as much as ever a monk, and expressly insisted that this freedom must not be restricted in any way. But on these terms, as in no way binding him, but simply an 'honorary promotion', his new rank was welcome to him. Jerome always thought and taught, even regarding the ministry, in tones of an uncompli-cated 'Catholic' piety. The priests 'make' the Lord's body, they guard the Bride of Christ in her chastity, only by them can we be Christians at all (*Ep.* 14, 8). Yet he was far from ignoring their weaknesses, and—despite his assurances to the contrary—from keeping his sharp tongue in check where they were con-cerned. Whenever he was personally upset or provoked in his vanity, any form of affront and insult seemed allowable to him even against spiritual—in such cases only apparently 'spiritual' —enemies. All this needs to be taken into account if we are to understand his human and theological attitude in later struggles.

Jerome stayed in Constantinople from 379 to 382, years im-portant in world history, as the great change under Theodosius was modifying the appearance of the whole Eastern church in favour of the Nicene Creed. He was presumably a witness of the famous 'theological speeches' of Gregory of Nazianzus, he ex-perienced at close quarters the turbulent Council of 381, later called 'ecumenical' and stayed on for some months afterwards in the city. In spite of this, he never mentioned these happen-ings. This is characteristic. To be sure, Jerome, as a Westerner and adherent of Paulinus, could not be very pleased with the result of this Council; yet on the other hand he was in the closest personal relationship with the leaders of the victorious, Neo-Nicene party. He repeatedly designated Gregory of Nazi-anzus as his 'teacher', who had disclosed to him the under-standing of the Holy Scriptures. In the days of the Council

Gregory of Nyssa, Amphilochius of Iconium and others came into the circle of his acquaintance. But Jerome was not concerned with the controversies of church politics. He wanted to advance his theological studies, and this meant above all, even then, instruction about the correct interpretation of the Scriptures, a solid knowledge of Biblical exegesis and philology. Under the overwhelming impression of the superiority of Greek theological education, he became for the first time aware of his calling and his real life-task, of which he would never again lose sight. 'I wanted'—he confessed at the end of his life —'to dedicate myself completely to the exposition of Scripture, and to impart Hebrew and Greek learning to the people of my tongue'; but the devil, he added bitterly, did not wish it, and interrupted and again and again disturbed his longed-for peace (*Hierem*. III, 1, 2). It was as much as anything the devil of his own perpetual unrest, of his quarrelsomeness, and vanity. But we will speak later of the scholastic achievements of Jerome.

At first Jerome occupied himself with the modest task of a translator—an activity to which during his whole life he returned time and again, an activity second only to his own writings inspired by Greek theology. He attempted to translate into Latin the chronicle of Eusebius, or, more strictly, the second part with its table of parallel dates, and so to create a solid source-book and manual, particularly for Biblical history. According to his own testimony, this was a pure translation as far as the fall of Troy; for the later centuries he sought to amplify and correct the work with the help of Latin historians, and finally he carried it on independently up to his own time. He chose to conclude with the year of the dreadful battle with the Goths at Adrianople (378); for now 'barbaric hordes rage through our lands, and everything is uncertain' (*Chron.* prol.). Jerome was at all times a naïve Roman patriot. It is to his credit that he now immediately applied his scholarly passion to such decidedly delicate and difficult material. Unfortunately, the characteristic weakness of almost all his scholarly enterprises is already revealed here. He himself called it a 'tumultuous' work, and one not completely organized on account of his haste, and he excused himself on the ground of the special difficulties of the subject-matter. As a matter of fact, he adduces an abundance of scholarly data, but it is hasty and full of errors. In the later parts the subjective partisanship of the author in praise and blame alike is obvious at once. His assurance that if necessary he was not afraid to tell the truth about living personalities could have been omitted. Jerome envisaged also a history of his own time—but this was one of the many plans of his life never accomplished. About the same time he began, perhaps at the instigation of his 'teacher' Gregory, the translation of certain homilies of Origen. Origen was for Jerome, as he was for Ambrose, indeed even more than for the latter, simply the great Biblical scholar, the only one who like himself was master of the Hebrew language, and who always carefully observed the differences in the textual tradition. Jerome followed him without hesitation even in the allegorical method of interpretation, which was to him, especially in the Old Testament, the accepted bridge to deep understanding and 'edification'. On the other hand, the methodical and systematic presuppositions of Origen's hermeneutics scarcely interested him; even as a follower of Origen, Jerome was primarily concerned with the material. Concrete questions of exegesis were to his philological mind the real theological problems.

After Gregory of Nazianzus and the various members of the Council had left Constantinople, the city lost its attraction for Jerome. He decided to follow the two bishops whose sympathies looked to the West, and who for this reason had failed to make their case at the Council. He travelled with Paulinus and Epiphanius from Salamis to Rome. Here a new Council was to meet which was to do them justice. Already his knowledge of languages must have given Jerome some importance, and he was no longer the unknown hermit of earlier days, but a personality of literary renown, whose connections with the East must have recommended him as an adviser. With a sure eye Pope Damasus recognized the importance of the man whom he had not answered some years ago. He appointed him his private secretary to prepare difficult letters, and at the same time custodian of the papal archives and of his library. Ecclesiastical rank played no role in this: it was medieval legend which first exalted Jerome into a cardinal of the Roman Church and adorned him with the broad-brimmed red hat. But now began the happiest and at any rate outwardly the most splendid and richest years of his life.

Damasus loved the grand style and presence. He was a great builder, and under him the papal household first assumed a 'princely' appearance. He was no narrow-minded Maecenas, and he placed the keeper of his archives and counsellor in an appropriate position, with suitable remuneration. Thus Jerome for the first time participated in luxury and the social life of the great world. Although he had a hard despotic nature, and was ruthless with his adversaries, Damasus nevertheless had a feeling for human intercourse, and was by no means without intellectual interests. He enjoyed the society of a man like Jerome, who was soon complete master of the manners of the curia. We still have some of the long and short letters exchanged between them. The Pope demanded books or precise theological information; he asked with condescending humour why Jerome was so long silent, whether he was 'asleep' or hugging his books. Jerome sought to satisfy his impatient master as far as possible, and promised him the dedication of his latest translation. But Damasus knew also how to put tasks before his protégé which were appropriate to his abilities. We have him to thank for the first impulse towards an enterprise which has made Jerome's name immortal in the Western church: the renewal of the Latin Bible, the text of the philologically reliable *Vulgate*, which put an end to the chaos of the older traditions. In these days at Rome, it is true, Jerome hardly went beyond a first revision of the gospels. He added to it a translation of the Eusebian *Canones*, i.e. synoptic tables which made it much easier to find the parallel pericopes.

Jerome was also soon drawn into the contests of church

politics against sects and theological parties, and his skilful pen and his extensive knowledge proved themselves useful. At this time (?) he therefore wrote a pamphlet against the Luciferians, a small rigorist sect of extreme anti-Arians, whose obstinacy gave the Catholics in Rome much trouble. In this he cleverly found the happy mean between the tone of breezy popularity and the calm superiority of objective and learned argument. This little *Dialogue* between a Luciferian and an 'orthodox' is written as though it were an official report of a disputation which really took place. All the emphasis is laid upon the 'objective' side of Catholic churchmanship, which not only forbids a deliberate schism, but also, when correctly understood, makes it senseless and unnecessary. The sacraments of the church, her ministry, and her apostolic tradition are efficacious, even if, like Noah's ark, she also contains impure animals. This should be understood even by the 'snarling eloquence' of the Luciferians, although experience shows that 'they are easier to refute than to convince' (*Dial. c. Lucif.* 28).

A deeper matter was his controversy with Helvidius regarding the perpetual virginity of Mary. This pamphlet was probably likewise instigated by Damasus, or at least, as Jerome emphasized, explicitly approved by him. Helvidius was a layman who by reference to the Scripture, which knows and mentions the 'brothers of Jesus', disputed the theory that Mary remained a virgin even 'after the birth' of her first Son. He was conscious of defending along with this the older Western tradition, which had certainly declined in popularity since Ambrose, and he protested against a more recent one-sided prizing of celibacy at the expense of matrimony. Here Jerome was in his element. His whole Biblical scholarship came into motion in order to save Mary's honour against all alleged distortions and forgeries of the text by the slanderer. The exegetical proofs he brought out are essentially the same as those the Catholic church still maintains today. They were effectually reinforced by a drastic caricature of the opposite point of view. Behind this stood the real, personal concern: the conviction of the clear religious and moral superiority of virginity. It was justified by the entire tradition and practice of the church, as Jerome saw it. Already the 'virginal Christ' and the virgin Mary had laid the foundation of virginity for both sexes. The apostles were celibate or, if they had been married, abstinent in their matrimony. Bishops, presbyters, and deacons are chosen from the celibate or widower's class, or at least they live in perpetual chastity after becoming priests (*Ep.* 49, 21). The whole idea of merit depends for the ascetic on this distinction between the two modes of life according to achievement and rank. It would be a peculiar God who punishes sins, but will not also reward good works! (*adv. Jov.* II, 3). Jerome guarded against prohibiting marriage as such, but it was a matter of course to him that it was of minor value, and consequently receives less reward. Marriage is to virginity as the mere avoidance of sin is to doing good, or 'to express it a little more mildly: as good to the better' (*adv. Jov.* I, 13). 'Why should we lie to ourselves and make ourselves angry? If we are continuously greedy for the embrace of women, the reward for chastity must naturally be denied to us' (*Ep.* 49, 21). This is the answer he gave to a later critic of his inflexible ideal, which all his life appeared conclusive to him in its logic. He lacked any faculty for the more serious problems of the monkish idea of sanctification, which other Western theologians of that time did nevertheless recognize. Jerome was the most zealous, but also the most indigent ascetic theologian the ancient church produced. Yet in what he said in these controversies he was completely serious.

Moreover, Jerome did not restrict himself to propaganda with his pen for the ascetic life. He also made a personal stand for his ideals. Soon we find him as the intellectual centre of a circle of aristocratic and wealthy ladies, to whom he became teacher and counsellor. His special liking for a female audience which admired and understood him, and which he could instruct, educate, and admonish was, as already stated, a lasting feature of his nature. Next to the protection of the Pope, the circle of aristocratic ladies in Rome evidently constituted his strongest support. Otherwise, his ascetic preaching and learning seemed to have found little echo. The palace on the Aventine in which the widow Marcella lived with her mother and her daughter Asella was the centre of the new ascetic movement. A number of other young women and widows who were no longer satisfied with the social life of Rome congregated around them. The earnestness of the ascetic demands gave their life a new meaning. They all felt themselves to be more or less like nuns who wore the veil, and renounced adornment and the vanity of the 'world'. They rarely appeared in public, fasted much, held devotions, and were very generous to charity, to the annoyance of their relatives and heirs. Even before Jerome's arrival, some had decided to make pilgrimages and a settlement in the Holy Land. The new ideas he imparted to this circle were, besides a more intimate knowledge of the strict Eastern exercises, the concentrated and regular pursuit of Bible reading and Biblical studies. Soon Jerome delivered before a select female audience his own lectures which found enthusiastic acceptance. Some began to learn Greek and even Hebrew themselves. They assailed him with more or less learned exegetical and theological questions. They borrowed books and translations, so that he had trouble in doing justice to all their wishes. To Marcella alone he wrote no less than sixteen letters which, from their content, were of course aimed also at a wider public. Jerome edited them himself, and considered them to be a complete 'book'. This evidently important woman dared on her part to educate the uneasy man a little, and tried to win him from his delight in slander and polemics. Paula was primarily interested in a 'mystical', i.e. allegorical-devotional interpretation of the Scripture. To her daughter Eustochium Jerome dedicated his famous letter on the right form of ascetic life.

At first Jerome had barely the courage, he asserts, to raise his eyes in their presence, such was his respect for these high-born ladies (*Ep.* 127, 7). But with time the relationship became more cordial and unconstrained. Jerome felt increasingly at home in the 'house-congregation' of his students, who were 'truly happy in their bodily and spiritual virginity'. 'The teaching made us stay together continuously; being together made me unself-conscious, and unselfconsciousness gave me confidence' (*Ep.* 45, 2). For Saint Peter's Day, Eustochium sent to Jerome, with a 'spicy' little letter, bracelets and doves which he did not reject, in addition to a little basket 'full of cherries, blushing with virginal modesty'; Lucullus could not have offered them better (*Ep.* 31, 1, 3). Another time, Marcella gave him a new robe, an arm-chair, candles and chalices. It is amusing to see how Jerome every time combined in his answer (of the elegance of which he is obviously proud) social and personal thanks with edifying reflections. The hairshirt, he thinks, signifies fasting; the arm-chair points to domestic decency; the candles to the light with which we await the bridegroom; the chalice to mortification and martyrdom. In his case this interpretation, however, is too favourable—here the arm-chair is rather a sign of laziness, the chalice signifies revels, etc.! Yet in respect to the donors he nevertheless believes himself to have revealed the 'mystery' of that which is veiled (*Ep.* 44). We see that the allegorical method, once learned, could be made useful for any purpose. With Jerome begins the dubious history of the theologian's 'professional joke'. What shall we say for instance, when he gallantly greets Paula, whose daughter had taken the veil, and now had become 'the wife not of a soldier but of a king', as the 'mother-in-law of God' (*Ep.* 22, 20)?

Jerome appears as the first example of the spiritual counsellor and confidant, almost in the manner of the later domestic chaplain of noble and aristocratic society. This too is a sign of the times, and lends his candid descriptions a more general interest. He had all his life avoided concerning himself with simple people. Being himself of common descent, in his social intercourse he always sought connections with those above him. But we must not adapt the picture too much to the analogies of modern times, for example, to the French salons of the *ancien régime*. The world-renouncing atmosphere was too strong for this and the gloom of a by no means aesthetic asceticism

11

brooded over the whole. It was supposed to be an expression of a special love to Christ, but the physical side of virginity was primarily emphasized, and in a way highly embarrassing to modern feeling. To be sure, Jerome had at his disposal the entire assurance and flexibility of an ancient rhetorician and preaching pedagogue, but his rough ascetic cure of souls had not yet progressed into the more sensitive regions of feeling. 'If in Rome any respectable woman would conquer my heart, this is the only way! She would have to mourn and fast, she would have to be caked with dirt and almost blind with tears. Her song would be the psalms, her speech the gospel, her burden abstinence, and her life's occupation fasting' (Ep. 45, 3).

Despite this it was inevitable that in the course of time mistrust and rumours arose out of these meetings and this correspondence. They were borne on a wave of opposition which the new ascetic propaganda was arousing everywhere. We detect it at the same time in Milan, in Gaul and throughout the West. The Romans were furious about the 'disgusting brood of monks' who gave themselves airs with their ascetic demands, the 'impostors and Greeks' who entrapped rich matrons, but otherwise were satisfied with nobody and nothing. Jerome was unwise enough usually to meet his opponents only with haughty wit and sarcasm. The critics of his Biblical text are 'two-legged asses'. Anyone who 'throws stones at' his ascetic tracts must be a dissolute person, a worldling and a hypocrite, and there are more than enough of those, he assures us, even among the monks and clergy. If anyone felt himself touched, things became even worse for him. We still have a letter in which Jerome makes fun of such a priest, with the ridiculous name 'Onasus': he will operate on his evil-smelling nose, and can only give him the advice not to let himself be seen any more if he wished to maintain his reputation as a handsome, eloquent man (Ep. 40). Even this little satire is, like everything with Jerome, embellished with a flood of classical and Biblical quotations.

It seems that Jerome scarcely had any real friends among the men of Rome besides the Senator Pammachius, the son-in-law of Paula, and Damasus himself, 'who has my lady's ear', as his enemies said. Of course, Jerome's quarters were daily visited by many; they kissed his hand in public, and struggled for the favour of a man who was esteemed the right hand and mouthpiece of the Pope, but they did not forgive him 'that he exposed with his filthy invectives the whole of Christian society, every rank and class, in short the whole church', so that everything appeared to be far worse even than their pagan opponents claimed (Rufin., *Apol.* II, 5). And so, when Damasus died on December 11, 384, catastrophe occurred. On all sides hostility burst out. The change was all the more bitter to Jerome, since he, as it appears, was at times naïve enough to have had his own hopes for succession. The new Pope, Siricius, had no understanding of his scholarly work. It even seems that the 'Senate of Pharisees'—as Jerome called the Roman presbytery—had explicitly expressed itself against him. At any rate, he was out of his profitable position. Unfortunately the young Blaesilla, whom Jerome had converted to a strict asceticism, died during these weeks. It was said that fasting had broken her. Her own mother, Paula, was near to collapse. The letter of condolence, which Jerome then wrote to her, praised the deceased to the skies, and at the same time met the mother's grief with barbaric harshness. This is probably understandable only in the light of the difficult situation in which Jerome actually found himself. Blaesilla, it says, is now blessed and enjoys the company of Mary and Hannah! How hurt would she be to see that her mother is provoking Christ by not controlling her sadness! Paula must not in any circumstances appear weak. Tears on account of such a happening are not allowable to a Christian, and even less to a holy nun. The Scripture teaches us the right behaviour. Moreover, a traditional theme, the remembrance of the departed will live on, and in this lies an earthly consolation too. With every line that Jerome will write in the future, Blaesilla's spirit will be before his eyes, and with his books her name will travel through the world and can never more die (*Ep.* 39, 8).

At times Jerome thought of navigating his 'leaky ship' into a calm harbour, and awaiting the storm on some near-by country estate. Why should he be concerned, he wrote, about Rome, her luxury and theatres, and even about the pious circle of his dignified friends? To cling to God—that is sufficient. And again a picture emerged before him, gleaming in Virgilian colours, of the happy rural life. There he may be satisfied with cabbage he has grown himself, with country bread, and fresh milk, and be frugally happy in the shadow of the trees and the meadow-bank dotted with flowers (*Ep.* 43, 3). Yet then he realized that such an evasion could not serve him. For the second time, Jerome made the decision to go to the East—and now finally: 'he returns from Babylon to Jerusalem'. His farewell letter to Asella (*Ep.* 45) is a true reflection of his mood at that time. He is evidently determined to silence his envious enemies, the 'priests and Levites' of the ungrateful city, and to refute especially the slanders concerning his female company; yet at the same time his whole personal exasperation and irritation once again forces its way in. He is supposed to be a libertine, a filthy sneak and intriguer! And even the people, who had once treated him with so much love and respect, say this! But the hypocrites, the worldly-minded society ladies may ridicule his holy life! He has learned to enter the kingdom of heaven 'in ill repute and good repute' (II Cor. vi. 8). Before Christ's tribunal it will some day be revealed who has had the right way of thinking. In its impulsive candour this letter is an astonishing document. The West had hardly known anything like it until then. It is as though Ciceronian cultural expression had combined with Paul's passionate scorn of the world. We hear the language of a reckless ascetic, who in his bitterness is neither free nor great, yet is at any rate a man really alive, through and through.

At first Jerome went to Antioch, where he again took lodging with Evagrius and Paulinus. Yet it was not for long. It was probably agreed from the outset that Paula and Eustochium should follow him by another route. He presently called for them at the house of Epiphanius, Bishop of Salamis, and then travelled in their company through Palestine—a pious pilgrimage which was quite customary in those days. Furthermore, this was for Jerome a new opportunity to broaden his Biblical knowledge. Jerome was the first theologian to emphasize the scientific importance of archeology and personal inspection in this way. 'He who has seen Athens learns to understand Greek history better, and he who has sailed from Troy, by Leucas and Acroceraunia to Sicily, and farther to the mouth of the Tiber, understands the third book of Virgil (i.e. the *Aeneid*). In the same way one looks at the Holy Scriptures with different eyes, if one has visited Judea and knows the old sites and landscapes, whether they have kept their old names or changed them' (*Paralip*. prol.). We owe to Jerome the revision of an old dictionary of Hebrew proper names, and above all of the Eusebian *Onomasticon* of Biblical geography which, supplemented by his own observations, is still an indispensable source today. Besides Palestine, the monastic settlements in Egypt were no less popular as a destination of spiritual and educational journeys. To these places also their learned guide joyfully accompanied the ladies and 'thus learned much, which was unknown to him until then' (*Apol*. III, 22). Above all, he now came to know Alexandria, the last metropolitan centre of theological education which Jerome had not yet visited. He made the acquaintance of the blind Origenist Didymus, his 'clairvoyant' teacher, whom he 'could ask about everything that seemed to him doubtful in the Scripture' (*Ephes*. prol.). Didymus' work on the Holy Spirit is the only dogmatic writing Jerome translated from Greek into Latin; he himself, however, seems to have questioned him primarily about exegetical problems.

In the summer of 386 the travels came to an end. They decided to settle down finally not in Jerusalem, but in the quieter Bethlehem. Jerome had means of his own, and later converted into money the property he had inherited from his parents, in order to help finance the colony planned, and 'not to be laughed at by his envious slanderers' if the enterprise failed

(*Ep.* 66, 14). The greater part, however, was without doubt paid for out of the immense fortune which his women friends put at his disposal. In the course of the years a large convent arose under Paula's leadership, divided into three departments in which the nuns were accommodated according to their social position. Jerome was head of a monastery, smaller than the convent, but in time also counting about fifty inmates. Besides all this there was a hostel for pilgrims and a school in which Jerome also imparted secular education in rhetoric to students. He had again refused to take over regular religious duties: the cloister had a chapel, but for worship the monks went to the church in the town. Jerome was satisfied to preach occasionally before his monks, at times even in Greek. Almost all the monks were Westerners. From the West came more and more visitors and pilgrims, with recruits for the cloister as well. Others occasionally travelled back into their home-country for visits, or on business. Permanent residence (*stabilitas loci*) was not yet considered by the monks of that time as an inescapable obligation, and there was still no question of strict solitude and silence either.

For thirty-four years, i.e. almost half his life, Jerome lived at this place, and did not leave it except for short visits in the neighbourhood, until his death. Besides new polemical treatises, all his long Biblical writings and translations originated here. This was his real life-work, in comparison with which his earlier scholastic achievements appear negligible in extent and weight. Undoubtedly the favourable external conditions contributed a great deal to this productivity. Almost like a modern scholar, Jerome complained, to be sure, of the many disturbances and the crowd of visitors who left him no other choice but to close either his books or his door. He says he does not want to boast of his hospitality—but he must excuse himself, that his work does not make better progress. Only in 'stolen' hours of the long winter nights, burning the midnight oil, does he find time for his commentaries (*Comm. Ezech.* VII prol.). Furthermore, he complains as ever about his weak eyes, which

especially while reading the Hebrew manuscripts refuse to
work; and in principle it is only possible to formulate thought
correctly if one writes down the words oneself (*Ep.* 21, 42).
On the other hand, he had in Bethlehem everything he needed
at his disposal: his countless books, readers, secretaries, and
assistants, students eager to learn, and not least important the
interest and sympathy of his devout women friends who clung
to him and cared for him with ever constant devotion. Whoever visited him received an indelible impression of his restless
energy at work: 'He is constantly at his studies, completely
absorbed by his books; neither by night nor day does he grant
himself relaxation; he is constantly engaged in reading or
writing' (Sulp. Sev., *Dial.* I, 9, 5). That Jerome nevertheless
could not find permanent repose is due less to the small disturbances and dissensions, which even in a monastery cannot
fail to arise, or to the slanders and envy of enemies, whom he
imagined always and everywhere to be at work, but above all
to the uneasiness of his own incorrigible temper, which could
always be provoked to controversy and defence.

Jerome's greatest remaining accomplishment of these years is
the translation of the Old Testament from the Hebrew. This
was probably begun in 390, and substantially concluded about
406. Besides this, he was engaged in other work which was
partly related to it. He had earlier started upon a new translation or revision of the text by use of the Septuagint, the old
Jewish-Greek Bible which in the church had replaced the
original text, and which was very much in repute and honour.
In the library of Caesarea in Palestine Jerome had come across
the original copy of the *Hexapla*, in which Origen had in his
time put together the text of the Septuagint with further translations, and with the original Hebrew text. Jerome started off
with the Psalms. This, his first translation from the Greek
Septuagint, is even today occasionally used liturgically. Further
books followed. Then, however, it became clear to him that
for his work, as he planned it, only the original 'truth' of the
Hebrew text could be determinative. With admirable energy

he set about thoroughly to refresh and deepen his remarkable
Hebrew knowledge, which manifestly was not sufficient for
such a project. He secured—as he did not forget, with his own
good, hard money—as teacher a learned Jewish rabbi, who
dared visit him only at night for fear of his co-religionists.
Beyond purely grammatical knowledge he owed to him also
many an important hint for the interpretation as such. The new
translation which resulted turned out—like everything Jerome
created—uneven. Upon the large historical books he generally
did excellent and precise work; upon others, more superficial.
For the translation of Tobit Jerome claims to have spent only
one day, for Judith only one night; moreover, both are translated from the Aramaic. A useful innovation, not until then
used for prose Biblical texts in Latin, was the arrangement of
the text in lines corresponding to the sense, which to a certain
extent form a substitute for our modern punctuation. Having
perhaps found the suggestion for this from the Hexapla, Jerome
referred to corresponding editions of Demosthenes and Cicero
and emphasized that these 'cola' must not be understood as
'verses'. Naturally, he could not help relying for his translation to a considerable extent on older Latin translations. This
was done in part consciously and on purpose: the faithful reader
of the Bible should not be offended by too radical innovation.
There is, of course, no lack of faults and errors in the work as a
whole—this could hardly be avoided with such a difficult and
novel task. Nevertheless Jerome's translation signified a tre-
mendous advance in every aspect, as compared with the state
of affairs up to that time, and it remains for those days a very
respectable and, on account of the continuous reference to the
Hebrew, unique achievement. With regard to the style, Jerome
repressed the many vulgarisms and barbarous neologisms of the
Old Latin Bible without sacrificing to a dull purism its popularity and vigorous expression. Consequently, the *Vulgate* has
justly remained up to the present day the classical Latin Bible.
There is hardly a later ecclesiastical translation into a modern
language which is not at least indirectly influenced and moulded

by it—even the translation of Luther not excluded.

Certainly it was at first far from immediately becoming the *Vulgate*, i.e. the commonly used ecclesiastical edition of the Latin-speaking church. Not until the early Carolingian epoch was this achieved. The new translation could only gradually establish itself against suspicion and all kinds of opposition. His contemporaries felt little gratitude to Jerome for the greatest work of his life. Even Augustine, who still complained about the chaos of older translations, and who tried to control it to the best of his ability, regretted that Jerome had not adhered more firmly to the Septuagint, in whose miraculous, inspired origin he firmly believed. This was, of course, painful to Jerome, who had at one time believed this legend himself. Others went even further in their criticism. As usual, the new and unfamiliar was at first regarded as merely perverse. But having once convinced himself of the *Hebraica veritas*, i.e. of the superior claims of the original text, Jerome could not give way on this point, at least in principle. Finally he attempted also to define the limits of the Old Testament canon on the basis of the Hebrew. Those books and parts of the Old Testament originally written in another language, in Greek or 'Chaldean' (i.e. Aramaic), have no right to be regarded as God's Word in the strict sense. They are 'apocryphal' and are pushed into the margin as more or less 'legendary'—a decision followed later by the Protestant churches, while the Roman Catholic church finally rejected it at the Council of Trent.

What caused Jerome most trouble was the narrow-mindedness of those who found fault with his translations, because, as he says, in their lack of education they had no conception what translation really means. One cannot simply transfer a living sentence word for word from one language into another. Every language has its own spirit and—without being therefore the poorer or more rigid—because of this also its own laws and possibilities. The 'verbal monstrosities' of the earlier translations are simply ridiculous. The problem is not to replace each word with the same word, but to rewrite the sentence in accordance with its meaning. Jerome, however, was cautious enough to defend the liberty which he takes primarily for his other translations from Greek into Latin, and not for the translation of the Bible, although the Latin language is far closer to Greek, as he well knows, than to Hebrew. In the Holy Scripture, he says, the precise sequence of words as such has in certain cases a deeper meaning, and must be preserved (*Ep.* 57, 5). This again is one of the safeguards which Jerome laid down to protect his ecclesiastical impeccability. Fortunately, he did not in reality by any means always act accordingly in his translation of the Bible. Jerome also referred to the freedom which the New Testament authors themselves display when quoting Old Testament passages, and with regard to the general principles of translation he relied, along with Horace, above all on Cicero, yet he was actually more cautious than either. In his translations taken as a whole, Jerome turned out to be a prudent and experienced scholar, who knows his business and makes no radical experiments. More profound problems of the philosophy of language did not occur to him. Here also, only the material with which he dealt was 'theological', and not the spirit in which he appropriated it. It would be doing him an injustice to compare him in this respect with a thinker like Augustine, who himself ungrudgingly acknowledged the superiority of Jerome's linguistic talent.

The largest part of Jerome's heritage comprises expositions of the Holy Scripture. They are in part detailed commentaries, in which he tried to present and expound every point, but in part also more concise comments or glosses, which are restricted to the brief explanation of the more difficult passages only (*Comm. Dan.* prol.). In addition we have the letters devoted to special problems, the extensive exegetical portions of his dogmatic writings, and the sermons which, though preached before monks, nevertheless have a similarly scholarly character. Jerome could not, for instance, refrain from going into the various readings in the Greek translations of the Psalms. Even as a preacher he expressly refuses to present mere declamations,

but offers real 'expositions'. Most of his commentaries are on
the Old Testament. The explanations justify and at the same
time confirm the underlying translation. The prophets pre-
dominate, and Jerome commented on them all in succession.
On the other hand, he did not deal with a single historical book,
but only some *Hebrew Questions on Genesis* (i.e. of translation)
in a special treatise. This seems at first sight remarkable; but
Jerome is no historian, only an 'historical-philological exegete',
who regularly uses historical information only in order to
elucidate the background, the hidden allusions to the history
of the time, and above all, of course, the 'fulfilment' of the
promises. From the New Testament, apart from a short exposition of the gospel of Matthew dictated in two weeks, which
is restricted admittedly to 'historical' matters, he expounded
only four of the shorter Pauline epistles. Here Jerome reflects
the contemporary Western interest in Pauline theology. Nevertheless, this was only a comparatively modest work done in
haste, which is essentially a catena of passages from older Greek
exegetes. The projected complete commentary on all the Pauline epistles was never written. By contrast, Jerome's 'Work on
the Prophets' had kept him busy for thirty years.

Jerome was a rapid writer, or rather a rapid dictator. He
describes to us how once his amanuensis became nervous, and
began to play with his fingers and to wrinkle his brow when
Jerome stopped in the dictation and tried to reflect. 'I dictate
what comes into my mouth' (*Comm. Gal.* III prol.). 'As the
hand of the writer runs, so also my speaking' (*Comm. Is.* V
prol.). There remained barely time to revise the dictation. It
was not without vanity that Jerome was pleased to apologize
with the excuse that he had finished this or that work under
the pressure of circumstances in so many days, or during one
night watch. In such a case, the circumstances are responsible
for the fact that he could not concentrate better, that this or that
side of the subject could not be more extensively or better dealt
with. As mentioned already, Jerome needed these excuses. Almost every one of his works is somehow an *opus tumultuarium*,

and bears the marks of his manner of working—not exactly uncritical, diligent in its way, yet always hasty and not very conscientious. It is not at all easy to evaluate Jerome adequately as a scholar. Where his statements can be checked, we again and again come across carelessness and oversight. Yet, although modern exegetes have complained about this loudly and legitimately—they nevertheless cannot get away from Jerome! The material he provides is so rich and manifold that nobody can miss it. Without his countless notes, haphazard and scholarly, there would today be lost to us forever any amount of information, allusions, and philological explanations. However, there is no possible doubt about one thing: Jerome produces his astonishing knowledge chiefly at second hand. Various later Greeks are drawn upon for the older information, and Eusebius particularly for the historical material, and above all again and again it is Origen of whom he takes toll, often repeating him almost verbatim for pages on end. Occasionally Jerome frankly admitted his dependence: 'They say that I made excerpts from Origen's works, and that it is illegitimate to touch the writings of the old masters in such a way. People think that they gravely insult me by this. For myself, however, I see in this the highest praise. It is my express desire to follow an example of which I am convinced that it will please all men of discernment and you too' (*Comm. Mich.* II prol.). In other cases, Jerome carefully concealed his dependence. He manages, for instance, —it may be from sheer hastiness—to present things which Origen had learned from his Hebrew teachers as if he himself had discovered them. The worst thing is the obvious exaggeration of his own knowledge of the sources. Jerome undoubtedly knows a great deal, yet he had not really read or even handled one half of the books to which he refers in the proud tone of a man with intimate knowledge. He can be excused in individual cases. It was then a common literary custom not to cite explicitly more recent authorities from which one drew. Nevertheless, the overall picture of Jerome's personality suffers from his thorough unreliability, coupled with his arrogance. Even in scholarly literature, the 'style' of the man reveals his character.

The exegetical method of Jerome is not uniform. He adopted the allegorical method of the Origenist-Alexandrian school, as well as the realism of the Antiochian philology, and he followed neither consistently. Yet on the whole it is evident that as time went on the 'mystical' interpretation of the texts was increasingly crowded out by the historical-philological exposition. It fitted much better the whole manner and bent of Jerome. He was primarily interested in the concrete meaning of a statement, less in its timeless and allegorical meaning. He was concerned to grasp the natural 'literal' sense, and to understand the special purpose of the text 'in that way in which it was understood by the author himself, who wrote it' (*Ep*. 37, 3). What mattered to him was the so-called 'historical' or 'literal' sense, the content of which he rightly defined so broadly that the figurative and metaphorical meaning also was included in this, so far as it was still aimed at the original, historical context. This did not yet mean to Jerome, however, that he had therefore rejected the 'higher', allegorical interpretation, or even that he considered it superfluous. Like all exegetes of the early church, and like his master Origen, Jerome affirmed the twofold or threefold meaning of the Scripture, and repudiated an exclusively historical interpretation as 'Jewish'. The mere letter 'kills'. What he demanded with increasing emphasis was only that the literal, historical exegesis should not be found inferior to the allegorical speculation, and in principle should precede it. One must not interpret a writing allegorically without any knowledge whatever of the historical content, as he himself had done in his youth (*Comm. Abd*. prol.). It is also significant that the 'mystical' explanations Jerome offered on his own are far more typological than allegorical in the strict sense. That is to say, they do not attempt to deduce general religious knowledge from the words and events of the Old Testament, but take them only as pointers and 'types' of the future New Testament history, which had 'fulfilled' them. Basically, the 'historical' method was to Jerome the really scholarly mode of interpretation, while allegory met rather the devotional, practical, and ecclesiastical needs, and had to be adapted to these. 'History (i.e. the historical interpretation) is precise, and does not permit arbitrary deviations. Tropology on the other hand (i.e. the higher, 'moral' interpretation) is free, and subject only to the one law that it must have a pious meaning in view' (*Comm. Abac.* I, 11). Accordingly, it allows different ways of interpreting one and the same text. When Jerome proceeded 'historically' he basically followed the original text, while he unhesitatingly based the higher, allegorical understanding upon the Septuagint, although at times somewhat 'against his conscience' (*Comm. Nah.* i. 14). But what else can he do, in view of those who consider any interpretation made without reference to the usual translation (i.e. the Septuagint) to be simply incomplete and defective (*Comm. Is.* xxx. 33)? 'We have', he suggests, 'the obligation to expound the Scripture as it is read in church, and yet we must not, on the other hand, abandon the truth of the Hebrew (text)' (*Comm. Mich.* i. 16). This is the genuine Jerome, who did not like carrying arguments on principle to their logical conclusion, and wished always to remain in contact with the ecclesiastical mind and tradition.

Independent theological decisions are not very common in his commentaries. His own judgement was often practically stifled by the many contradictory opinions he reported, and it was left more or less to the reader's discretion. The teachings and expositions of the heretics, or of heathens like Porphyry, were indeed always sharply repudiated (for the books of the Holy Bible are of course dictated by the Holy Spirit, and he who does not have the Holy Spirit, is naturally not capable of understanding it correctly), but the 'correct' understanding itself was equated with the teaching of the church. A critical examination is found only in regard to details. The basis question is never really asked or answered, what the inspiration of the Scripture actually means in relation to critical and philological knowledge, and whether this conception was to be understood literally or in a more general sense. Jerome contented himself with the general acknowledgement that the Scripture contained no contradictions and was infallible, but he was not able to develop a Biblical hermeneutic of his own. Accordingly, his explanations of the Bible fluctuated between dull philology and unauthoritative edification. Useful as these were, they lack theological substance. Only in moral and especially in really ascetic exposition did his personal temper break through. This corresponds to the picture also revealed by his later letters, so far as these have an instructive character. Often in the form of small essays, they discuss specific questions of Biblical exegesis, or as admonitions (and obituaries) glorify and illustrate above all the ascetic 'virginal' ideal.

From time to time Jerome still intervened with his own treatises in the theological controversies of the West, particularly when they were of practical ecclesiastical importance. He remained in later years also consistently silent regarding Trinitarian Christological problems, in face of which he had already been somewhat perplexed at the beginning of his career, as we have seen. It is as if these questions, which kept the whole East around him in ferment, did not exist for him. He had probably not even read the numerous new works on this subject. Everything which happened, however, in Rome, Gaul, or Africa, immediately provoked his excitement, and it was not difficult for his friends there to elicit letters and essays from him, which then produced the natural response. 'I only have to write something', says Jerome in self-satisfied complaint, 'and at once my friends or my enemies are out to circulate my writings among the masses. The intention is surely different, yet the zeal of both groups is identical, and both exaggerate whether in praise or blame' (Ep. 48, 2). Conversely, it was felt in the West that Jerome was often lacking in due moderation in his polemic, that he distorted his adversaries' opinion, and that he argued from personal irritation—objections which he always repudiated with indignation. When the views of Helvidius found a certain revival in the 'books drunkenly vomited' by the 'Epicurean' monk Jovinian (adv. Jov. I, 1), the two-volume refutation turned out so violent that the effect threatened to be the opposite of that intended. Jerome's praise of virginity shocked many circles, appearing as a defamation of marriage. Pammachius vainly exerted himself to withdraw from circulation the copies published. Things went no better in the case of the priest Vigilantius, 'The Vigilant', than they had with Jovinian. Jerome in his attack called him 'Sleepy head', *Dormitantius*. After Jovinian had 'belched out his spirit between pheasants and roast pork' (*adv. Vig.* 1), Vigilantius represented not only a repetition of his immorality and intemperance, but even aimed his spittle at the holy martyrs also; i.e. Vigilantius had criticized new forms of the martyr cult, and the abuses related to it, which even Jerome could not completely deny without doing some justice to the underlying serious concern of his opponent. He was especially bitter against Vigilantius because he had himself lodged him earlier in Bethlehem, and now presumed him to have secret connections with his Roman enemies.

Such violent invective has done no little damage to Jerome's reputation in the eyes of a more sensitive posterity. It cannot be denied that, like the coarse statements on sexual matters, it belongs to the figure of the man. Jerome in anger readily displayed a vulgar and malicious disposition, which stood in singular contrast to the elegant form and culture of his writings. Nevertheless, it would be unjust to take his methods of controversy as the expression of an unrefined or impure habit of mind, and completely to ignore the contemporary presuppositions of his polemical style. In this, also, Jerome was the successful product of the academic training he had enjoyed. The various forms of bellicose insinuation and mockery, including the exaggerations, misrepresentations of names, and manifold zoological terms of abuse conform to the rules of ancient, and particularly of Ciceronian polemic, in both the juristic and literary field. Tertullian also served as an example. Jerome was not deficient in wit when he was using such weapons. He possessed an innate talent for striking characterization and telling caricature. His descriptions of the vices of society, of the bad habits

of the monks, and of the manifold profanities of the Holy Land
are convincingly life-like and perspicuous. The disturbing factor
is simply that he used his sharp eye, his amusing sarcasm, and
his polemical tricks no longer as a pagan rhetorician, but in the
essentially different profession of a Christian, and that he did
not, like Tertullian, compensate for the all too human side of
his method by deep and truly original thought, and a genuine,
objective passion. His controversies stayed on the level of the
petty, the outward, and the personal. Despite his learned display, his ascetic zeal, and his occasional spiritual unction, they
remained basically inappropriate and not really satisfying; they
were edifying only for his partisans. Jerome was not equal to
the spiritual requirements of his subject-matter, and much too
self-satisfied to recognize the limits of his nature. Thus, for
instance, he let himself be moved in old age to compose a
Dialogue against the Pelagians, from which the modern reader
must conclude with astonishment that Jerome had not the
slightest understanding of the real issue in the controversy, and
stood much nearer in his attitude in the matter to Pelagius than
to his alleged confederate Augustine!

In the permanent private warfare and quarrels the constant
confusion of factual and personal issues had a most embarrassing
effect even on his contemporaries. He was unable to look away
from himself, and his veracity failed whenever his own reputation seemed to be jeopardized. Jerome could not bear to have
any person of rank placed at his side. Basil the Great, whom he
never knew personally, he did not acknowledge because of his
wicked 'arrogance'. Ambrose, his predecessor in appreciation
of the Greek theologians, he declared for this very reason to be
a writer without strength or savour, and he compared him to
an ugly crow trying to adorn himself in borrowed plumes.
For a time he even pursued Augustine, who had approached
him by letter without flattery but with respectful politeness,
with damaging insinuations and treated him as an impertinent
young man. Apart from a small circle of friendly woman
ascetics and blindly devoted adherents, hardly anyone
12

succeeded in living continuously at peace with Jerome. Once the quarrel started, it was almost impossible again to reconcile this suspicious, choleric and, as an opponent, unscrupulous man. He felt that all means were justified that helped him to achieve moral annihilation of 'the envious'. In one case, this unfortunate disposition not only hurt himself, but also had very serious implications damaging to the whole church—in the so-called 'first Origenist controversy'.

In reality, these struggles which lasted for years, and details of which can hardly be untangled, do not at all represent a unity of subject-matter. Incidental personal and political differences were artificially transferred by Jerome to a dogmatic basis, distorting the real connection, simply because he could best defend himself in the role of the persecuted witness for the truth. In this way, there was a break-up of old friendships, traditions, and convictions which must really have been dear to him, and which in different circumstances would have enjoyed his protection. We must here be satisfied with a short sketch of these disgraceful incidents.

Origen, the great Alexandrian theologian, had not remained immune to attack in his lifetime, and during the century and a half which had elapsed since then, opposition had again and again been registered against individual doctrines of his system which was, strictly speaking, more Hellenistic and philosophical than Biblical. His opinion regarding the origin and end of the world, his teaching on the soul, and his theory of universal salvation and redemption, could hardly as a matter of fact be brought into harmony with the early Christian tradition. Added to this was the use made of his writings by the 'Arian' theologians, and the quite general suspicion aroused against the extremely spiritualizing tendencies of his exegesis and speculation with their various layers, tending to sublimate and evaporate every concrete, historical, and visible element. On the other hand, however, Origen was the real creator of a 'scientific' theology. He was the great systematic Biblical expert and interpreter, on whose immense life-work the following generations lived. In the fourth century the study of his writings and his theology underwent a revival in the East, and thus Jerome was in his early years won over to this master. He saw in him the Doctor of the Church *par excellence*, the like of whom had not been seen since the days of the apostles. Jerome dreamed of an almost complete translation of his works into Latin, and began with the Homilies. During his Roman stay he praised and recommended Origen in enthusiastic terms, and based almost all his own writings on him as the most weighty authority. There is not a word of qualification of his theological authority; on the contrary, the hostility Origen had had to endure from churchmen was to Jerome just an example of the ingratitude of the world, which has always pursued the best with its envy (*Ep.* 33, 5). While Origen was still virtually unknown in the West, this judgement coincided with the conviction of almost all Greek theologians of rank. Only the narrow-minded enemy of all dubious teaching, Epiphanius, Bishop of Salamis, had already declared Origen to be a heretic to be condemned—and with him Jerome had co-operated. At first, however, this produced no repercussions upon his relationship with Origen. The only circles besides this hostile to Origen were in certain monks' colonies in Egypt. The monks felt themselves disturbed in their crude religious notions by his spiritualizing interpretation of the Scripture, but this 'anthropomorphism' was then still despised as a primitive superstition and the patriarchs of Alexandria themselves deemed it important that its adherents should not become too powerful.

The change of position which Jerome made in 393 on the basis of a rather unimportant incident thus appears even more puzzling. Certainly we do not know the background from which a certain Atarbius, otherwise unknown, at that time stepped forward in Palestine and carried on propaganda against Origen. While he was flatly rejected by John, Bishop of Jerusalem, and his friends, he was successful with Jerome in Bethlehem: and the latter was willing without more ado to anathematize all errors of Origen, lock, stock, and barrel. It may be that, his interests being primarily exegetical and ascetic, he had not until then considered it necessary to examine more closely the disputed teachings of the master, and to ponder their theological rightness or wrongness. He had certainly never himself consented to these false teachings. All the same, this indiscriminate condemnation, the moment it was demanded from outside, was irresponsible. Jerome was certainly always anxious to be seen in the foremost ranks of ecclesiastical orthodoxy and prone to condemn more or less without examination what was accounted doubtful, suspicious, and undesirable. To be added to this is his allegiance to Western presuppositions. He was only willing to learn from the East academically, not dogmatically. Jerome hardly imagined what implications this first, and almost incidental, expression of opinion would have. Later, he explicitly declared that the theological condemnation had by no means been intended to justify the Philistines who did not read Origen at all. As a matter of fact, Jerome never ceased to base his work on Origen, but from now on he necessarily became increasingly cautious not to refer to him by name, and he no longer dared to complete the translation of the *Homilies*.

When in the next year the aged Epiphanius visited Palestine, and unpleasant scenes took place between him and Bishop John on the question of Origenism, Jerome was already considered to be his declared partisan. Among the monks at Bethlehem Epiphanius stormed against the Origenist heresy, and called for a decision. Here also there were controversies. These disputes would probably have been forgotten again after a time, had he not simultaneously undertaken a canonical step which Jerome welcomed for completely different reasons. Epiphanius ordained his brother Paulinianus presbyter of the monks of Bethlehem, in order to make them ecclesiastically independent of the Greek clergy of the town, and at the same time also of John. By canon law, this was an affront which the bishop of Jerusalem could not possibly brook after all that had happened. He refused to give approval to this encroachment upon his rights, and, when this did not succeed, changed to means of coercion by barring

access for the unruly monks to the churches of Bethlehem altogether. Jerome now had no alternative, unless he would give
in and admit his guilt, but to transfer the quarrel completely to
the dogmatic field, and to renounce obedience to his bishop
on account of doctrine. He drew up against John a frenzied
pamphlet, in which he presented the case—by no means in
accordance with the truth—as though John, because he had not
permitted the anathematization of the illustrious dead, approved
of all Origen's errors. But, meanwhile, John had turned to
Theophilus, Patriarch of Alexandria, for help and intervention.
The latter substantially took his side, and the government also
threatened Jerome with expulsion on the grounds of continuous disturbance of the peace. Nothing was left to him but
to accept the 'paternal' intervention of Theophilus, and, with
loud praise for his love of peace, and faint complaints about his
'credulity', to reconcile himself again with John (396/397).
That the old relationship was not so easily re-established can be
imagined; yet, fortunately, the discord seemed to have been
resolved outwardly.

The quarrel had another and more intimate and personal
side for Jerome. His old friend and compatriot Rufinus had also
travelled to Palestine, some years before Jerome, likewise
accompanied by a wealthy and aristocratic Roman lady. He
lived in Jerusalem, just like Jerome in Bethlehem, in pursuit of
his ascetic ideals, and the study of Greek theology. However,
when Atarbius appeared, Rufinus behaved very differently
from Jerome. Being an Origenist like him, he at first tried to
keep away from the conflict, and then, when he did not succeed, he came out resolutely on John's side. This firm attitude
must have been all the more embarrassing to Jerome, as a comparison between the two friends was natural. The admiration
which Rufinus reaped from activities similar to those of Jerome
had perhaps already earlier aroused his jealousy. Of course, the
official steps of reconciliation re-established the outward relationship between Rufinus and Jerome, and both friends again
shook hands. Yet, since Rufinus soon afterwards left Palestine

and settled in Rome—Rome which Jerome had left under such unfortunate circumstances!—it is understandable that Jerome's suspicion against a rival barely reconciled to him soon began to stir again. All this constitutes the background for the rapid revival of the unfortunate controversies.

Rufinus had found in Rome, as he thought, the appropriate place to work for the promotion of Greek theological education, and especially for the knowledge of Origen, in the way indeed which Jerome had originally intended, and in a certain way still practised. The Palestinian disputes, however, had meanwhile aroused suspicion against Origen in Rome also. Rufinus tried at first to dispel this by translating the *Apology*, formerly written by Pamphilus and Eusebius in defence of Origen. He then added a revision of *De Principiis* itself, Origen's main systematic work. At the beginning of 398, the two first volumes of the *Beginnings* or *Chief Articles* of the Christian teaching were published for the first time in Latin. Rufinus admittedly proceeded by simply leaving out the dogmatically disputed portions, or by 'supplementing' with orthodox passages from other writings of Origen, a procedure which Jerome in his commentaries largely followed in just the same manner. Rufinus felt himself even more entitled to do this, since he did not consider the questionable passages to be authentic, but— doubtless mistakenly—as later interpolations inserted by the heretics. In the prolegomena to this edition he mentioned, without name, the older and meritorious translation by Jerome which Pope Damasus had formerly sponsored. Since Jerome had meanwhile turned towards other and original projects, Rufinus, urged on by his friends, had now to decide on the continuation of these works despite his own more modest talents. It is not necessary to suspect spite concealed behind these words which are respectful in tone. Rufinus could not very well avoid some mention of the works of his predecessor, and he hardly could have imagined that Jerome would now simply take as tactless any reference to his earlier efforts upon Origen. On the other hand, it is evident that Rufinus with this reference simply

wished to protect himself against the new anti-Origenist sentiment, and the cool tone in which he mentioned his old friend
no longer reveals any trace of the former intimate confidence.
Be that as it may, Jerome, who in this whole matter could not
have had a completely good conscience, felt himself compro-
mised, and he attached the worst construction to Rufinus'
reference, and to the whole work. He took the prolegomena
as a more or less malicious attempt to damage his reputation,
and to cause him new trouble by unwelcome reminiscences of
his former attitude.

Nevertheless, he tried to keep his temper, and his only wish
was if possible not to be connected any more with the regret-
table disputes about Origen. It was the clique of his Roman
friends and associates who first opened the conflict, and who
would have liked to put Rufinus in the prisoner's dock as an
Origenist. The Christian community of Rome had obviously
been split for a long time, and the rival parties were fighting
for influence in the church. After all that had previously
occurred, Jerome, however, could not keep silent for long. If,
as Rufinus maintained, Origen was no heretic, but actually
entirely orthodox, then his own noisy attacks upon John, and
Epiphanius' condemnations which he had translated, were evidently unjust. Such a suspicion he could not let go unchallenged!
Hence, Jerome hastily made a second translation of Origen's *De
Principiis*, complete and literal, which admittedly had no other
purpose than to unmask the author as a notorious heretic. This
made it inevitable that Rufinus' translation and defence appeared unreliable and untrue or at least partial and extremely
questionable when compared with it. A half-hearted concilia-
tory letter written to him by Jerome was intercepted by his
Roman adherents. Rufinus only knew his polemical remarks
from third parties, and must have felt himself attacked with
bias. Threatened from all sides, he on his part now put up a
vigorous resistance. His *Apology* against Jerome expresses the
whole bitterness and indignation he felt at his two-faced attitude. On the one hand, it is charged, Jerome reproaches Rufinus

with his Origenism; he renounces, on the other hand, his own old love to Origen, and tries to conceal the change of position which he had quietly made. Rufinus makes a good case in defence of his method of translation, his personal behaviour, and his orthodoxy. He no longer shows any consideration toward Jerome: with painstaking accuracy the unpleasant features of his character, and the contradictions of his statements, are proved by verbatim quotations. Rufinus is almost completely in the right in his claims. Moreover, his personal honesty is not to be doubted. Yet Jerome was now driven to extremities: his moral standing was at stake.

Among the many polemical writings composed by Jerome, the three-volume *Apology* against Rufinus, which did not originate at a stroke, is the most passionate and spiteful. The manner in which he hurls at his adversary charges of malicious intent, conscious lying, and every kind of baseness, is most displeasing, and shows sufficiently how bad a case he really had. So is his unvarying prejudice, and the way in which he gets tied up in his own contradictions and half-truths. It would have been far better for him to take a stand by the distinction he had attempted between Origen the exegete and Origen the theological heretic and, in addition, quietly to concede certain distortions in his own evaluation. But Jerome was incapable of this. Everything Rufinus had enumerated had to be shown up as utterly untrue, and his behaviour shown to be determined entirely by the most sordid motives. Fear for the reputation of his own orthodoxy now combined with the insulted vanity of the scholar. The quarrel was theological as well as literary and personal, and threatened repeatedly to lose itself in mere insignificant corrections, insinuations, and trivialities. Rufinus is now an ignoramus, with not the slightest idea of how to translate. He is not even able to express himself at all like an educated person. In his personal life, too, there is not a word to be said for him. It is simply not true, maintains Jerome, that he ever had stood up in the church's warfare and suffered for the faith. Even now this alleged ascetic in reality lives in magnificence and pleasure. Above all, he is and remains an Origenist, who committed forgeries to protect his heresy, and brings in the most dubious heretics on his side. In the third book, added later, Jerome indignantly rejects Rufinus' olive-branch, and declares further proposals of reconciliations attempted by other parties to be totally unacceptable. So long as the faith is in danger, there would be no peace for him, and least of all would he let himself be intimidated by threats. Jerome wrote letters in all directions, and sent his *Apology* as far as Africa in order to check Rufinus' abominable intrigues, about which, as Augustine disapprovingly informs him, until then nothing had there been heard. Nobody was really interested in this quarrel. The heresies of Origen were still virtually unknown in the West, and Rufinus was the last to attempt to circulate them. When despite this an official condemnation finally took place, it is to be attributed only partly to Jerome's activity. A double change which occurred in the politics of the church as a whole was the decisive thing.

Until the year 400, Theophilus, Patriarch of Alexandria, had protected the Origenists in accordance with his own conviction. He was, however, now confronted with the pressure of the anti-Origenist monks, and was at the same time exposed to serious personal charges raised against him by these monks. This sufficed to cause a complete change of mind. Theophilus condemned Origenism, and since his accusers had turned for help to John Chrysostom, Patriarch of Constantinople, the matter soon attracted further attention. Almost at the same time, a change of pope took place in Rome which also signified a shift in attitude. The deceased Pope Siricius was, as we know, not too well disposed toward Jerome; the new pope, Anastasius, was elected by the opposition, and was also supported by Jerome's friends. So he was readily willing to endorse the condemnation pronounced by Theophilus and compelled the bishops of Milan and Aquileia, to which Rufinus had retreated, to take up the same position. There was no intention to persecute Rufinus personally; Jerome, however, was triumphant at his victory and tried to extend it on all sides. So he put himself in other ways also at the disposal of Theophilus' unscrupulous policy. Even old Epiphanius, who had all along participated in the struggle, finally refused to take part in the intrigues against Chrysostom, yet Jerome did not hesitate to translate into Latin the shocking pamphlet, full of atrocious slanders, which Theophilus had written against Chrysostom. He thereby sided with the mendacious propaganda against one of the purest figures of the old church. His attitude toward Rufinus is similar. The latter had been wise enough not to continue any longer the undignified conflict with such an opponent. For years he peacefully produced his translations of Origen and other literary works, and never again mentioned the name of Jerome. Jerome, by contrast, could never let an opportunity pass without needling anew and complaining about the fat 'grunter', as he calls Rufinus. He was the 'poisonous and dumb beast' like a scorpion, the voluptuous 'Sardanapalus', the wild 'Nero' who outwardly carries himself as a puritanical Cato. With his classically-draped but mean sarcasm his former friend persecuted him even beyond his grave. How far Jerome himself believed in the truth of his invective is difficult to decide. In the bitterness of the controversy he finally lost all feeling of decency and veracity. Disregarding these personal differences which occupied the foreground, the first condemnation of Origenism remains the permanent result of this controversy. However, at first the practical consequences of the official anathema were small. The final proscription of the 'heretic' took place only a century and a half later, at the fifth Ecumenical Council (553). There can undoubtedly be different opinions about the rightness and necessity of this delayed censure—even by the criterion of the dogmatic attitude of the ancient church. For Jerome's agitation, however, there is hardly any real excuse. It was just in the West, which he tried to stir up against Origen, that there was not the slightest ecclesiastical cause for this. The 'danger' of a theological heresy existed only in his head. It was only his own interests, by no means unselfish, his private embarrass-

ments, entanglements, and whims which forced him, almost
against his will, to this public polemic and heresy-hunt. Jerome
cannot be excused in this case. We can only explain his attitude
up to a point in the light of the circumstances, and make it to
some extent understandable on the basis of the known facts of
his weak character.

The last years of Jerome also were filled with controversy.
It is as if he subsequently wished to justify his own behaviour
by trying to bring into an artificial connection with Origenism
new enemies with whom he had to deal, Pelagius among them.
Out of revenge the Pelagians set fire to his monastery in 416.
Already before this, however, there were external troubles: the
Bedouin of the desert and the turmoil resulting from the beginning of the barbarian invasions were threatening Palestine.
Refugees from the West deluged the country, and for a time
an escape by sea was even considered. The dangers, however,
always passed by. A serious blow for Jerome was Eustochium's
death in 419—Paula had died earlier (404). At last his physical
strength began to diminish. It is said he had become so weak that
he could rise from his bed only by aid of a rope which was
fastened to the ceiling beam. Yet his energy was unbroken. His
last commentary, on the Prophet Jeremiah, shows no sign of
senility; even the continued polemic against Origen's arbitrary
allegorism is here well-founded and entirely pertinent. Jerome,
now more than seventy years old, was able to carry on his
dictation as far as the 32nd chapter. Then he died on September
30, 420 (419?). His bones were buried in Bethlehem. They are
supposed to have been brought to Rome in the Middle Ages,
but are missing today.

If we wish correctly to understand and classify Jerome's historical significance, we have above all to see and hold to one
fact: Jerome was a Westerner, a typical and conscious representative of Latin Christianity. This sounds rather paradoxical in
respect to a man who lived the greater part of his life in Greek
surroundings, who everywhere carried on propaganda for
Greek education, and who became famous primarily as a

student and translator of the Greeks. None the less, the man who called himself ironically a 'half-barbarian', and who in distant lands had virtually forgotten his Latin (*Ep.* 50, 2), remained always a *homo Romanus* in nature and purpose (*Ep.* 15, 3). The Greeks were his 'teachers'; but Latin compatriots remained his associates, his friends, and his correspondents. In all Jerome said, wrote, and did, he looked exclusively to the West, and gave his attention to the response he found there. Thus in church politics too he always adhered to the party of the 'right', to the extreme group of Western-oriented old-Niceans who in the East formed a diminishing minority. The problems of theological metaphysics dealt with in the East did not interest or concern him at all. In this, Jerome was far more backward than other Western theologians of his century, like Hilary, Marius Victorinus, Ambrose, or the deacon Chalcidius who had even translated and partly commented on Plato's *Timaeus* for Hosius of Cordova. By nature he was as entirely un-philosophical as any previous Latin theologian, even if he occasionally boasted of his philosophical knowledge: 'What has Aristotle to do with Paul? or Plato with Peter?' (*adv. Pel.* I, 14). His austere moralism, his practical church sense, his real-istic liking for the visible, the actual, and the concrete, his sar-casm and rude wit were also a Western heritage. As theologian, Jerome stuck to his church, to her firm teaching, to the Scripture, and, above all, to the Old Testament. This was completely sufficient for his inner religious life. Yet with a clear view Jerome recognized what his home church lacked, when her modest literature was compared with the rich theological, and above all the exegetical, tradition of the Greek church. Jerome sensed the need for Western Christianity to catch up with the East intellectually, and he summoned all his strength to fulfil this need. The hasty nature of his writings, unbalanced and rushed, can be partly explained by this. He thus imparted to the West a knowledge of the Greek commentaries and homilies. By his own works he aroused scholarly interest in the exposi-tion of the Scripture and acquainted his fellow-countrymen with the literary, archaeological, and above all, with the linguistic prerequisites for such work. Jerome was, of course, not the only man to attempt this sort of activity, but he far outdid all his friends and enemies who were striving for the same goal, and looked at as a whole completed an imposing life-work. He gave to Latin Christianity its Bible anew, and provided the possibilities for further study of its language. Yet one seeks in vain to find in him solid methodological and theological principles, on the basis of which such research should be conducted. His own attitude, the perpetual fluctuation in principle, and the many practical, ecclesiastical, and polemical considerations he incorporated were not very promising as a theological model.

We do Jerome an injustice if we try to view him as a creative theologian, as a great teacher of the church, and judge him as such. In a way it was his misfortune to have been pushed into this role by the situation of his time and his own convictions. What kept Jerome all his life bound to his spiritual calling was his ascetic decision, gained after a painful struggle, and passionately maintained. This ascetic pattern changed his intellectual world and made him the teacher of an ascetic education, the theologian of the Holy Scripture. But even in the monk's habit, he remained himself the late classical scholar and rhetorician, who with his literary ambition could never get free from himself, and who valued the world and men according to the success of his own productions. Jerome believed in his ideals, but his faith remained superficial and never penetrated to the depths. All his ecclesiastical and theological achievements were ambiguous and remained problematical in their effect. He lacked all round the decisive requirement for lasting greatness: character.

It is different if we evaluate him as a literary figure in the general history of ideas. Jerome was a successful scholar, the founder of Western Biblical philology. In his cultural aims, despite his asceticism, he was almost a humanist. The stimulus his writings gave to scholarship has had a lasting effect through the centuries. In their formal skill his letters remain a model of the elegant art of correspondence, such as the older Christian literature did not yet possess. The whole picture of his personality, never dull, always lively, has made an unforgettable impression upon posterity. Therefore all good humanists, and most humanistically-inclined theologians, have always treasured a measure of friendship for Jerome, in spite of his human limitations.

CHAPTER VI

AUGUSTINE

AUGUSTINE is the only church father who even today remains an intellectual power. Irrespective of school and denomination he attracts pagans and Christians, philosophers and theologians alike by his writings and makes them come to terms with his intentions and his person. He also has an abiding indirect influence, more or less modified and broken, as a conscious or unconscious tradition in the Western churches, and through them in the general heritage of culture. It is therefore not easy for the historian to find the necessary distance and correct criteria for the study of Augustine. We still stand on the many-fissured spurs of that mountain-chain, the ridge of which seems almost to cut off behind us the horizon of church history. If one approaches it, however, as we do now, from the opposite side, the impact of the steep height and of the precipitous summit, of the breadth of intellectual and religious power in this one figure, so far above all his predecessors, is even more surprising and, at first sight, overwhelming. The older Western theologians appear, compared with Augustine, small in stature, unproductive, almost insignificant. Yet this impression too is deceptive, or at least one-sided. On closer examination, one realizes that the colossal massif is still based upon the old solid strata of the early Latin church, and that the lesser peaks which we have so far crossed have often pointed in the direction where Augustine emerges before us, though still suddenly and independently.

Pre-Augustinian Western Christianity—this has shown itself time and again—had a fundamentally 'Jewish' character. It was moral, legalistic, and rigorous. It demanded subjection, it asked

for accomplishment, and affirmed ecclesiastical order and discipline. In its earnestness and practical energy it was great, but
it dwelt upon the rational consideration of the divine precepts
and promises. It lived on the institutions of the past and hope
for the future—a religion without a genuine present, without
full freedom, and without final dedication and blessedness. It
was therefore also lacking in freedom in its relationship toward
the natural and the intellectual world. Western asceticism was
until Augustine exclusively negative, violently renunciative and
defensive in spirit, and the dry rationality of Latin thinking did
not tolerate any real philosophy. This means that at the same
time it did not tolerate any attempt to come to terms with the
spirit of Hellenism, or with the theological vitality of the Greek
church. Yet it is obvious that already prior to Augustine this
inner seclusion and intellectual inadequacy of Western Christianity had begun to change, so that new vistas were increasingly
opened up. Jerome was a straggler of the old brigade, and even
he in his own way sensed the necessity of a renewal. With
others of his generation, above all with the great Ambrose, a
dialogue with Greek theology was already bound up with a
deeper understanding of the Biblical proclamation itself. The
Old Testament lost its autocratic position, while the individuality of the 'gospel' gleamed and waxed bright. The previous
formulation of the anthropological problem, and the old Latin
interest in virtue and merit, in forgiveness of sins, penance, and
justice, changed meaning in this light. They were united with
faith in Christ, and acquired an evangelical direction. The most
important symptom of this change was the new interest in
Paul's theology which came to have a decisive influence on
Ambrose, Marius Victorinus, and the so-called 'Ambrosiaster',
sometimes in quite different ways. In the East Paul remained, as
with the Gnostics of the second century, primarily the theologian of spiritual and 'mystical' cognition, of speculative enthusiasm, of vision and the purified life. The anti-Judaizing
Paul who broke through the law and established 'righteousness
by faith' was first discovered by the Western theology of the

fourth century, and never again lost. In Augustine's theology of grace this movement reached its climax, and found a formulation valid for a long time. The period which followed varied in its attitude to his Paulinism; only the Reformation went beyond the Augustinian understanding of Paul, and to that extent in a fundamental sense beyond Augustine himself.

Augustine was a genius—the only father of the church who can claim without question this pretentious title of modern personality-rating. All attempts to find some explanation of the greatness of this man from his milieu, from his intellectual heritage, or from his undoubtedly extraordinary natural talents lead nowhere. Augustine developed more than others. This ability to develop, i.e. to take up new ideas, to change and remould himself, was perhaps the most essential requisite of what he became. His own story and this inner capability he himself understood as no natural gift, nor as his own accomplishment, but as the work of divine grace, and of the inward and outward guidance which was granted him. We will not attempt to analyse his 'nature' in this introduction, but proceed immediately to follow the course of his life, and to mention briefly the accomplishments in which his actions and his 'nature' found expression.

Augustine's background—his ancestry, environment and the first stages of his career—is reminiscent of Jerome. Augustine also came from a middle-class, perhaps even a lower middle-class, provincial milieu. He was born on November 13, 354, in Thagaste, a small town with a veneer of Roman culture, in which nevertheless the national Berber traditions were still strong. To outward view, his youth appears banally commonplace. What his family and he himself strove for was rapid advancement, wealth, and reputation. For this reason, the gifted son had to receive the best possible education, yet the circumstances were more straitened and depressed than they were for the son of a notable from Strido, who hardly ever knew serious financial problems. Patricius, Augustine's father, must have been the descendant of some Roman veteran who

13

had been settled in what is now Algeria, in the interior close to the Tunisian border. He was a member of the city-council of Thagaste, and possessed a vineyard and a small competence; but it was not sufficient to enable his oldest son, who had finished his schooling in the neighbouring Madaura, to continue his studies in Carthage. A friendly patron and relative, Romanianus, had to assist. Patricius probably thought of making his son a lawyer, but Augustine decided to enter the more intellectual, and, so to speak, 'academic' career of a professional rhetorician. The ideal created by the Greek Sophists, and transplanted by Cicero on to Roman soil, of the rhetorician who had mastered language and classical literature was still central in the idea of those who cared for culture and general education. Though rhetoric had long ago forfeited its old political power, and had become a purely literary activity, its cultivation, which was then restricted to a small stratum of urban society, was still a part of public and political life. The intellectual content of its rhythmic and vocal devices, of its arrangements, definitions, and etymologies, of its dialectic and polemical dexterity, seems to us today chilly, formal, and wearisome. Nevertheless, this school developed and refined both the ear and grammatical sensitivity, with the result that it offered the most attractive possibilities to a man like Augustine, of linguistic talent and artistic ability. With his gifts he was quickly able to attain rhetorical self-assurance, and soon became a master. At nineteen Augustine became a teacher of rhetoric in his native town, in the following year in Carthage, the capital, and rapid advance continued during the decade following. Augustine was well on the way to becoming a celebrity in his department. He took his calling seriously, finding it hard to bear the crudity of his students when they disturbed his lectures with their ill-manners and only assimilated what he wanted to teach them superficially, if at all. He could, nevertheless, be satisfied with his successes. In 383 he was called to Rome, where the intellectual conditions were more propitious. Here he was upset only by the fact that the students, though listening diligently, absented themselves from classes at the end of the term, and 'forgot' to pay their fees. To Augustine this was by no means of secondary importance. He was consumed by a burning intellectual ambition, and wished to become renowned and admired for his abilities; but he also wanted to become wealthy, and dreamed then of an aristocratic marriage, to complete the happiness of his position. For the time being he contented himself with a concubine for the satisfaction of his desires and of his need for more intimate companionship, and this kept him from grosser excesses. Augustine was faithful to his mistress for fifteen years, and the words with which he remembered her love and faithfulness even as an elderly man and a bishop indicate that this irregular association really meant much to him, although he passed over her name in silence. Before he was 18 years old she bore to him a wonderfully gifted boy, as Augustine assures us, who received the name Adeodatus, 'given by God'. He remained until his early death the joy and happiness of his father, and this relationship was in no way changed by their joint conversion to a strict Christian view of life.

Unlike Jerome, Augustine did not interrupt his secular career prematurely, but pursued it to the climax. But with him the change signified much more than the more or less arbitrary result of a moral decision; it prepared for itself gradually, and progressively and irresistibly made itself known. This, at any rate, is how Augustine himself later saw and described his youth. Parallel with the external history of rise and success ran a history of his inner life which lay beneath the surface and often almost disappeared, but pushed up and emerged again and again, finally seizing upon his entire existence to give it a new meaning. Augustine has described this development in his *Confessions*, and interpreted it as the secret action and guidance of the ever-victorious divine grace. The *Confessions* are not an autobiography in the modern sense, but a new, extremely personal, kind of work of edification, composed with high literary aspirations and written in the appropriate style. Nevertheless, it is not fiction. Augustine expressly maintained that the book was to contain exclusively, and even in detail, nothing but the truth, and wherever we are able to test it, this claim proves to be justified. Mistakes have no bearing on this, and the light in which his own past is seen in retrospect is no deception, but an interpretative unlocking of his life by him who knew it best. Once its purpose is understood we can safely trust ourselves to the guidance of this book. In any event, there is no other, better guide.

Unlike Jerome, Augustine did not stem from the pagan Balkans, with their lack of traditions, but from the soil of Africa, soaked for centuries with the blood of Christians, the only Latin-Christian region which had long possessed an intellectual profile and, in addition, a distinct ecclesiastical individuality. Already in childhood he knew what living Christianity was in the person of his mother Monica, the only one 'not to be imagined as absent' from his development (Guardini). Augustine has depicted her personality in the *Confessions* with tender love, and even reported many trivial features of her life; yet he has not really idealized her. Monica is essentially nothing more than the wife of a typical bourgeois, herself the product of a country-town, intellectually alert yet without higher education, practical and gentle yet at the same time full of womanly energy and determination whenever she wished to follow her motherly instinct and religious conviction. Devoted love for her eldest son became her fate. Only in her care for him and for his eternal salvation, did she rise to true inner greatness and complete freedom. Up to his conversion Augustine's history can be understood, as it was by him, as a story of mother and son, of their indissoluble relationship persisting despite every alienation until they finally came together in the faith. It was a faith which Monica had confessed from the beginning, and affirmed vicariously for her son throughout, while Augustine came to it only late, by long travels and laborious détours. Yet in a certain sense, he was always a Christian. Monica had already taught him to pray in his childhood, and had made him familiar with the customs and practices of the Christians. Augustine could never efface these early impressions, and they had not only to do with externals. The Bible was all along a holy book to him, and, according to his own testimony, he had already with his mother's milk sucked in and preserved the name of the Saviour so intensely that nothing could really delight him later that was deprived of this name (*Conf.* III, 4, 8). As Augustine the child desired baptism when he had indigestion, or prayed that he would not be beaten in school, so also in later life praying was a natural thing to him. Yet all this lost its importance at the beginning of his manhood; Augustine no longer took either the faith of his childhood or his mother's complaints and reproaches seriously. As a student he plunged into a whirlpool of love affairs and would like to appear a little more shameless than he actually was. He began to work intellectually and make progress, and in this he saw the meaning and content of his life.

The first time this attitude was shaken, it was the result of an intellectual experience, not through a person, but through a book. In the same way Augustine's further stages of development were never to occur without some new intellectual perception which then brought in motion his whole personal life and activity. The curriculum of his studies led Augustine to the reading of the *Hortensius*—a dialogue, lost today, in which the ageing Cicero called his readers away from political rhetoric to philosophy. Philosophy alone was able to make life meaningful, to make death gentle, and to prepare the soul to pass over to immortality. The effect on Augustine was striking. In contrast to the great variety of opinions of the various schools, as he considered philosophy to be until then, for the first time the seriousness of the one object of life, the Real and Whole which is wisdom, dawned on him. 'Suddenly every vain hope became worthless to me, and with an incredible warmth of heart I yearned for an immortality of wisdom', and thus I, continued Augustine, 'began now to arise that I might return to thee' (*Conf.* III, 4, 7; *LCC*, 7, 65). This is not a later, reflective interpretation: according to his own testimony, Augustine was only disappointed by the fact that there was not to be found any word about Christ in Cicero, and the first effect of this experience, which was shattering in both its philosophical and its religious effects, was that he reached for the Bible, and began to read it seriously. But the attempt failed. Its words seemed unpalatable, 'unworthy to be compared with the dignity of Tully (Cicero)' (*Conf.* III, 5, 9). We might think we were listening to the young Jerome! At this moment, the spiritually inexperienced and helpless Augustine needed personal guidance and living fellowship. Among his acquaintances up to now he was unable to find it, and hence he soon joined a sect widespread among the intelligentsia of Carthage and also elsewhere: he became a Manichean.

This fellowship, founded by the Persian Mani in the third century, was the last great religious creation of the East between Christianity and Islam. It rejected Judaism and the Old Testament, but had accepted Christ among its forerunners, and in the West claimed to be a higher and spiritualized form of Christianity itself. This was how Manicheism appeared to Augustine too. Always prohibited and suppressed in the Roman empire, its conventicles were thereby surrounded by the attraction of secrecy and mystery. The basic teaching was a rigorous dualism. In Manichean mythology the present world was considered to be an outcome of an original fall, of a fatal mixture of light and darkness. The souls of men were only dispersed sparks of the one divine substance of light, which require to be rescued and liberated from the dark imprisonment of their corporeality. This bringing together and leading home of the elements of light was understood as the real redemption of men, and of God himself. A total separation, attempted by all sorts of fantastic methods, will finally bring about the end of the world, and the consummation of all that is light into the unity of light. The practical implications of this message of salvation could only be a strict asceticism. Yet only the very few set foot on this radical way; these were the elect and perfect. Augustine was satisfied with being a mere 'hearer', i.e. to remain like the majority a member of the broader fellowship, with few commitments. They were fully aware of the value of their new acquisition, and treated the young rhetorician with the greatest politeness. The tragic analysis of his own incompleteness and weakness, the possibility nevertheless of rising up above them intellectually, and the enchantment of the services of common worship, with their psalms and hymns, their liturgical confessions and utterances, all this appeared to Augustine as release and exaltation over mundane everyday activity. It appeared as the true religion glorifying ordinary life. Soon he himself was active as leader and missionary: under his influence his pupil, the son of Romanianus, and he himself became members of the Manicheans, and his relationship to his mother, who was almost at the point of despair over this development, became increasingly unhappy. She could not think of following her son in his new way, and irritated him by her unshakable hope that she would yet see him one day return to her in the haven of the Catholic church. Monica had been a widow for some years, but continuous life with Augustine proved impossible in these circumstances. Temporarily he moved into the house of his patron, Romanianus.

It is a question how far Augustine ever accepted Manicheism without reservation. Its aesthetic and emotional attractions, and its fantastic proclamations and promises could not in the long run cover up the inner difficulties of the system. Augustine was no half-educated enthusiast. He demanded clarity and closely reasoned thought. Instead of the primitive prejudices and superstitions of ecclesiastical Christianity, he had expected to find in Manicheism, as it promised, a real, spiritually-based outlook. Now question after question emerged to which it gave no convincing answer. By this time, 'at twenty-six or twenty-seven', Augustine published his first study, *On Beauty and Propriety*. It seems that he here sought to relate himself to the Manichean metaphysics; but this work, which was soon lost (in his later years it was not available even to him), was already truly Augustinian with respect to the topic and posing of the problem. The nature of beauty remained for Augustine at all times a genuine metaphysical problem, and even then it drove him beyond the consideration of mere appearance. Everything that is appropriate to its purpose is appropriate only in relation to something other than its 'purpose'. The beautiful, however, is beautiful through itself. It is spiritual and thereby lies beyond the visible, corporeal world. Yet what is spirit and spiritual truth itself? The materialistic thought of the Manichean metaphysics of light could not solve this problem. Besides, there were the contradictions of its cosmic and astronomical theories. These philosophical and scientific objections remained unsolved. For a long time, the Manicheans consoled Augustine with the prospect of the visit of Faustus, a bishop with a reputation for great learning. When at last he came, he proved to be an amiable, rhetorically educated cipher. All that remained was a fundamental disappointment, which occasioned an increasing alienation from the sect, and a hopeless discontent with his own intellectual situation and condition. Augustine now occupied himself with astrological writings which, on close examination, likewise turned out to be empty. Finally he came upon the literature of Scepticism. The denial in principle of any certainty of knowledge seemed to him the most honest attitude open to us. But this attitude is really one of despair. Augustine decided to pray no longer; he forced himself into the sceptical attitude, against which his whole nature rebelled. The truth he sought in his sceptical broodings was in reality no theoretical matter at all: Augustine was looking for a secure centre of gravity, the basis and meaning of his life itself, and he was unable to find it. He never actually doubted that there was this saving truth. It was only that access to it seemed to be forever barred to human reason. Basically Augustine was still looking for the truth which he had known as a child: he wanted to obtain knowledge about God, about divine providence, and judgement, and about his own immortality, and he felt that all this had now become unattainable to him as an intellectual possession. His life no longer had any direction, and drifted along. The picture of his mood may have been painted unduly dark in the *Confessions*. At all events, it is certain that Augustine suffered as a result of his unsettled state of mind, and all outward successes offered no effective solace for these secret troubles.

In the autumn of 384 Augustine reached Milan, with a recommendation from the city prefect Symmachus, and thus he
came to the imperial residence itself. When leaving Africa, he
had meanly deceived his mother: he wanted to be rid of her,
and had departed secretly. Now she followed him to Milan. He
restored their life together, and peace was re-established. The
victim of this reconciliation was Augustine's mistress. Monica
succeeded in having her dismissed, a step which seemed justified
in view of a future marriage, and which in any case had to be
undertaken some time (to marry a concubine was entirely
impossible for legal reasons). Yet Augustine suffered under
this separation: 'My heart which clung to her was torn and
wounded till it bled' (Conf. VI, 15, 25; LCC, 7, 132). While the
girl, who returned to Africa, remained faithful to him all her
life, Augustine presently took into his house a new concubine,
as though in defiance of his mother. He himself felt this con-
cession to his sensuality to be disgraceful, but he could not resist.
Monica was also obviously unable to help in his deeper spiritual
miseries. The same was true of his friends who loved and admired him, but whom he knew only too well not to be his
equals. Augustine felt frustrated and wretched. A brief scene,
described in the Confessions with extreme artistry, reveals his
mood. Augustine was entrusted with the delivery of a panegyric upon the emperor (Valentinian II) at a festive occasion.
Full of uneasiness and stage-fright on the evening before, he
took a walk with his friends through the suburbs. There, a
drunken beggar got in their way, and launched forth into foolish jokes and seemed to feel extremely merry in this. The sight
overwhelmed Augustine. 'What do all our plans and ambitions
mean?', he exclaimed. 'By them we only increase our miserable
burden, which we have to carry in any case! We do not want
anything else but to be happy, after all. The beggar has
achieved it: and we perhaps never shall!' Yet this temperamental
outburst had no results. Augustine went on living in the old
way and, inwardly unsatisfied, continued 'to be greedy for

honours, money, and matrimony' (*Conf.* VI, 6, 9).

Milan brought Augustine more than reconciliation with his mother and new professional successes. The church and Catholic Christianity, which he thought he knew from infancy, met him here in a new form which surprised him, impressed him, and finally urged him to a decision. The decisive thing was the personality of the great Ambrose. Augustine himself describes to us how he first wanted to get to know the famous preacher as a rhetorician, and attended his sermons for this reason alone. But soon the preaching fascinated him also by its content. Augustine realized with astonishment how the seeming absurdities and 'old wives' fables' of the Bible could be understood in their deeper meaning by the allegorical interpretation, and that a powerful and comprehensive idea of God, the world, and man became visible behind the anthropomorphic statements and the apparently primitive ideas of the texts. So Christianity was a spiritual reality which evidently had something to say not only to uneducated and childish spirits; and it was at the same time the reality of an actual fellowship which could lay hold of, transform, and determine men. In his undivided devotion to the service of the church, and in the impact and composure of his commanding appearance, Ambrose appeared the antitype of Augustine, the problem-ridden intellectual, who was still undecided and immature, uncommitted and yet dependent in so many ways. Nevertheless, he was also a person of rank, whom Augustine had to regard as an intellectual equal, indeed, an entirely new experience to him, his superior. In his figure the authority of the church was embodied, firmly established beyond arbitrary opinions and sceptical objections, and demanding that one accept and obey her teaching as the truth of God. With this claim she could face an intellectual test and hold her own under a critical judgement. Augustine still hesitated to give complete assent to her claims; such a *salto mortale* into faith would have appeared to him as capricious and irresponsible. But he slowly began once again to draw near to the church, and decided to remain in the waiting class of catechumens until such time as 'something certain should shine forth' to him, by which he could then finally direct his way (*Conf.* V, 14, 25). Several times he tried to speak to Ambrose personally. There were no external difficulties about this; for, in spite of his countless duties, Ambrose never locked his door, and anybody could visit him without announcement. Yet one knew that actually he had not time. Every time Augustine found the bishop so deeply absorbed in his work and his books that he did not dare to disturb him, and after a period of silent waiting returned home unsuccessfully. The pious Monica, however, had met the great man some time ago. She realized very well the inner crisis of her son and followed it with intense hope. Perhaps this was a reason why Augustine could not overcome his final hesitation regarding Ambrose. Or was he perhaps afraid that the busy pastor of the congregation would not consider and understand his complex doubts and anxieties as carefully and personally as seemed to himself desirable and necessary? Once Augustine turned to Ambrose's old teacher, the priest Simplician, who aptly referred him to the example of the Neo-Platonic philosopher Marius Victorinus. The latter had sacrificed his teaching appointment and publicly confessed Christ in the time of the Julian reaction, and had then become an important theologian.

This was the time of Ambrose's fight against the Arian policy of the empress Justina. The whole city was excited and sided with its bishop. But it is characteristic how superficially these events are mentioned in the *Confessions*. They constitute only the shadowy background of the real history of his soul, which for Augustine went on entirely in the inner sphere of responsible knowledge and spiritual decision. At that time, he began to study Neo-Platonic philosophy, from which Ambrose also was not far. He read the writings of Porphyry, and above all of Plotinus, in Victorinus' Latin translation, and the knowledge he encountered here released him from the intellectual blind alley in which he had remained for so long a time. It brought him all at once into the open air! Here finally the difficulties of his

conception of spirit and of God were really solved. God in his
infinitude and perfection cannot be thought of at all as long as
he is imagined materially, be it as a spiritual substance, as with
Tertullian, or as a substance of light, as in the view of the Manicheans. The transcendent reality of the spiritual lies beyond all
natural analogies. Spirit is not 'the abstract', but rather appears
as the essence of all which is sensible and real, from which one
has to proceed philosophically. In contradistinction to God, the
world is not original, but derived, restricted, and virtually
unreal. The problem of evil which distressed Augustine finds
a corresponding solution. This too has no original, indeed,
strictly speaking, no real substance at all. It exists only in the
estrangement from the good and true. It is the destruction of
sensible reality. Actually it appears only negatively in relation
to real being as its perversion and deprivation. Neo-Platonism
had changed these Platonic notions in an increasingly religious
direction. God is the origin and goal of all that is true. He is the
eternal One who reflects and 'reveals' Himself in many ways,
but never Himself enters into this manifold existence, nor is He
to be found in it. True philosophy therefore calls man to contemplation and conversion. It calls him to step outside to an
intellectual transcendence of the multiplicity of the phenomenal world, to cognition and experience of God in His unity,
beyond the limits of the finite. In adopting these ideas, Augustine certainly felt himself to be only at the beginning of his
intellectual and philosophical journey; but his sceptical helplessness, his doubt-ridden absorption in the temporary and
transitory, were now overcome. There is an attainable truth of
God, the possession of which would make 'life precious and death
gentle'. As formerly after reading the *Hortensius*, Augustine
now without more ado understood this truth also in a Christian
sense. Again he had recourse to the Bible, and what once had
failed seemed now to succeed. The Bible spoke to his heart.
Above all Paul confirmed the one great truth of pagan philosophy as the revealed truth of God. But he offered at the same
time more than this. He not only testified to the transcendent

superiority of the Absolute. By speaking also of Christ, and of God's active redemptive participation in history and, on the part of man, of the spiritual necessity to respond to this God in humility, repentance, and new dedication, he testified also to the personal gracious will of the merciful Creator.

Augustine was now confronted with a personal decision: he must change his life, and reform it to meet the new Christian demand. This seemed to be possible only by a determined break with all these previous ties which for so long a time had disgusted him, and which he considered basically vain and sordid. As long as the truth was still half-hidden, it was comparatively easy to evade the decision. Where could he hope to find the books, the helpers, and the time to go deeply into the new? Was it really necessary to make the break now, just at the moment when he had at last reached the point where he might at any moment obtain perhaps a governorship, or some other profitable and distinguished office, and perhaps make an advantageous marriage? We can see how the choice one way or the other had come to a crisis demanding a radical and ascetic decision. The striving for a career and human admiration, the desire to become rich, the sensuality which could not be held in check even for a short time, in fact, the whole of Augustine's manner of life contradicted with its empty activity both the Christian and the philosophical ideals. There was no third solution or middle course, which would allow him to do justice simultaneously to studies and to women, to outward advancement and to inner truth. Again and again this was considered by Augustine, and time and again rejected as half-hearted.

The development which ensued is described by him in detail, in a stylized form certainly, yet with an incomparable truth of psychological observation. We cannot reproduce the whole story in full; it is known to every reader of the *Confessions*. 'Thus with the baggage of the world I was sweetly burdened, as one in slumber, and my musings on thee were like the efforts of those who desire to awake, but who are still overpowered with drowsiness and fall back into deep slumber. And as no one wishes to sleep forever (for all men rightly count waking better)—yet a man will usually defer shaking off his drowsiness when there is a heavy lethargy in his limbs; and he is glad to sleep on even when his reason disapproves, and the hour for rising has struck—so was I assured that it was much better for me to give myself up to thy love than to go on yielding myself to my own lust. Thy love satisfied and vanquished me; my lust pleased and fettered me. I had no answer to thy calling to me, "Awake, thou that sleepest, and arise from the dead, and Christ shall give thee light" (Eph. v. 14). On all sides, thou didst show me that thy words are true, and I, convicted by the truth, had nothing at all to reply but the drawling and drowsy words: "Presently; see, presently. Leave me alone a little while." But "presently, presently", had no present; and my "leave me alone a little while" went on for a long while' (*Conf.* VIII, 5, 12; *LCC*, 7, 165). The difficulties did not exist any more in the intellectual realm, where they once had lain. The moral demand, also, appeared to be clear. God had 'encircled' Augustine from all sides, as he expressed it; yet the last, decisive change of will could not be forced—it was still lacking. Evidently, Augustine himself was now looking for a solution, but only an impulse from without, the definite example and model of a conversion, brought him the decision.

One day, an African compatriot, a high official named Ponticianus, visited him on some occasion Augustine had later forgotten. He found Paul's epistles lying on Augustine's card-table and showed his surprise at finding a Christian brother in a professor of rhetoric. He thereupon told him about Anthony, the first 'monk', whose biography, then translated into Latin, was at that time beginning to cause a stir in the West. It was still unknown to Augustine, who was impressed by the fact that such a renunciation of the world was possible not only in the remote past but even now in the present, 'in our time so to speak'. But Anthony did not remain an isolated case. The conversation turned to contemporary monks, and the guest said that he had recently been witness in Trèves when two of his acquaintances found Anthony's 'life' in the cell of a monk, and then without more ado had renounced their promising careers in order to direct their heart from now on to heaven. (This description perfectly matches Jerome and his friend Bonosus, who had been converted in Trèves in the seventies of the fourth century in just this way). Ponticianus, however, had returned with tears in his eyes to the imperial palace, in order to drag out his life in the usual secular way. This report shook Augustine. He thought he saw his own fate before his eyes, and 'while the man continued his narrative' it seemed to him as though he himself 'was taken from behind his back', and unwillingly forced to look himself in the face (*Conf.* VIII, 7, 16). When Ponticianus had left, and only his friend Alypius stayed, he burst out, highly excited, into furious self-accusations: 'What did you hear?' he shouted at Alypius. 'The uninstructed start up and take the kingdom of heaven by force, and we—with all our learning but so little heart—see where we wallow in flesh and blood!' (*Conf.* VIII, 8, 19; *LCC*, 7, 170). Augustine left the room and dashed into the adjacent garden, of which the friends enjoyed the use. Here, struggling step by step forward, he fought the last 'frantic' battle 'between me and myself'. The dreadful tension finally relaxed into a 'flood of tears': Augustine left the faithful Alypius alone and threw himself sobbing under a fig-tree. 'Suddenly I heard the voice of a boy or a girl —I know not which—coming from the neighbouring house, chanting over and over again the same words, "Take up and read! Take up and read!" (*tolle, lege; tolle, lege*).' Augustine came to himself and began to think earnestly whether he had ever heard anything like this, whether there was perhaps a children's game with such a jingle; but this was not the case. Thus he decided to take the words as a heavenly challenge. For the third time Augustine had recourse to the Bible at a decisive moment,—i.e. the copy of the Pauline letters left with Alypius. He was resolved, according to Anthony's example, to accept the first text he laid eyes upon as the ultimate order for his life. He chanced—in the middle of a sentence—upon a passage in the epistle to the Romans (xiii. 13 f.), which he read not aloud, but like Ambrose 'silently' for himself: '. . . not in rioting and drunkenness, not in chambering and wantonness, not in strife and envying, but put on the Lord Jesus Christ, and make no provision for the flesh to fulfil the lust thereof' (*Conf.* VIII, 12, 29; *LCC*, 7, 175 f.). This was the text which spoke to his condition. Augustine read no further, but simply gave the book without a word to Alypius, who read on at the marked place, and humbly referred to himself the following passage 'Him that is weak in faith receive'. He too was now ready to enter the new Christian way at the leading of his friend.

Now, everything was decided. The thunderstorm had passed, and radiant joy spread abroad. Both hurried to Monica, who jubilantly learned the good news. Augustine wished to avoid a public sensation. Since the vintage holiday was near at hand, he finished his teaching work. Then he pretended to have a 'chest-complaint'—it seems to have been a harmless bronchial catarrh—in order to resign from his office. Next a friend and colleague placed at his disposal a charming country estate, protected from the wind, the *rus Cassiciacum* (Casságo?) south of Lake Como, where he could spend the vacation with his mother, his son, some friends and students, and where he could breathe freely. After half a year, they returned to Milan, where together with Adeodatus, Augustine was baptized by Ambrose on Easter Eve of the year 387. Now Milan could offer nothing more. The little family decided to travel back to their native-land, together with a young fellow-countryman, who had also been converted, and to settle down there. The time of searching was over, a new period of life began.

What was the meaning to Augustine himself of this conversion, and what is its actual content and significance? The first answer is clearly laid down in Augustine's confession and report. It must neither be effaced nor softened down. Augustine was not converted from paganism to Christianity or from unbelief to faith, nor from philosophy to theology and from intellectual license to the authority of the church. Rather was he converted from worldliness to a new, a really Christian course of life. After a long and hard struggle, he renounced marriage and pleasure, money, glory, and the admiration of men. All this counted from now on as worthless, vain, and hollow. The breaking with his promising career and resignation from his former life were the essential signs of this change. As was frequently the case in those times, baptism was the seal of a decision already accomplished, and also outwardly marked the start of a new life. So far, Augustine's 'conversion' bears a practical character, and has an unequivocally ascetic meaning.

Nevertheless, Augustine did not think of becoming a monk, and retreating as a hermit to the desert or cave. The life of the cloister under ecclesiastical supervision, as it had just been commenced at Milan, was also out of the question. He became a follower of Anthony only with regard to his absolute, total break with the former life. What Augustine actually desired was a quiet, 'philosophical' life with friends, outwardly frugal and withdrawn, dedicated exclusively to God and to the search for true knowledge. To that extent, it was to be also a life of intellectual work. Even in Cassiciacum Augustine began, as a matter of course, to engage in philosophical writing, after having until then—apart from that unimportant little tract—exclusively taught and worked by word of mouth. These first dialogues, composed according to the tradition of the schools, also describe the idyllic surroundings in which they were conducted and recorded. We are almost reminded of the garden discussions and 'Platonic' academies of the Renaissance. Monica took charge of the household, the men only occasionally doing a little gardening. Everyone had leisure for contemplation and private studies. The communal conversations occasionally began early in the morning, but usually only in the afternoon or toward evening, in bad weather in a bath-house, otherwise in the open air on the lawn in the shadow of a beautiful old tree. The proceedings were vivacious, at times even gay. Occasionally, Monica interjected a word, and was then admired by all for her 'wisdom' and religious understanding. Augustine of

14

course took charge; he remained the guiding professor in the new milieu also. As before, they read and discussed the classical authors and poets, the beloved Virgil for choice; but essential philosophical problems had now become decisive, dealt with primarily in connection with Cicero. It was no accident that Augustine sought to direct his friends particularly to the *Hortensius*. The questions with which he had struggled so ardently himself occupied the central place: the problem was that of the possibility and certainty of knowledge of the truth, the problem of real happiness, of providence and God's world order, and of the immortality of the soul.

Coming from the *Confessions*, one is surprised at the academic and wholly unenthusiastic spirit of these early writings. It is remarkable what a secondary place the expressly Christian elements occupy, but, on closer examination, one realizes that they nevertheless always constitute the background and are not emphasized more strongly partly because the dialogues are composed on the classical model. The 'oracles' of the Bible are authoritative to all who are present. The words of 'our priest', namely Ambrose, are remembered, and Augustine is happy now to subscribe to the same 'philosophy' to the summit of which Monica had long ago climbed. The dialogues were interrupted by the chanting of hymns and common prayers. A welcome supplement to the dialogues are the *Soliloquies*, Augustine's 'monologues' with his soul, a peculiarly interesting early form of the later *Confessions*. Here the newly converted man, after a solemn prayer to God, undertakes a self-examination of the stage attained in his inner life. He confesses that certain temptations could still exert a dangerous power upon him, that his heart in particular still clung too much to certain who were dear to him. Yet he now lived ascetically; wealth and honours, matrimony and sensual enjoyments were no longer any serious enticement to him. In this early work comes the famous definition of his intellectual aim: 'God and the soul, I desire to know. —Nothing more?—Absolutely nothing' (*Solil.* I, 2, 7).

At first sight, the sociological picture of the circle of friends

and scholars at Cassiciacum reminds one of the ideal life that
Jerome also longed for after his conversion, and later realized
in a more monastic form. But the new element lies in the intellectual aim of this ascetic community. To be sure, Scripture
study and common devotions, the main thing for Jerome alongside ascetic exercises, were also by no means neglected by
Augustine; but the philosophical search for the truth, the question about 'God and the soul,' has now become decisive. The
answer was sought and found in a truly 'maieutical' conversation. Augustine's dialogues were no lectures in dialogue form.
In this respect, they were something new and unique in
Christian literature. Philosophy, despised by the older Westerners and still suspect to Jerome, now flowed as a broad stream
into the church and into Christianity. Until that time, it had
remained an almost exclusively Greek interest in the West; in
Augustine's Latin dialogues it found for the first time a con-
spicuous recognition and acceptance. It was the Neo-Platonic
philosophy, amalgamated with older elements of the Aristotelian ontology and of the Stoic-Ciceronian academic tradition.
According to Augustine, the Platonists alone have reached the
climax of cognition of that truth which leads immediately to
the threshold of the Christian and Biblical revelation, and which
can be perfected in the Christian theology as the true philosophy. In this he is thinking primarily of the central position of
the conception of God, which he, as a Christian, always understood in the strictly theistic sense, and affirmed in his practical
and personal dedication. God, from whom everything proceeds, the knowledge and acceptance of God's thoughts and of
His eternal truth,—that is the real meaning and content of any
true life. The longing for religious fulfilment, aroused by Manicheism, found its intellectual clarification and perfection in the
similar striving of Neo-Platonism, as understood in a Christian
sense. The conceptions of divine light, of purification, and of
ascent have lost their half-mythological, hollow, materialistic
meaning and are elevated, in the spirit of Platonic dialectics,
completely into the sphere of the spirit. Augustine was no mystic

and no pantheist. He knew no immediate 'ecstatic' absorption in the divine being, yet his enthusiastic feeling of dedication to the knowledge of God, to the submission and elevation of man to Him remained unaltered, lively, and strong. It was as though this dedication were only purified by philosophical thinking, and gained further warmth, depth, and moral responsibility to the extent that it was permeated by Christian, and especially Pauline and Johannine, thoughts. The philosophical religion had become personal. It was no longer a matter of intellectual knowledge for its own sake, but of satisfaction of the inner longing of the heart for the living God, of dependence on Him in faith, hope, and love. On his path of exuberant longing, Augustine broke through beyond all things created to immediate life in God. The peace which was to be purchased by the overcoming of all worldly desires realized itself in a calm rest in God.

Yet this final religious goal also cannot be understood apart from the presuppositions of Neo-Platonic spiritualism. The traditional ascetic decision won a new and permanent significance and power in Augustine's life. From now on, asceticism changed the nature of its demand, as compared with the early Western view, and attained a deeper spiritual function. The meritorious or disciplinary meaning of the demand for individual ascetic acts diminished, and no longer interested Augustine for its own sake. Asceticism now meant the basic attitude of the life of devotion itself. It was the practical presupposition of the ascent toward truth and God, and so gained a positive meaning. As the overcoming of the 'world', with its sensuality and diversions, asceticism was, as it were, only the reverse side of spiritual contemplation and dedication to God. 'This was the whole matter,' the Confessions run, 'not to want what I wanted, but to want what thou didst want.' With this the 'doing without all sweet trifles' all at once became 'sweet' itself (Conf. IX, 1, 1). He who wishes to live entirely with God gladly renounces worldly desires. To be sure, he will use the good things of this world, but he must not wish to 'enjoy' them, that is to

say, to love and desire them for their own sake. The older
Augustine became, the greater the determination with which
he emphasized that creation was not evil as such, even the
material creation and the bodily nature of man. Rather as God's
gifts were they good, and to be affirmed in their proper place.
But his world-renouncing idealism sought to transcend and
abandon this modest, provisional acceptance of their value as
rapidly as possible. Setting aside all external acts of renunciation, Augustine remained an ascetic by nature and innermost
volition. He always understood the Christian commandment of
obedient love to God, and the total surrender of his own self as
a demand to overcome the lower world and its sensuality altogether, and to rise to the spiritual realm of eternal and pure
being. Here only did God encounter him in his full perfection.

This peculiarity stamped Augustine's entire theology and
ethics, and imposed its idealistic philosophical character on his
thinking even when he was interpreting the Scripture. This is
particularly evident, for instance, in his aesthetics, especially in
his theory of music (for the rhetorician thirsty for beauty had
hardly any independent interest in the fine arts). The mathe-
matical laws of harmony and beauty reflect the eternal order
of the world of ideas, i.e. the thoughts of God. Everything depends on this, and the real goal therefore is not to experience
'phenomenal freedom', but on the contrary to leave the sensual
appearance behind and to enjoy 'beauty itself at its source'. But
Augustine also interpreted the highest values of friendship
and love ascetically and theocentrically, in accordance with the
hierarchical grading of the philosophical doctrine of goods. The
final goal of all love is God. Love for one's neighbour is not
co-ordinated with love to God, as originally in Christ's double
commandment, but is only an emanation and effect of love to
God, derived from it and bound to it. It is therefore 'true' and
really desirable only when included in the movement of the
soul to God and experienced as part of love to Him. This is the
explanation of the convert's coolness with which Augustine, for
instance, spoke of his pagan father, who was baptized only

shortly before his death, or the passionate intensity with which he attempted to win over to the ascetic life his patron Romanianus, and Romanianus' son—and likewise the silent indifference with which he ignored both after this attempt had failed. This breach of human contact is the more striking, as Augustine by nature possessed a strong need for fellowship, had many friends at every period of his life, and was in his way almost a virtuoso in friendship, as his letters prove. It is not really surprising in view of his times, surroundings, and personal development that he accounted the entire sphere of the erotic, in which he himself was at home for so long a time, merely as 'sensuality', not prohibited within permitted limits, to be sure, but to be eliminated from his life, and from the lives of all the fully converted. Nevertheless the ascetic curtailment of life can be felt here too.

The question has often been put, how the Christian and Neo-Platonic elements are really related to one another in his conversion, and how the influence of the two forces is to be differentiated. In his old age, Augustine himself retracted the exuberant praise of Plato (and Cicero) found in his early works (*Retr.* I, 1, 4), and already in the *Confessions* (VII, 9, 13 ff.) he had emphasized clearly enough, besides what he owes to the *Books of the Platonists*, also what was missing there and was found to be missing in comparison with revelation. The Platonists have in truth known of God's transcendence, the dependence of the soul upon His light, and even the glory of the Son existing in the substance of the Father. Nevertheless they did not know of the really redeeming event of Christ's incarnation, of His death for us, or of the whole loving and active descent of God into the world, and of His active mercy, which falls only to the lot of the humble and poor, not to the proud and wise. They did not know the way by which they could really have reached the goal of their striving. It is not to be assumed that Augustine, who had already found Christ's name missing in the *Hortensius*, and who let himself be led from Plotinus to Paul without further ado, only discovered all this long after his conversion. The question of Christian and Neo-Platonic elements is meaningful only when we analyse the early and later writings of Augustine from this point of view. As a biographical question it is scarcely to be answered, and basically the question is probably wrongly formulated. The truth which Augustine believed he had found philosophically was immediately understood by him as a confirmation and recovery of the faith of his childhood, which had never been lost completely. In so far as it was the truth, it was for him identical with the revealed Biblical truth. It thus actually led him back to the Bible and the Catholic church. What Augustine experienced had been learned in a similar way, though less decisively and consciously, by Marius Victorinus, Simplicianus, and Ambrose before him. Neo-Platonism in other ways too was the force which broke through the Judaistic narrowness of the old Latin Christianity, overcame its legalistic moralism and primitive rationalism with its teaching on the Spirit and God, and opened the way from an Old Testament to a New Testament Christianity. Augustine, who in his thinking was more of a real philosopher than his predecessors, also surpassed them in his appropriation of this 'evangelical' element, that which is genuinely Christian in Christianity. The imperfect expression in his younger days of the purely Christian element, and his criticism in old age of the Neo-Platonic element, do nothing to alter the continuous movement of his life which turned the Christian Neo-Platonist into the Biblical theologian, who, however, never ceased even then to be a Platonist and a philosopher. The loftiest testimonial to this are his *Confessions*, which are the prayerful recording of his former life by Augustine himself, and form the ultimate interpretation of his life and his conversion, as testimony to the undeserved guidance and unfathomable grace that come from the almighty God.

Today, the *Confessions* are the best-known of Augustine's writings, and it is understandable that they have always aroused interest, particularly for their autobiographical material. They were written in 397–398, more than a decade after the occurrences at Milan. It was the criticism of opponents who reproached Augustine for his Manichean past which made the occasion for their composition. The structure of the work itself is surprising, and retains an element of the enigmatic, despite all the interpretations which have been attempted. Of thirteen books in all, nine deal with the course of Augustine's life until his departure from Italy, one with the mode of new life he had finally attained, and three offer a speculative interpretation of the account of creation at the beginning of the Bible. The main part of the book is powerful confession, a testimony to scrupulous self-examination, and to intense and acute self-criticism. At the same time there is no sign of torture or despair in this, because it is accompanied by the perpetual praise of God's mercy which in spite of all did not forsake his life, but precisely by the experience of sin and guilt brought him through hidden ways to the knowledge of salvation, and to the peace of forgiveness. He who confesses his sins, Augustine considers, must always accompany this confession with the praise of God. Only then is he 'pious' in a Christian sense, 'when it happens not in despair, but in appeal to God's mercy' (*Enarr. Ps.* xciv. 4). Therefore, a 'sublime peace' covers all. The impression this book leaves 'can be compared to the impression we get when after a dark, rainy day, the sun finally again prevails, and a pleasant sunbeam brightens the damp land' (Harnack). It is the ultimate truth which is to be acknowledged in a wholly personal manner, not even sparing the most intimate facts. Both the moving effect of this book, and the offence it again and again gives to more reserved modern feeling, consist precisely in this. Are such literary confessions, such self-revelations, really possible at all? The undeniable art and occasional artificiality of the highly developed form have increased this suspicion. Is not this still the old rhetorician, speaking with self-reflecting vanity? Can such an exaggerated feeling of sin be genuine, such a self-description and self-exposure be true at all? Augustine has anticipated this criticism. 'What is it to me . . . that men should hear my confessions. . . . People are curious to know the lives of others, but slow to correct their own. . . . And how can they tell when they hear what I say about myself whether I speak the truth, since no man knows what is in a man "save the spirit of man which is in him"' (I Cor. ii. 11) (*Conf* X, 3, 3; *LCC*, 7, 202)? By their very nature, such confessions have to be made before God, and this explains the almost voluminous character of the whole work. It is one single uninterrupted prayer, a laying out of reflections and reminiscences before Him who has created this whole life, and holds it in His hands from start to finish. Nevertheless, people shall hear this prayer, for its purpose is to thank God for the guidance of his own life, and in this way to praise Him and to glorify His name. In conformity with the language of the Latin Bible, the title of the work, *Confessiones*, has to be understood first of all as 'praises'; yet the praise and glorification of God here occur precisely in the 'confessions' which Augustine makes about his life, his sins, and the experiences of his faith.

This theme of the book is indicated from the very beginning. '"Great art thou, O Lord, and greatly to be praised (Ps. cxlv. 3); great is thy power, and infinite is thy wisdom" (Ps. cxlvii. 5). And man desires to praise thee, for he is a part of thy creation; he bears his mortality about with him, and carries the evidence of his sin and proof that thou dost resist the proud (I Peter v. 5). Still he desires to praise thee, this man who is only a small part of thy creation. Thou hast prompted him that he should delight to praise thee, for thou hast made us for thyself and restless is our heart until it comes to rest in thee' (*Conf.* I, 1, 1; *LCC*, 7, 31). The starting-point, purport, and goal of human existence is indicated by the mysterious way in which man is surrounded by a God who creates and sustains everything, and to whom man is personally allowed to turn after having once found him in this earthly life. It requires a special skill to describe how this human will, which seems to make itself independent and go its own way, free from God, must nevertheless again and again fit in with God's higher guidance and plans, encounter His call, and finally yield humbly to His unfathomable omnipotence. 'Man's confession is man's humility; God's mercy is God's majesty' (*in Joh.* 14, 5). A peculiar fascination of the narrative, which occurs nowhere else in Augustine, comes from the direct amalgamation of Biblical quotations, particularly of words from the Psalms, in his prayer. They flash up afresh, lively and bright, as never before in his usage. The strange Biblical illustrations and phrases deepen the classical eloquence, and attach to the clear and perspicuous rhetoric a mysterious, as it were exotic, charm. Much misunderstanding and dislike of the *Confessions* is due to the reading of translations. The text cannot be translated. The sentences, always clear, mostly concise, only occasionally of a more elaborate structure, have a firm and pure sound in the original language. In their 'Romanesque' beauty they have a well-formed and musical effect. In translation, on the other hand, they easily become inflated and stilted, their emotion is wearisome and at times almost boring and sentimental. One is tempted to forget that the author of the *Confessions* was an ancient thinker skilled in expression, and far from being a modern Pietist.

The *Confessions* were intended by Augustine as what they have been accounted throughout the centuries: a book of devotion. 'When they are read and heard, they stir up the heart . . .' (*Conf.* X, 3, 4). Countless Christians have recognized their own spiritual lives, and their own destinies before God, in the story of this life, and of that unique Augustinian ego. A mere biography could never have effected this. Herein the book proves its inner breadth and depth, and the peculiar combination of its personal and objective elements which constitute its theological uniqueness. With the *Confessions* there begins a new period in the history of human self-consciousness, of psychological understanding and anthropology. A relationship is established between man in his real nature and God, and so with an infinite being outside man himself. This means that the old, 'classical' uniformity of the conception of man has been abandoned. In the presence of God and of his real definition man becomes aware of his 'unreality' and hopeless disunity. The old definition of man as a rational being hampered only by some insignificant sensual 'passions' is transcended. Here are exposed the strange limits of freedom in the decisive realm of the will itself, the mysterious complexity of human nature to the very frontier of the unconscious. In so far as in his life and time man is encountered by God, and finds or loses his salvation, the whole area of history is seen as the decisive anthropological dimension. All this, of course, not proclaimed by Augustine as a new teaching. He is surprisingly conservative in all academic matters, and the new ideas appear as though spontaneously in the contemplation of his life and himself, and are then developed, to his own philosophical amazement, in the grand reflections on self-consciousness, memory, and the nature of time. By the way in which the problem of time is seen as a theological problem of God's creation the two main parts of the book are linked together.

The biographical part of the *Confessions* ends with Monica's death in Ostia, shortly before the proposed return to Africa. The last great conversation between mother and son concludes with anticipation of the joy to be found in the eternal blessedness of perfection, completely filled with the experience of God. It is one of the high points of the whole work in which in a wonderful manner the ultimate hope of the Christians permeates the Neo-Platonic vision of the One. Augustine himself admits that he had not exactly used 'the very words' in his report, but vouches once again for the full material accuracy of his account. This accords with the circumstance that in this passage, as almost everywhere in the *Confessions*, Christ is not mentioned. Monica knew she had reached the goal of her life: 'There was indeed one thing for which I wished to tarry a little in this life, and that was that I might see you a Catholic Christian before I died. My God hath answered this more than abundantly, so that I see you now made his servant and spurning all earthly happiness. What more am I to do here?' (*Conf.* IX, 10, 26; *LCC*, 7, 194).

When he arrived in Thagaste, Augustine tried to live as he had done in Cassiciacum. With a circle of studious friends, he made his home a refuge of the monastic and contemplative life.

They renounced all private property, and established themselves in permanent community. Augustine remained the intellectual leader of the circle: 'When the brethren saw that I had time they put different questions to me'. The answers were immediately written down, as had already been done in Cassiciacum, and were later worked up into a book (*Retr.* I, 25, 1). As previously, the problems were still mostly those of the philosophy of religion: on the nature of the soul and happiness, on the origin of evil, the knowledge of truth and suchlike questions. Augustine himself, however, now began to give his work a more definite direction, whereby it assumed a momentous significance for the church. After his repudiation of academic scepticism, he began to settle matters with the still extremely active Manichean sect. This task impelled Augustine to study the Bible more intensively, especially the Old Testament, which the Manicheans repudiated. Controversy with his former fellow-believers occupied Augustine for decades, and was occasionally not without embarrassment to him. On the whole, it did not benefit him personally. It was merely a problem which earlier he had touched upon lightly, but which was now to be treated thoroughly, and which remained important beyond its immediate occasion. The basic meaning and necessity of faith compared with fully conscious knowledge had to be clarified and justified. The catch-word of Manichean propaganda ran that it 'would be absurd to believe without reasonable grounds' (*Util. Cred.* 14, 31). The charge was that while the Catholics let themselves be intimidated and seduced by sheer authority, the Manicheans were able to convince all-comers on clear rational principles of the truth of their teaching. This was indeed a somewhat ludicrous pretension, and Augustine, who had experience of this very matter, did not miss his chance of tearing to pieces the theosophic nonsense of the Manichean speculation and explanation of the world. It was important to demonstrate that the demand for faith both prior to and along with perceptual knowledge was by no means absurd, but was rather entirely reasonable and unavoidable. It was therefore com-

pletely in order, and was indeed necessary for salvation, that the
Catholic church should above all demand faith from those turning toward Christianity. In consequence, authority precedes
independent cognition.

In spite of the apologetic aim, it would be entirely wrong to
see in these thoughts of Augustine an apologetic invention, de-
vised in the interest of the church. With him they had already
been formulated earlier in complete independence of any
ecclesiastical purpose, and they cohered with his philosophical
epistemology and anthropology. 'Faith' in this connection contained no specifically religious meaning. It denoted at first
simply the acceptance of an opinion or piece of information,
for the time being unverifiable, passed on by another and better
informed person. Such a thing happens constantly, and quite
rationally. If we were to maintain the standpoint of accepting
only that which we ourselves had experienced and completely
apprehended, no human life or community could exist. The
result would be general and frightful chaos. Besides this, it is
precisely true wisdom that is not available to any man from the
beginning. He must first find it and come to know it, and this
is only possible by joining those who already possess it, and by
first listening trustfully to it. To be sure, everything depends on
meeting with the right mediator of the truth, with Christ, who
is God's Wisdom itself, and this takes place by the assistance of
the church which testifies to Him on the ground of those Scriptures which themselves testify to Him. Both Scripture and
church are endowed by God with such obvious privileges—
Augustine is thinking here of the proof from prophecy and
miracles, and of the Catholic universality and the apostolic succession—that it by no means runs counter to reason to put confidence in their leadership, and, for the time being, to 'believe'
what the church authoritatively proclaims. It is perhaps possible in exceptional cases to see the truth without her mediation.
There may be a stage of knowledge which renders sheer faith
dispensable. In Augustine's early period such questions remained open, but most men would quite certainly never attain

to the truth without authority, and to him who knows the truth it does no harm if he nevertheless joins the church, and acknowledges the sure way which she is willing to show to all, in keeping with her commission.

This whole way of thinking now underwent an essential deepening, so soon as Augustine dropped the initial and purely theoretical conception of faith, and, following the Bible, applied it no more to single truths, but to God who has revealed Christ as the truth. Faith thus received an existential character, and was joined essentially with love and hope. 'Faith' now means accepting with the will, and 'loving', as much as it does affirming. Only by this attitude can the living truth be experienced and 'known' at all, and it is known the more, the more intensively a man binds and dedicates himself to it. In order to know the truth, one must be open to the truth, and increase in purity and goodness, and not vice versa, as abstract intellectualism has at all times maintained. For this, Augustine time and again refers to Isaiah vii. 9 in his Latin Bible: 'Unless ye believe, ye shall not understand'. 'If thou art not able to understand, believe, that thou mayest understand'; to that extent, faith precedes knowledge (*Serm.* 118, 1). On the other hand, we must always already know something of an object, that is to say, we must have learned from the 'authority' of others, in order to be able to believe in it at all, and 'if we did not have rational souls, we could not believe' (*Ep.* 120, 3; *LPNF*, 6, 465). Faith and knowledge are continuously interwoven. One must therefore comprehend the Word of God in order to believe, and believe in order to comprehend. This does not mean that faith, as the Middle Ages tried to make it, is turned into an inferior form of knowledge. Augustine is not thinking of any kind of ability to know, but of an inner 'assent', which is the willingness and openness of dedication, without which experience of 'truth' is not possible at all. In contrast to an abstract epistemological theory, Augustine understands faith as an act of volition of the whole personality which, when it is a matter of a man's own being and his own 'truth', can never be detached from his ethical powers and his personal attitude to God and the Good. When in this context Augustine speaks of the church, it does not imply that her authority is a substitute for the perception of truth, but that she is the leader and way in which one comes to the truth. She is at the same time the place at which truth has to prove itself, and where it is to be exercised in love, because God's truth leads us into fellowship, whereas in arrogant self-sufficiency it perishes. 'Thy truth is neither mine nor His nor anyone else's; but it belongs to all of us whom thou hast openly called to have it in common; and thou hast warned us not to hold on to it as our own special property, for if we do we lose it. For if anyone arrogates to himself what thou hast bestowed on all to enjoy, and if he desires something for his own that belongs to all, he is forced away from what is common to all to what is, indeed, his very own—that is, from truth to false-hood' (*Conf.* XII, 25, 34; *LCC*, 7, 290).

The new ascetic and theological writer swiftly attracted attention in his home town. Despite his secluded life, people increasingly turned to him in spiritual and at times even in purely secular matters. Understandably, his friends felt such disturbances to be unwelcome; Augustine himself suffered under the burden, but considered it his duty not to refuse advice whenever it was sought. Occasionally he had even to decide to travel overland. Then he carefully avoided places in which the bishop's see was vacant. As always, there was a certain shortage of really competent men, i.e. theologically educated, and powerful in preaching. Augustine could naturally be regarded as suiting the episcopal office better than others, but he preferred independence. There might be, he wrote to a friend, churchmen who succeed in sustaining inner peace amidst the storms of daily work in the congregation, but to him it would be impossible. 'Believe me, I need complete detachment from the tumult of transient things' (*Ep.* 10, 2). Only in this way did he think he could remain faithful to the real truth. In the spring of 391, Augustine stopped in the northern seaport of Hippo Rhegius, where he hoped to win a friend for his ascetic community, and went to divine worship there. He did not know that the local bishop Valerius, a Greek by birth, had for a long time been looking for an assistant who could help him with his Latin sermons. As he now again uttered his old lament, some men noticed Augustine in the congregation and dragged him, on a sudden impulse, to the front. The man was found! Augustine must be ordained priest, and henceforth take over the preaching. When they realized his consternation they presently added that they would surely make him bishop later. All reluctance, all desperate resistance was in vain. Valerius laid his hands upon Augustine, accommodated him in a house with a garden near the cathedral, and ordered him to begin his service at once. The only thing Augustine could secure was a leave of absence for a few months in which, as he said, he wished to strengthen himself for his new office with prayer 'and by the remedies of the Holy Scripture'. Augustine did not deny that he knew the Christian doctrines of salvation, and affirmed them personally without any reservation; but he did not know as yet 'how to communicate them to other people'. For this he expected, as at all turning-points of his life, advice and assistance from the Bible (*Ep.* 21, 3 f.). Then he began his new activity without fear, and worked out his first sermons and catechetical instruction. These found an immediate response. In the Africa of that day it was quite unusual for an ordinary priest to preach instead of the bishop, but soon he attended synods also, and arranged disputations with dissentients. Five years after his appointment, the ageing Valerius consecrated him joint-bishop—despite Augustine's misgivings this was then still possible—and when soon afterwards he died, Augustine became his successor as had been foreseen.

We must not doubt that the tears which Augustine tried vainly to suppress at his ordination really came from his heart. The surrender of his previous ideal life appeared to him as a sacrifice, and even as a punishment for his sins. He knew why he had been of a resolution never to return to the disturbances of a public office. 'Yet the Lord laughed at me and wanted to show me by reality itself what I really am' (*Ep.* 21, 2). 'A slave must not contradict his master' (*Serm.* 355, 2): Augustine submitted himself to his destiny without joy. The former possibility that he might do philosophical and theological work entirely according to his own plan and wishes, and free from any external obligation, was gone once for all. The countless duties of a bishop henceforth occupied him day in, day out. There was no more leave of absence. Augustine intended to be a conscientious bishop, and remained such for thirty-five years until his death. Hippo Rhegius, the modern Bône, which lies a little farther to the north, was no quiet country town, but the most populous city of the province of Numidia, second in importance only to Carthage. There were several churches, chapels of the martyrs, other church buildings, and pagan temples, a circus and a theatre. The schismatic Donatists were stronger than the Catholics, and moreover, there were other sects as well, while a considerable percentage of the population was still non-Christian. There were controversies and quarrels with all of these. The Catholic congregation itself was not undivided, and contained great contrasts, from the poor Berber or Punic-speaking inhabitants of the dock-side to the luxurious villas of the ruling class. For all of them, the bishop had to be available—he was indeed not only preacher and counsellor, but, in accordance with the system of the time, also judge, advocate, and representative of the people. The ecclesiastical interests dealt with here had little to do with the problems which had previously occupied Augustine. Quarrels, gossip, and sordid intrigues were an everyday occurrence. Augustine's consecration as bishop had almost fallen through because his opponents had spread abroad the rumour that he had provided a wife with a love-potion for adultery (in reality it was the usual gift of consecrated bread). In addition, there were the cares of the neighbourhood, and of the whole church. Soon from all sides they turned to Augustine for help. Countless times we find him travelling to councils and meetings in Carthage and other places. His correspondence went overseas into almost all the provinces of the empire. He was, however, already dead when

15

the imperial invitation to the great Council of 431 summoned him to Ephesus.

We may be indignant when we see how much time and effort he had to spend in settling trivial quarrels, bringing to reason pugnacious theologians, or discussing all sorts of problems brought up from outside. It cannot be denied too that the permanent strain of his ecclesiastical duties had an effect upon his nature. In the course of the years, Augustine became less kind and versatile, dogmatically more rigid, ecclesiastically sterner and more 'Catholic'. But pressing duties and advancing years always change a man. All things considered, however, the ministry gave Augustine much more than it took. Indeed, only in his office and by his service to the church did he really become the man he was. Despite his great ability as an organizer, Augustine was by nature no pure theoretician, who takes up problems and solutions without a personal stimulus, and pursues them for their own sake. In spite of their dry academic form, his first attempts at a philosophical theology were already concerned with questions decisive for his personal development, for Augustine was trying to assure himself intellectually of his new way. The refutation of the Manicheans can be seen from the same point of view. Now he was finished with himself and his past. Should he spend the strength now released simply in spiritual service in untroubled peace, surrounded by a small circle of friends who readily followed him, and explore 'the truth'? This was obviously Augustine's own desire—the desire of a writer and philosopher who appreciates the value of intellectual activity, and therefore feels his need for a peaceful life to be fully justified, and defends it with ascetic and devotional arguments. But even before his election, the duties which came along unbidden drew him gently beyond the self-drawn circle, while his sudden appointment had the effect of a second life-changing conversion, which at first he did not want and hardly understood. The work of a bishop, the endless and difficult tasks in the service of the Catholic church, brought Augustine back to real life, and led his intellect increasingly to real and historically pressing questions which had to be decided in everyday life, and for this very reason had to be answered seriously. Augustine did not succumb to these things: he mastered them. And the unity of life and spirit which he had found for his personal existence thus appears even deeper and greater in the broad realm of the church, for which he must speak and teach.

At first sight, it seems almost impossible to imagine how Augustine could manage to remain uninterruptedly busy with intellectual problems amidst the current business of the ecclesiastical office. He wrote an extraordinarily large number of letters, sermons, essays, and some voluminous theological treatises. Most of his literary work was done while he was a bishop. Augustine himself was surprised when he realized at the end of his life that he had published 93 'works' or 232 'books' (there were in fact even more); and already his pupil and biographer Possidius gave it as his opinion that in all probability no one person could read them all. To be sure, Augustine was no modern scholar in his method of working, and also no historical polymath like Jerome. He conceived his ideas rapidly and independently, while their formulation caused no trouble at all to a trained speaker. The books (often several at the same time) were dictated directly to his amanuenses. Nevertheless Augustine loathed carelessness. He certainly did not extemporize his writings, but considered them carefully and subsequently revised them many times and emended the text. He made eager use himself of the church library of Hippo, which grew swiftly under his supervision, and even as an elderly bishop set about refreshing and improving his knowledge of Greek. Among Augustine's works there are of course some dry and rather flat pieces, but they are few. As a rule, one recognizes him at once by the vigour, directness, and relevance of his clear train of thought. Even when he must occasionally become more detailed and unfold material on a broader basis, one never gets lost. Augustine always knew why and to what end he was writing. His ideas at times digressed, but they never became detached; they always remain in the context, for they are related to the great realm of truth, which as such is God's truth and the truth of the Christian church. This was to him a personal help: 'When I am bowed down under my load, I am equally lifted up by your love' (*Ep.* 101, 1; *FC*, 10, 144). Even on the highest peaks of intellectual life, Augustine did not live for himself alone, and the miserably depressing daily round remained meaningful because it was the daily round of Christ's body. This ultimate unity of his life-work is the secret of his never tiring creative power.

He who wishes to know Augustine in this unity of his spiritual activity must read his sermons. Particularly in the original tongue they are still readable today, and grip the reader not only as documents of church and cultural history, but also immediately by their form and spiritual content. Like Ambrose, Augustine preached regularly, and his sermons were similarly in part written down as books; but the revision with respect to style and subject was more intensive than with Ambrose. So he began his episcopate with an exposition of the psalms which originated partly from sermons actually delivered, partly from exegetical notes. The famous work on the Gospel of John originated later in a similar fashion. But we still have any number of Augustine's sermons in their original form—as they were written down in the church service, or as they were dictated subsequently by Augustine himself. Before the service Augustine made no notes, but only prepared for his exposition with prayer and meditation—*orator antequam dictor* (*de Doctr.* IV, 15, 32). Depending on the occasion, time, and audience, the sermons were entirely different. The speaker, Augustine thinks, must not bring a ready-made idea along, but must continuously have an eye to his hearers, and according to how well they understand him, must either proceed or repeat in other words what has already been said. The essential thing is that his sermon reach the congregation, i.e. be heard with understanding, joy, and obedience. In order not to tire it must not be too long— after all, the hearers must stand whereas the bishop may sit! Above all, it must be clear and really lead to the word of the

Bible. This last is the crucial point: even more important than popularity is the demand for substance and relevance, and from this point of view the whole ancient attitude toward speech underwent a basic revision. True, the sermon also is a rhetorical task, and Augustine seldom neglected to embellish it and make it more attractive by impressive antitheses, pleasantly constructed rhythms, and an occasional sparkling play on words or rhyme. Yet this cultivation of style becomes evil so soon as it becomes the main concern, and detracts attention from the content, on which everything depends. One might learn from Cyprian, Augustine thinks, 'how sound Christian teaching restrains the tongue from rhetorical excess, and places it under the discipline of a more dignified and moderate eloquence' (*de Doctr.* IV, 14, 31). Anyone who tries to see Augustine as only an artificial orator has not understood him, or has applied a wrong criterion. One must compare the old Augustine with the young, the preacher with the writer of letters, and compare him above all with his contemporaries. Then one realizes the extent of the self-training to which he has subjected himself, and one understands the power to rejuvenate language which he as well as others derived especially from his regular preaching. Augustine did not create the style of the Latin sermon, but he perfected it, and became the accepted model for future generations.

Besides, despite its short sentences, its direct intelligibility, and its closeness to life, the language Augustine uses in his sermons is by no means 'popular', and is not meant to be. When he rejected exaggerated purism he was thinking primarily of the Latin Bible, with its various linguistic oddities. With the word of the Bible he did not find fault. Moreover, the charm of his style lies in the very fact that the simplicity at which it aims is not based upon helplessness. The driest sentences Augustine composed still display something of the character of 'shot silk which, however folded, always glistens somewhere' (v.d. Meer). In content, too, what Augustine offered never sank below his level. He had the rare gift, arising from inner freedom and sureness, of saying the deepest things intelligibly, the complicated simply, and never being banal even with what is simple. Undoubtedly the concise train of thought in his sermons occasionally demands much of his hearers, and must certainly have been above the heads of a part of the congregation. But they always led back to the spiritual possession common to all, and appealed not in vain to the charity which dwells in the congregation, and connects all its members. In his handbook on *Christian Learning*, with which we will deal later, Augustine himself expounded his teaching on homiletics. With his charming little book *On the Instruction of Simple People* he also composed the first book on catechetics. In spite of this he confessed to being 'almost always' discontented with his own achievements. 'I desire my hearers to understand everything as I understand it; and I feel that my words are not achieving it.' This is primarily due to the fact, as he explains in a mood of philosophical reflection, that an intellectual perception flashes up like lightning and is then complete, whereas its expression in words and syllables always has to pass through a long and laborious process. Yet the preacher may take solace in the knowledge that experience shows that the hearers often feel themselves edified even when he himself is distressed by a feeling of failure (*Cat. Rud.* 2, 3; *ACW*, 2, 15).

Even as a priest Augustine personally maintained the ascetic mode of life. On the estate assigned to him a cloister (*monasterium*) was immediately built. Some of his friends from Thagaste moved into it. The number of residents increased swiftly. In part they travelled from afar, but the majority came from the common people. The former pronouncedly 'intellectual' character of the community was thus changed. Admission was not denied even to the illiterate, only they had then to be instructed in reading and writing. Augustine had to emphasize more than previously his own position as prior of the monastery, and firm rules were issued. The rule composed by him is the oldest Western monastic rule; even Benedict of Nursia knew it. When Augustine was promoted to the bishopric, he had to entrust the prior's office to another, and himself to move into the bishop's palace. The crowd of visitors and guests he received, invited, and often had to put up would have disturbed the monastic peace too severely. Yet Augustine did not wish to give up his ideal, so he now asked his clergy to live with him. All the clergy of the town under his leadership founded a *vita communis*, and everyone newly elected had henceforth to pledge himself also to join it. Otherwise he would not be ordained. Such an order had occasionally been attempted in Italy and Gaul even prior to Augustine, but it is a question how far he knew anything about these precursors. In any event, Augustine's 'clergy-house' (*monasterium clericorum*) served as a model for the future. In Africa this institution was at the same time a kind of nursery for bishops. Priests called for service abroad rapidly made the new order known, and in medieval times all cathedral and collegiate chapters were based on Augustine's rule. In the priestly mona-stery, the manual work which Augustine highly esteemed in general had to give way to the activity of the cure of souls, yet the spirit of fellowship and of intimate association of all was not to suffer in consequence. 'The first goal of your fellowship is to live together in concord and to have one heart and soul in God' (*Regula*, I, 1). Its model is the primitive community as described in Acts (iv. 32). Intention is the decisive factor, not ascetic achievement as such, the spirit and not the organiza-tion. The set order of the day, the hours for meals and prayers, only mark out the framework. True charity does not treat all and everything alike; rather it knows to take into account indi-vidual differences and needs. Only one demand was inflexible for Augustine: there must be total poverty. Where this com-mandment was violated, he took ruthless measures. As a fixed rule he himself gave away or sold every donation presented to him; he would be ashamed, says he, to wear a better garb than the rest of his brethren (*Serm.* 356, 13). 'We desire to live according to the manner of the apostles' (*Regula*, I, 4).

The monastic community realizes what the Christian congre-gation should be: a fellowship of perfect love. In that way it will serve as a model to the congregation; it is the outstanding portion of the whole, as it were the hem of the Lord's garments (*Enarr. Ps.* cxxxii. 9). Isolated disappointments occasioned no change with regard to this. Augustine confessed that even though he 'hardly found any men better than those who have done well in the monasteries', it was also the case that many of those who had 'broken into' the cloisters belonged to the worst kind he has ever known (*Ep.* 78, 9). In principle, all monks in the clergy-house should be willing to serve in the congregation. The tension must be endured between the contemplative and the active ideal of life, which Augustine himself had experienced so painfully. We must be Mary and Martha at the same time, must love God and our neighbour equally. This last tension will be resolved only in the life to come: 'It is love of truth that prompts the search for holy leisure (*otium sanctum*), while it is the compulsion of love that makes men undertake a righteous activity in affairs. If this burden is not placed upon us, we should use our freedom to discern and contemplate truth; but if it is placed upon us it must be accepted because of this compulsion of love. But even so, delight in truth is not to be wholly abandoned, lest when that satisfaction is denied, the compulsion in question may crush us' (*Civ. D.* XIX, 19; *LCL*, VI, 205).

Philosophical activity in the strict sense now took a back place in Augustine's writings. His work was directed towards the understanding, exposition, and proclaiming of the Bible. Criticism of the philosophers, their vanity and 'arrogance', grew sharper. The positive significance of their assertions was now seldom mentioned. But this impression might be deceptive. Augustine avoided direct reference to the works of the philosophers; after having once found the full, unrestricted, and infallible truth in the Bible, he did not need them any more. Nevertheless, he did not cease even as a theologian from being a philosopher. Augustine knew neither the medieval grading nor the modern separation of theology and philosophy. To him there is but one truth, which has shown itself to the pagan philosophers imperfectly and to the Christians perfectly in Christ. If this Christian truth is to be understood, intellectually adopted, and confirmed, he has no hesitation in turning, consciously or unconsciously, back to the modes of thinking and logical laws, to the conceptions, expressions and traditions he had learned from Cicero, Aristotle, and the 'Platonists', which have there proved to be right. The most imposing outcome of this attitude is his *Fifteen Books on the Trinity*. He began them in 399 'as a young man' and did not conclude them until twenty years later 'as an old man' (*Ep.* 174). Even the external structure shows the concern of Augustine: after the first eight books have presented the Biblical teaching on the Trinity as such, its scientific, i.e. logical and metaphysical, justification and foundation follow in an even more voluminous second part. Without knowledge of the Neo-Platonic teaching on God, and of other findings of ancient philosophy, it cannot be understood.

In this attempt to treat the Trinity philosophically, Augustine had had a forerunner in the West. He was Marius Victorinus, the pagan philosopher who had become Christian, in whose translation Augustine came to know the writings of Plotinus. The starting-point for the philosophical interpretation of the dogma was Plotinus' teaching regarding the self-emanation of the deity, which had already led in his teaching to a kind of 'trinity', expressly differentiated from the further world of inferior spiritual realities. Nevertheless, it always remained difficult to prove from these Neo-Platonic presuppositions the 'unity' and 'equality' of the three divine entities, on which now everything depended theologically. At this point Victorinus still stood in a direct front against the Arians, whose power had since been crushed. In complete calm Augustine now brought the debate to a conclusion. The manner in which he assimilated and corrected the philosophical ideas has nothing to do with a merely external or forced accommodation to the needs of the situation. On the basis of an outline of the Christian teaching Augustine was trying once again independently to think over the correlations of the system, and to bring them

to a conclusion. In careful accomplishment of his design and
in precise treatment of over-subtle conceptions, he may have
fallen below the standard of his philosophical teachers. His researches, nevertheless, have their own proper importance, and
under the pressure of his new concern were repeatedly advanced
to new logical understanding. When in contrast to the classical
and static definition of spirit and the divine perfection, as consisting in the conception of pure vision, Augustine, taking
Victorinus further, began to stress the dynamic and volitional
aspects of 'love' for the life of the Trinity, this was certainly
also due to the special nature of the Christian and Biblical
impulse.

Augustine approached the doctrine of the Trinity not by way
of its historical origin—the sending of the 'Son of God' in the
flesh, and the experience of the 'Spirit' in the primitive Christian congregation—he started off, as did the whole theology of
the early church, 'philosophically' with the eternal being of the
Godhead in itself. He was aware, more than were his predecessors, and above all more than the Greek theologians, that the
mystery of the Deity transcends all imagination, and that any
attempt to comprehend it conceptually of necessity therefore retains something of the symbolic. This gives him a certain broad-
mindedness and freedom compared with other attempts at
comprehension. Yet, on the other hand, the new spiritual philosophy of the 'Platonists' permitted him in fact to overcome certain weaknesses of the older, materialistic picture-language, and
to define things more appropriately than hitherto, yet at the same
time not, as so often happens, to be satisfied with sheer assertion.
According to Augustine, it belongs to the nature of the spiritual
itself that it has a 'trinitarian' character, that it appears in a
threefold form and is in itself such. This is observable already
in the simple act of perception of the human self-consciousness,
in that the self simultaneously experiences itself as the thought,
as the thinking subject, and as the ego directing itself to itself;
a phenomenon which Augustine described with a variety of
expressions, and expounded very clearly. The trinity of our

spiritual self refers back to the triune God who has created us, but we become God's image only if we find Him again in His Trinity and are able to love Him. God the Father, Son, and Holy Spirit are the prototype of all spiritual existence as personality, inasmuch as we have here too an indissoluble 'self-consciousness', 'self-knowledge', and 'self-assertion', the mutual relationship of lover and beloved through the third, which is love itself. A subordination or separation within the Trinity is now out of the question. The unity of God—an old theological concern particularly in the West—now appears with such emphasis that the divine 'Persons' really become mere elements within the one living being of the Deity, and are not to be isolated one from the other even in their external activity. At the same time, the personal character is also more clearly defined than previously. Augustine criticizes the traditional concept of the one divine substance, the bearer of the divine being and its 'attributes', to which the three 'Persons' of the Deity are then held in contradistinction. Carried to its logical conclusion this is a downright blasphemous anthropomorphism. As a person God has no attributes distinguishable from Himself, according to which one could think of Him like a human being, or on the basis of which one could standardize His 'Person', but His being is essentially His own personal being itself. God is not good because He possesses the attribute of goodness, but He is goodness itself in Person, with the consequence that all that is good can be called good only by Him and in Him.

We cannot here develop Augustine's teaching on the Trinity. He himself stated that his work was 'extremely difficult', and in his opinion 'understandable only by a few' (*Ep.* 169, 1). From now on it dominated the Western doctrine of the Trinity almost exclusively. Even Thomas did not really go beyond Augustine on this question. Even the later disputes with the East regarding the Spirit's relationship to the Son followed lines determined by Augustine. In other respects, the close connection of the divine Persons with each other inevitably resulted in complications in Christology. The divine and human natures of

Christ can be united only with difficulty, and the difficulty of
proceeding from the intrinsically consistent doctrine of God to
the basic dogma of the incarnation was much greater for Augustine than it had been for Ambrose, precisely because he tried
to explain and 'understand' it philosophically. As we have seen,
Augustine was aware that the decisive boundary between
philosophy and revelation comes precisely here. The longer he
was occupied with the problem the more he was concerned
with the reality of the incarnate Christ, with the 'humility' of
God, who wanted to redeem our pride by surrendering His
divine abundance for our poverty, in order Himself to teach us
the way of humility as the way to happiness.

The work on the Trinity occupies an exceptional position
among Augustine's major works, in so far as it originated without a pressing cause and was written for the most part unpol-
emically. That is why its composition took up so much time:
again and again other, more urgent, tasks intervened. The long
quarrel with the Donatists was the most obstinate that occupied
Augustine. The controversy with this typical 'sect' had repercussions upon his ecclesiastical thinking, and caused it to develop in a particular direction which was originally far from his
thoughts. It is astonishing that in his early years the Donatists
were entirely disregarded and unmentioned by Augustine,
although they were found everywhere in Africa, and particularly in the interior were actually dominant. Outside Africa,
however, they were of no importance and intellectually they
were of no interest to him. Once he had entered the service of
the church, no year elapsed in which Augustine did not write
pamphlets or sermons against Donatism. For Augustine as a
bishop, and even as a presbyter, there was no evading this problem—he had immediately to engage in the struggle and
controversy. The Donatists were in a majority even in Hippo
Rhegius. They possessed the finest basilica in the town, and
influenced Augustine's congregation on all sides. Mixed mar-
riages between Catholics and Donatists were not infrequent,
conversions, rebaptisms, and petty irritations were everyday

occurrences. Once even a clergyman went over to them when
he had had a difference of opinion with Augustine, and was
naturally received with enthusiasm by the opposition. Actually
rebaptisms were prohibited by the state as sacrilege, and the
primacy of the Catholic church was protected by law in other
ways also, but in view of the actual balance of power the police
hesitated, and avoided as far as possible provoking the easily
aroused sectarians, who in any case complained on every occasion about earlier persecutions and the injustice done to them.
There was scarcely any difference this way or that in ritual and
doctrine, which at first glance made the unexampled animosity
with which the two churches opposed each other all the more
puzzling. Quite often it degenerated into bloody violence.

.The origin of this unhappy situation lay far back. After the
end of the last great persecution, at the beginning of the century, a bishop had been elected in Carthage who was unacceptable to the party of the uncompromising confessors, and it was
said that one of the ordaining bishops had himself shunned
martyrdom in the persecution. The schism having once started,
it swiftly spread, obviously owing to more general causes.
Accustomed as they were to persecution, resistance, and isolation, wide circles of African Christianity, which had all along
inclined to rigorism, were unable to adjust themselves so rapidly
to the changed situation. They mistrusted the new union with
the ruling classes, and after Constantine had rejected the Donatist
complaints, they presently resumed their old attitude of opposition. By contrast to the tolerant and allegedly lax Catholics,
the Donatists proclaimed themselves to be the sole 'pure' representatives of the true church of the saints, and they stiffened
themselves into an exclusive particularism. The animosity of
the Berber rural population against the Romanized society in
the towns joined with this, and the more the social differences
increased in the fourth century, the more easily did this hostility
at times also assume politically dangerous, revolutionary features.
Gangs of Donatist 'fighters' were actually formed, who sacked
the manors of rich landed proprietors, burned Catholic churches,

and forced the population willingly or unwillingly to support them. Yet along with this the Donatist congregations displayed real orthodox zeal and sacrificial devotion, which the Catholic congregations could no longer match. The different attempts of the government to suppress the sect by force achieved nothing, and only intensified the hatred against the ungodly, and an ominous readiness for 'martyrdom'.

Nothing could be effected against these people as a rule by theological argument. Indeed, since the days of the great Donatus who had given his name to the sect, outstanding literary defenders of its cause were not lacking in the Donatist camp. But what they put forward did not really touch the root of the passionate conflict, and shifted the controversy to secondary issues. It was not difficult for the Catholics to refute the Donatist contentions and complaints, convincing enough as such, and when they still did not achieve success they were the more disappointed and annoyed at the malevolence of the heretics. The claim, in opposition to the Catholic church which was 'spread throughout the whole world', to represent the sole true and holy Christian fellowship had something hopelessly stubborn about it, and the contention that the Donatist congregations consisted only of 'pure', real Christians, in contrast to the Catholic sinners, needed no refutation. Already before Augustine, the struggle had become focussed theologically on the problem of the sacraments in particular. The Donatists maintained, following Cyprian, that only the 'holy', i.e. persons free from serious sins, were able as priests to perform the sacramental consecrations, and administer efficacious sacraments. Since the Catholics had formerly violated this principle when ordaining the bishop of Carthage, and since that time had abandoned it completely, they were now no church, without baptism, without priesthood, and without the Holy Spirit. They were but a blasphemous society, which by the imitation of holy rites were even more defiled and worse than the pagans. Here, too, an originally quite serious concern had taken on a rather baroque appearance, and when logically pursued it could lead to nothing but impossible conclusions and contradictions. As a matter of fact, differences of opinion and schisms arose in the Donatist church also. But the Catholic contention that the sacraments possessed in themselves alone a sanctifying power if administered with correct outward form, also had its difficulties. The Donatists were not really concerned about a particular sacramental theory, but about concrete separation from the 'ungodly', and about resistance to the detested pressure of their 'persecutors'. It was precisely the favoured position of the Catholics and the corresponding detriment to the Donatists which made any reconciliation impossible.

At the time when Augustine began his activity, the earlier pressure upon the Donatists had declined considerably; only the exaggerated remembrance of former afflictions still poisoned the atmosphere. Not without reason, the Catholics on their part complained about excesses and encroachments of the sectarians, and so the prospects for a settlement were as slight as ever. It was essentially due to Augustine and his friend, the primate Aurelius of Carthage, that negotiations, theological activity and discussion were set in motion anew, in order to win back the schismatics. In contrast to the resigned attitude of many of his colleagues, the removal of a division both unfortunate and senseless was to Augustine a religious necessity. Why should it not be possible if both sides exercised good will? Is Christ really divided? (I Cor. i. 13). A church which acquiesces in schism ceases to be a church. Surprise has often been expressed at the determination with which Augustine embraced these convictions and acted accordingly the moment he assumed office. In view of his former, individualistic development he was the last man to be prepared for this. The new obligations and experiences which had of necessity come his way as presbyter were undoubtedly of the greatest importance in this, namely the preaching, pastoral advice, and work in the congregation of a confessionally mixed city, with all the unpleasantness with which it was attended. Yet this does not mean that Augustine's ecclesiastical thinking was based upon purely 'practical' considerations. It had spiritual presuppositions which reached further back, and which were essentially theological. Where there is life, where the Spirit and God reign, there discord is overcome. To Augustine unity is the token of truth and perfection—this is a conviction which went back to the Neo-Platonic level of his thinking, and which the study of the Bible had made concrete. Paul is above all decisive for the idea of ecclesiastical unity. Christ has redeemed us for unity—this no longer means for a mere unity of spirit, but for the unity and fellowship of His body which is the church. Through Christ all mankind was reconciled to God in the church and now partakes in his Spirit. In Christ, the 'new Adam', we find the way back from enmity and dispersion to union with God, and remain henceforward in the fellowship of unity one with the other worked by love. This love is the 'grace' of the New Testament; it is peace and the Holy Spirit Himself. Outside this 'unity' there is no life 'in Christ', no justification of the sinner, no sanctification and no salvation. This unity is no mere 'idea'; it is our new reality, the reality of service of the many members in the church which cannot but be one by its very nature, as Christ is one. Christ's church is the church for all in the whole world; it cannot be a specialist or separatistic church like the church of the Donatists. Upon this basis Augustine takes up readily the old anti-Donatist argument of catholicity; not for nothing does the Catholic church stand in firm connection and communion with the church in Rome, with the ancient churches in the East, and with the churches of the whole world—it is the only universal church, and therefore the true church from which nobody may exclude himself. Outside the catholic church no one finds salvation. This argument, at first sight rather external and brutal, now attains a deeper spiritual significance. The majority is not right simply because it is the majority, but because in its midst the will to unity and fellowship becomes visible. 'Nobody will be so foolish, I think, as to maintain that anyone whatever belongs to the unity of the church who does

not possess love' (*c. Crescon*. I, 34). The really evil and unchristian element in Donatism is the malignity of its inner attitude and disposition, the fact that it does not desire the unity
and fellowship of Christians at all, and in a spirit of hatred denies
it in favour of separation. It is perverse because it is opposed to
the basic Christian commandment of love. 'Love creates fellowship, fellowship loves unity, and unity preserves love' (*in Psalm*
xxx. 2, 1). By contrast, the Pharisaical affirmation of one's own
holiness and purity is completely untenable. The conventicle
ideal of the church is not feasible practically. Christ wanted the
wheat and tares to grow together until He Himself holds the
judgement (Matt. xiii. 24 ff.). We are not yet at the goal of our
pilgrimage through this age, but on the way. We must be satisfied with separation from evil people in volition and act; 'meanwhile, we can only await the final separation at the end of the
world faithfully, patiently, and bravely' (*Litt. Petil*. III, 4).

Augustine spared no pains in order to enter time and again
with endless patience into the particulars of what the Donatists
put forward. The matter of the election of the bishop of Carthage, decided three generations previously, was re-examined and
discussed anew. Augustine undertook laborious journeys in order
to provide himself with the complete record and documents.
He looked into all the theological misgivings item by item. He
sought to give to the Catholic teaching on the sacraments a
satisfying formulation by distinguishing more closely between
the validity, the legitimacy, and the efficacy of the sacraments.
Baptism can actually produce its full effect of blessing only when
it is received, or becomes alive, in the 'Catholic' community of
love, yet outside the true church it does not cease to be baptism.
Even there it is still the sign of attachment to the one Lord, as
it were the brandmark (*character*) with which each lamb of
Christ is branded. This claim of Christ's to ownership is valid
and indelible, and points at the same time back to the one flock
of the one Shepherd. Therefore there must be no 'rebaptism',
but also no persevering in separation. When the Donatists ask
about the moral uprightness of the administrator, they are

16

looking in the wrong direction. It is not the man, but the gift of God, that counts. 'Is the servant of the evangelical word and sacrament good? He becomes a companion of the Gospel! If, however, he is evil, he nevertheless does not cease to be a steward of the Gospel' (*Litt. Petil.* III, 67). The truth of God uses many instruments, for of itself it is powerful and fruitful.

All these reasons appeared to Augustine convincing and irrefutable. And, indeed, they were far superior to the more or less useless and obstinate objections which the Donatists brought against them. But what was gained by that? The issue was, how to bring them home to his opponents themselves, how to initiate a discussion with them, and how really to obtain their recognition at first intellectually, and then also in the practical consequence of reunion. And here lay the greatest difficulties. As always in such cases, it is the stronger party which is concerned about union and discussions of union. This very intellectual and moral superiority of the Catholic leaders took away from the Donatists any inclination to negotiate, and made them haughty and defensive. Negotiations and discussions, furthermore, were out of keeping with the intellectual tradition of a church of martyrs and pietistic moralists. Augustine certainly realized the awkwardness of the situation and did everything in his power to overcome it. Immediately after he became bishop, he sought an exchange of views with his Donatist colleague in Hippo. Similar attempts were repeated at other places. The opposition were allowed to choose the place, the circumstances, and the witnesses for the disputation. Augustine was willing even to withdraw, and to propose a less versatile partner to the discussion, in case the Donatists feared his rhetorical training. The practical regulations in case of union were also arranged as generously as possible. Augustine was serious in desiring only that the truth should prevail, and not that one party should triumph over the other. In contrast to the evil tradition of the struggle with heresy, he tried not to caricature and cheat the dissentients; he really wanted to understand them. He was willing also frankly to admit the past errors of his church. He admonished the members of his own congregation to patience, and checked his anger often when the opposition reacted rudely, dishonestly, or not at all. In fact, all was in vain. Augustine's sermons were heard by Donatists, to be sure, and again and again he was successful in converting individuals. But the great body, the leaders, the Donatist church as a whole, persevered in malignant opposition. Occasionally, when Augustine's kindness personally won over one or another authoritative figure for his plan, the possibility of discussion and of 'peace' seemed to be within reach. Then the opposition came to an understanding among themselves, retreated suddenly, and looked for excuses. In the end nobody appeared, and it came to nothing.

Taken as a whole, all Augustine's efforts for peace thus turned out fruitless. Whose fault was it? It has been pointed out that Augustine belonged intellectually and socially to a class, and accordingly also spoke a language, which was alien and hateful to the simple Donatists, especially those in the country. They would not, and could not, read or understand the writings of this 'Manichean' rhetorician educated abroad. They also scorned, it may be presumed, the cultivated townsman who associated with the wealthy, and seemingly did not know their sufferings. There is some truth in this. Even Augustine could not get away from his background, and despite all his personal renunciations remained a member of his society, a representative of literary education and cultured ideals from which the subject-masses of the late Roman empire had begun for some time to withdraw. He was a privileged citizen and spoke Latin exclusively. Yet Augustine took pains to achieve a popular style and be intelligible in his sermons and polemics, especially in dealing with the Donatists. His *Psalm Against the Donatist Party*, consisting of 300 verses, is a remarkable proof of this. 'I wished', he wrote, 'to bring the case of the Donatists to the knowledge of precisely the lower classes, and the uneducated and simple in general, and impress it upon them. For this purpose, I did not want to use any form of artistic poem, in order not to be compelled by the laws of metre to choose such words as are unusual among the

common people' (*Retr.* I, 19, 1). Augustine desired to speak
with complete plainness and clarity. So he threw completely
overboard all claims of literary culture, and composed a poem
which is certainly no 'poetry', though in its popular form it
nevertheless pointed to the future. The beginnings of the
stanzas are arranged consecutively according to the alphabet,
while a plain, singable refrain for the choir concludes them,
and all the lines have the same final sound -e (or -ae) and
so 'rhyme'. In place of the 'quantity', still rigidly observed
by Ambrose, we find, following the example of Punic (?)
poetry, the simple rhythm of the words. The melody, also,
which we do not know, was most likely adapted to the tunes
of Donatist hymns and chants. This primitive '*Psalm*' is sure
to have had its effect on the Latin-speaking population also.

The decisive difficulty in coming to terms with the schismatics was most likely not Augustine's education and social
position as such; it was due to the political position and tradition of his church which, in the opinion of the Donatists, had
been and still remained the 'church of the persecutors'. This
accusation was justified. Again and again, under Constantine,
and then above all under Constantius, the Donatists were punished, suppressed, and persecuted by the police, and even now
there were a number of regulations to their detriment, above
all the severe prohibition of rebaptism, which nevertheless continued to be performed. In this lay the decisive obstacle to any
Catholic attempt at winning them back, and likewise to a true
mission, which in conditions of freedom would have been
effective. Augustine was not blind to this endangering of his
'peace' work. With the candour which always distinguished
him, he tried to refute and invalidate the reproaches arising out
of this. First it is necessary to repudiate the Donatists' false pride
in martyrdom: sufferings and loss as such prove nothing of the
truth of a cause. Only true confession makes martyrs; for pagans,
criminals, and heretics are likewise persecuted. 'I have proved
countless times, both by debate and by writing, that they cannot
have the death of martyrs because they have not the life of

Christians, since it is not the pain but the purpose that makes a martyr' (*Ep.* 204, 4; *FC*, 8, 5). Besides this, the alleged martyrs permit themselves frauds, injustices, and abominations for which they are punished on good grounds, and with full right. Finally, however, there is actually a far-reaching freedom for the Donatists. They have their churches, congregations, and services—and it is not true that the Catholics thirst for their blood. Augustine prides himself that he is no extremist, that he repudiates denunciation to the police in certain cases, and had even pressed for a reduction of punishments already inflicted. This is honest, yet nevertheless somewhat naïve. Augustine did not think of disapproving the existing laws as such—it is only right that the heretics do not receive the same favours from the state as the servants of the truth. But he would nevertheless like to continue with and to succeed in discussion and conversion in complete freedom without interference; the last thing he wanted was to promote religious opportunism: but how could this be achieved in the given circumstances? We come here upon an ambiguity similar to that found in Ambrose and most of the fathers of this transitional period, who affirmed the right of freedom and the right of the state-church at the same time. Yet the development continued, and Augustine followed it.

Toward the end of the century, the situation of the Donatists again began to deteriorate. Their support of a rebellious governor caused them to fall into political disgrace. Above all, however, the notion of the Catholic empire, as framed by Theodosius, pressed by itself for an increasingly stricter realization. There were, of course, in the Catholic camp church leaders who welcomed this, and demanded a more rigorous enforcement of the laws against heretics. At the beginning of the year 405, the time came: the Emperor Honorius issued an edict which decreed the general repression of the Donatists by force. All their churches and properties were to be delivered to the Catholic bishops; their services were prohibited; those who broke the laws were threatened with confiscation and expulsion. Yet all this still could not break their resistance. Thus the state arranged a final official religious debate in 411. It is evident, and Augustine stressed this time and again, that at this council equality of rights and full freedom of discussion were actually granted to the Donatists. The Catholics did not let themselves be wearied by the desperate evasions and delaying actions of their adversaries: in negotiations which continued for days all their accusations and contentions were once more examined, discussed, and 'refuted'. Of course the result proclaimed by the imperial commissioner at the end was determined from the very beginning. The Donatists had come only because there was no other way out, and they refused to accept the decision. But now there was indulgence for them no longer. Imperial 'executores' took care of the enforcement of the 'Catholic peace', and took drastic measures against the obstinate dissentients. Catholic bishops who did not arrange the incorporation energetically enough were threatened in the same way, and were to be denounced. We hear of horrible scenes of suicidal resistance, of sanguinary measures, and of acts of revenge by the suppressed. Donatism was not dead, but vanished from public life. Entire congregations joined Catholicism in a body, sometimes with their clergy.

Augustine regretted the violence of these actions. Like Ambrose, he protested above all at the use by the government of capital punishment, which he considered to be wrong in all circumstances within the realm of the church, and in this he was successful. Even now he wished to win the reluctant by peaceful means, by preaching, by enlightenment, and by pastoral instruction. He made provision that the rights of those newly converted in the congregation were not curtailed, and disclaimed any military protection for his own person. Obviously, his endeavours had real success in some cases. Augustine's patient and friendly attitude succeeded in winning over, at any rate later, many former Donatists. Indeed, it was often only custom, innate prejudice, and lack of acquaintance with Catholic truth which had made these Christians resist reconciliation. Now, it appeared, they were actually thankful to have the opportunity to change their views, and in part accepted the new ideas gladly. It is shocking to see how it was exactly these personal successes which led Augustine to a revision in principle of his standpoint, the implications of which in world history he certainly could not then anticipate. 'Originally my opinion was, that no one should be coerced into the unity of Christ, that we must act only by words, fight only by arguments, and prevail by force of reason, lest we should have those whom we knew as avowed heretics feigning themselves to be Catholics. But this opinion of mine was overcome not by the words of those who controverted it, but by the conclusive instances to which they could point' (*Ep.* 93, 17; *LPNF*, I, 388). Such an 'instance', to which Augustine was referred by his colleagues, was first and foremost the changed situation in his own city, in which peace now finally reigned; and furthermore, the former dissidents were outspokenly happy regarding the changed circumstances. Was this not to be recognized and welcomed? The government actions were not in any case to be regarded as injustice, for the final negotiations in Carthage had proved with all clarity that the Donatist assertions were wrong, and that their resistance was unfounded, and explicable as merely due to stubborn ill-will, or simply factual ignorance. An energetic intervention was then imperative, after all. Thus Augustine came to his famous, or infamous, theological justification of force. Of course he considers it better if men voluntarily arrive at adoration and veneration of God in the right way; 'perfect love casts out fear' (I John iv. 18). Yet this does not mean that exercise of threats and force must in all cases be evil, or that it may not be actually indispensable in many cases. In conclusion, parents also force their children to obey, and teachers compel their pupils to work, for which they are grateful afterwards. 'You are also of opinion that no coercion is to be used with any man in order to his deliverance from the fatal consequence of error; and yet you see that, in examples which cannot be disputed, this is done by God(!), who loves us with more real regard for our profit than any other can.' Christ also himself exhorts us in the Parable of the Great Feast that we are to 'compel' everybody we can reach to enter his house (Luke xiv. 23 according to the contemporary, all too literal translation: *cogite intrare*, *Ep.* 93, 5; *LPNF*, I, 383).

Force is thus regarded as a short-cut only, and as a provisional means to the true goal of free and voluntary conversion, but this way must be employed in case of emergency. In the case of this schism, where things were clear as the day, proved and established, it would have been unjust to give way to the manifestly malevolent obstinacy of the Donatist leaders, and simply to leave to ruin the poor misguided people, who neither knew the truth nor ever would come to know it in such a way. If we wish to understand Augustine's decision rightly, and contrast it with the medieval ideals of the Crusades and the Inquisition, we must not forget that the whole Donatist question was to him in no way a matter of conscience, or of a difference in faith to be taken seriously. It was plainly a matter of inveterate prejudice, of incitement of the people, and of the power of bad habit, for the overcoming of which the assistance of the police therefore seemed in order. It is quite wrong to explain Augustine's attitude in this question in terms of a particularly exaggerated hierarchical consciousness, or the 'domineering' instincts of a churchman. Rather is the contrary the case. Augustine did not decide by political instinct, but let himself be persuaded and determined by the favourable aspects of the situation. With the unconscious arrogance of a man of theoretical training he put all his confidence in the power and persuasion of his reason. After all his personal and literary endeavours had failed, he let himself be pushed, rather angrily, in just the opposite direction, and accepted the assistance of the secular power. He was sadly mistaken about the successes attained in this way. With the forced conversions of the Donatists the decline of the once proud African church began. Finally, at the Mohammedan invasion, it was the only church of the Mediterranean area which disappeared completely. It seems that the former Donatists welcomed the Arabs as liberators, and, at any rate, the 'Catholic' heritage was not seriously defended by them.

He who wishes to become genuinely acquainted with Augustine's thought regarding the church, the world, and the state, must not stop at the anti-Donatist writings. The main work for these subjects is the ' *Twenty-four Books on the City of God*', *De Civitate Dei*, which is at the same time a kind of summary of the whole Augustinian theology itself. This is connected with the special intention of his *opus magnum*: it is the last great apology of the church against paganism, the final justification of her teaching and historical position at the end of time, and before the whole world. The whole material of traditional Christian polemic, collected through the centuries, is therefore expounded once more in a new and independent formulation. The repudiation of pagan religion and philosophy is combined with the positive exposition of the entire system of Christian doctrine and ethics. Yet this writing also originated in a specific cause; and this lends to it the particular manner, liveliness, and vivacity, in which the questions are posed. It took, however, twenty-two years to complete, proceeding from issue to issue according to a design drawn up at the beginning.

On August 28, 410, Alaric's troops had stormed and sacked Rome. This event had a shattering effect, far beyond its direct political importance. How had it come about that the capital of the ancient empire, the ruler of the world, the eternal city, had experienced such an overthrow? The world seemed to shake at its foundations, and the pagans knew the answer! In their eyes, the catastrophe was the recompense for abandoning the old guardian divinities and the traditional religion; the new Christian God of the empire had obviously proved impotent, and had failed. The Christians had no reply to this, for they had provoked precisely this criticism by their previous polemic. Since Constantine, and even during the later times of persecution, they had indefatigably propounded the view that the surrender of pagan superstition and the protection of true religion would renew and sustain the empire. Ambrose too had held to this, even though he temporarily developed other ideas under the stress of emergency (cf. p. 107). Theodosius had made the orthodox faith the foundation of his order for the empire on precisely these grounds. The embarrassment was now great. A serious moral set-back menaced the church. In this situation Augustine was urged from all sides to utter a word of aid, for he was regarded as the spokesman and theological adviser of all Latin Christianity.

The first hurriedly published books of his apology still reflect the acute danger of the religious and political situation. Augustine was concerned to show above all how ill-founded was the contention 'that human welfare must necessarily be promoted by adhering to the worship of the many gods venerated by the pagans' (*Retr.* II, 43). The old demons are simply unable to do this. It can be shown, at any rate, that they, whom people now seek to set in opposition to Christ, did not protect Rome in earlier years better than he is doing at present. For a direct refutation, more massive arguments are also not disdained by Augustine. So he points out in particular that only the asylum of the Christian sanctuaries had protected both pagans and Christians during the destruction of the city, and not the temples of the old gods. Nevertheless, it is clear from the very first that he does not really mean to base his main case on such obvious reasons, with which the pagans can be refuted at best by an external proof. Augustine has his eye also on the failure of his own fellow-believers, and takes up the whole problem on a deeper level. Why do so many who call themselves Christians face the new situation so helplessly, and think that their God should not have permitted all this? They have obviously no real understanding at all of their own faith, and therefore succumb to the deceptive logic of the pagans. In reality, one does not truly believe in God so long as one conceives of Him only as a means to provide the good things and happiness of this world, so that they may be enjoyed peacefully, and despairs of Him the moment external disaster occurs. One does not understand what life is so long as one expects its fulfilment in this age, and dares to demand this as a due claim upon God's government of the world. He only can participate in the meaning of life who is sincerely humble before

God, who accepts all that God sends, and who gladly and willingly continues on his pilgrimage because he believes in an all-perfecting eternity which will be just as much God's as are all the troubles of this present time.

The question is thus—in the context of an apology—that of the interpretation and foundation of the Christian faith itself, which has to distinguish itself from pagan idolatry not only by its object, but also by the manner of its devotion, and its inner relation to God and the world. But Augustine does not content himself with distinctions and postulates of principle. His theodicy is intended as pastoral guidance, and is to help the afflicted Christians. It plunges therefore into the whole perplexing misery which murder and rape, pillage and deportation have brought upon the individual, and the whole empire. And so he summons the whole art of his dialectics and rhetoric, in order not to evade any possible objection, and to give an answer to every question and doubt. He explains in detail that suffering is not mere suffering, but, depending on how one bears it, can be a curse or a blessing already in this life, in that it does indeed harden the ungodly, but it purifies and liberates the believer from his remaining inward burden. Furthermore, quite apart from all this, the seeming senselessness of this divine judgement, which befalls the wicked as well as the good, is rather in reality a religious necessity, to the end that God should be sought and found not for the sake of temporal welfare, but in truth, i.e. for His own sake. This statement also is divided further into regular cases and exceptions, and the exceptions also find an explanation, and have their apparently necessary place. Basically, all this is indeed not a matter of real 'proof', logical and conclusive. With relatively convincing proofs, Augustine appeals to the Christian conscience in the decision of faith to give up the empty scepticism, the instability, and the wretchedness of an unbelieving quarrel with God, and in the affirmation of God's will to find the way back to reality, truth, and the service of love. Toward the end of his work (*Civ. D.* XX, 2) he reverts once more to this whole range of questions. It is as if he wanted once again to secure the decisive thoughts against any possible misunderstanding and reduction, by pointing out with extreme pungency that faith, and nothing but faith, is the power which alone can pass all the tests of life. It is hidden from us why God now holds back something good from the virtuous, and now spares a criminal from suffering. We do not know why this too is not valid without exception, and why at times even its reversal appears to be the rule. It is given to us to know only this much, that in principle it depends not upon the disposition in this world of so-called luck and misfortune, but upon that which will one day eternally separate us one from the other, before God's tribunal. Then, at dooms-day, all enigmas will indeed be solved—even down to this last mystery why it is necessary that God's justice should still in the present life so often, and indeed always, remain hidden. That it nevertheless exists and determines all events—this much is even today certain to Christian faith and this is sufficient.

The favourite term Augustine uses to designate the basic Christian attitude is 'humility' (*humilitas*). The defence of Christianity against paganism is therefore the same thing as a correct exposition of the meaning of humility against the demonic pride and haughtiness of men, their *superbia*. That is what this book is about. 'I know, of course,' writes Augustine in his preface, 'what ingenuity and force of arguments are needed to convince proud men of the power of humility.' Humility is powerful not of itself, but by the grace of God which permits it to rise higher than all the trembling and vanishing heights of this world (*Civ. D.* I praef.; *FC*, 6, 19). Now it is the pride of the supposedly 'eternal' Rome, the pagan metropolis, which rises up against the peace of the 'City of God', which alone is in truth eternal. With reference to the old gods, and the departed Roman tradition, that same fundamental reversal of religion to make of it the servant of one's own greatness and glory, which already connoted the very nature of paganism in the individual life, is applied once again as on a gigantically enlarged scale. Augustine views paganism in its final state as a political religion. The old idols are not believed in any more. They serve the pagan Roman spirit only as the self-confirmation of its own haughty desire, of its own past and its own glory. Augustine is by no means unaware of the greatness of Roman attainments. They would have been admirable if they had originated in a truly devout attitude and not in the dark desires of ambition. As it is, however, they are to be viewed in connection with the fertile ground of evil will, from which they derive. They then have to be 'reckoned as vices, rather than virtues' (*Civ. D.* XIX, 25), 'as splendid vices', *splendida vitia*, according to the later formula. One observes this, Augustine thinks, in the nature of their historical effect. Virgil's famous epigram on the calling of the people to rule, '*parcere subiectis et debellare superbos*' (to spare the vanquished, and to put down the mighty) denotes a violation of the glory of God, who alone gives grace to the humble and has the right to punish nations. This mentality is the ultimate reason why there is never peace in this world. It is the origin of all the wars and conquests, which have made Rome the terror of her neighbours for centuries, and finally the all-devouring world empire.

Along these lines Augustine, taking his cue from Sallust and other classical authors, ventures to give a thorough and terrible rehearsal of the whole of Roman history, beginning with the fratricide of Romulus up to the last abominations of the Republic. It is a single-minded attack upon the sacrosanct tradition, never before attempted in this manner, wherein he tears off the mask from the face of Roman hypocrisy. He is not concerned with historical objectivity, but with a perception of principle, if one may say so, and likewise with a new political ethos, for which he would prefer to win nobody more than the descendant of the old Scipios and Fabricii. In the true faith, says Augustine, their traditional virtues also would shine with a new and purer splendour.

Hence Augustine is not concerned with the rejection of the political interest as such, or of all political activity; against this he expressly guarded himself. 'Pride' is not a necessary by-product of power itself, 'but of the soul that is inordinately enamoured of its own power . . .' (*Civ. D.* XII, 8; Oates, II,

186). 'And in action it is not honour, or power in this life, which should be prized, since all things under the sun are vanity, but the task itself that is accomplished through that same honour and power, if rightly and helpfully performed; that is, if it contributes to the welfare of those who are set below us. This is according to God's law' (*Civ. D.* XIX, 19; *LCL*, VII, 203). A vast disillusionment, a cool detachment from any political 'mythos', and from any express political passion is voiced in these words. The empire was sick, and offered little cause for political enthusiasm. One cannot reproach Augustine for not having considered himself called to be a political reformer, for which he would have been utterly unsuitable. Augustine restricts himself to the essential, and to what is valid at all times. The subordination of all passing and temporal purposes, to which politics must not be more than a means, to the eternal, spiritual, and transcendent purpose of existence with God has in him perhaps still an ascetic, philosophical, Neo-Platonic sound. Yet the over-all outlook nevertheless remains Christian and Biblical. In place of the timeless hierarchy of gradations of value, the prevailing idea is of historical movement toward a goal, namely toward the judgement, and God's eternal realm of peace. It is a definite community which carries this movement through time, the eternal church, the citizenship of the City of God. Indeed, in striving for worldly peace these have a common task which must be accomplished in co-operation with the citizens of this world. Nevertheless, they have no common goal. The attitude and direction of men's hearts, i.e. hope, and future, and not present existence, determine men's nature, and give it its meaning. History, which moves onwards, and historical volition, have become decisive. With Augustine a new, Christian evaluation of time began, which was not previously known in antiquity. He stands at the beginning of a Western 'philosophy of history'.

From the very beginning there are two human 'states' or 'cities', two human communities in the world which are stamped by their attitude. 'Two cities (*civitates*) have been formed by two loves: the earthly by the love of self, even to the contempt of God; the heavenly by the love of God, even to the contempt of self. The former, in a word, glories in itself, the latter in the Lord' (*Civ. D.* XIV, 28; Oates, II, 274). Pride and humility, 'faith and disbelief', in their coexistence and opposition constitute, as Goethe says, 'the real, sole, and deepest theme of the history of the world and man'. Both attitudes are as old as the history of the world. They found their origin in Adam's fall, and ever since that time the development of 'citizenship under God' or 'Jerusalem' runs down through the line of Abel and the Old Testament '*Heilsgeschichte*' (the history of the saving acts of God) until Christ, and from Him again through the church, to conclude only at the end of time in the eternal 'City of God', 'where victory is truth, where dignity is holiness, where peace is happiness, where life is eternity' (*Civ. D.* II, 29; *LCL*, I, 263). Contrary to it, though interwoven with it in many ways, there also takes its rise the state or citizenship of the 'City of Earth', the selfish and proud who once in Babylon, and now in Rome, gather around their great, demonic symbol. By injustice and violence they strive for their own glory, and for the earthly dominion and temporal peace which they can neither maintain nor keep. They end in eternal damnation. Despite all the conflict, God nevertheless remains the real and only Lord of this double historical process, which he guides according to his inscrutable counsel as he wills. One day the end will come, in fact, when the number of predestined citizens of God is reached, a number determined in order to substitute exactly for the number of originally fallen angels. Yet the date of this end is known to none, and Augustine expressly refuses to ascertain and calculate it in advance on the basis either of Biblical texts or of the philosophy of history. What matters to him is the inner analysis of the meaning of history, for from this is derived decision in favour of God's community and its true, everlasting goal.

This view of the framework of '*Heilsgeschichte*' was not created by Augustine himself. With many mythological details he simply followed in this the Biblical, primitive Christian, apocalyptic view of history, which stretches from the creation and original fall until the end of the world, and the irruption of the kingdom of God, and which takes its centre and meaning from the Christ who calls 'all peoples' to conversion and renewal. Augustine was fully aware of the contrast to all ancient views of history, 'cyclical', aimless, and in his opinion totally comfortless. The classification, also, of the two states, cities, citizenship—the Latin denotes all this with one and the same word (*civitas*)—had already been developed prior to him by the Donatist Ticonius, from whom he adopted it. But only with Augustine did it attain to real historical vitality, because he not only relates the two *civitates*—according to his apologetical intention—to Rome, and to the (Old and New Testament) church, but from this point on attempts to trace them throughout the whole course of world history. On the basis of the Bible and the ancient historians, Augustine gives a detailed description of both 'cities', of their origin, development, and progress through earthly time, in order to conclude with the expectation of the resurrection, and the completion of time in eternity. This procedure alone makes the theologian into a historian and, we might say, into the first 'philosopher of history'. We must, however, beware of false modernizations when using this expression. It goes without saying that Augustine was no independent, and certainly no 'critical' historian. Moreover the criteria and interpretations he uses are not 'historical' in the modern sense. The development of the two 'cities' has nothing whatever to do with the modern, immanentist conception of evolution. God determines history, and what results from it is precisely the incomprehensibility of the concrete event as it is given at any moment, which we have to accept but which we cannot possibly explain. The faith which understands the goal of history renounces any prophecy immanent to the world. Therefore, Augustine intentionally leaves open any decision about the future of the Roman empire. He certainly repudiates the panic which the conquest of Rome immediately threatened to unchain. He demands that everyone fulfil his duty at his post. He hopes that everything may turn out well once again. Yet no greatness of this world is 'eternal', and it is for God to decree when Rome will perish. Even in retrospect, Augustine sees no essential connection between the decisions ordained by God in accordance with his secret counsel and the causal-genetic deductions and connections sought by the secular historian. The historical judgements which Augustine makes on events, persons, and the supposed necessities of former times, are mostly furnished by the Bible and given an exclusively theological evaluation.

Nevertheless, world history for Augustine is not constituted by sheer accidental facts and details. The tension between the two warring communities constantly gives a deeper meaning to the apparently isolated fact, and this religious meaning can be grasped and clearly described with the aid of the Bible. This is the particular and surprising achievement Augustine accomplishes with the aid of his symbolism. But this too is at first a general phenomenon. The whole of antiquity, especially in its last phases, gave reality an interpretation that is not exclusively causal in the modern sense of the word. It discovered everywhere in nature the 'spiritual' laws of analogy, harmony, and sympathy, which also determine human life. In a similar way it understood the words of the poets 'allegorically', as reflections and manifestations of general moral and philosophical truths. This alchemy of thought acquired in the Christian church a special significance from the beginning, because it was now applied to actual history. Christ had to be proved to be the fulfilment of the Old Covenant. For this purpose not only was reference made to individual prophecies which fitted Him, but there was a growing attempt to interpret the whole ancient '*Heilsgeschichte*', with its real persons and events, in relationship to Him, and to understand them as exemplary 'types' of coming history. So, for instance, David is a type of Christ the king, or Isaac's sacrifice represents His death upon the cross. This old Biblical principle of exegesis is now extended by Augustine to

17

world history as such. The antagonism of the two *civitates*, which in Adam were still comprised by a single human being, for the first time emerges 'typically' in the two brothers Cain and Abel. It continues in Israel's struggle with the Gentiles, assumes a visible form in the cities of Babylon and Jerusalem, and finds its last, demonic expression in the pagan Roman empire persecuting the church. On both sides it is primarily a matter not of simple identification with the single-mingled community of the ungodly, or of the righteous,—they are, indeed, intermingled and outwardly inseparable—but of a symbolical representation which nevertheless designates what the powers are in their historical reality. Just as in Augustine's symbolical teaching on the sacraments, so also here the object and the symbol cannot be separated. For that reason, the typological connections and structures which he creates with the aid of historical illustrations and 'signs' do not produce, like many medieval constructions of history, the impression of a game, but possess a power to elucidate real history. At all events, a great deal of the peculiar aesthetic charm which Augustine's conception of history still displays, with all its strange restriction to the categories of Biblical theology, is derived from the mysterious fascination of the historical parallels and correspondences pointing forward or backward, and from the magical reflection and iridescence of images and ideas which nevertheless retain their depth and meaning.

The *City of God* was the favourite book of the entire Middle Ages, being a work then read far more than the *Confessions*. But change of time brought also a change of understanding. Against the background of the controversies of state and church in the high Middle Ages the basic ideas of the book were instinctively given a political or clerical colouring. One discerned in them a devilish devaluation of the secular and a sanctification of the ecclesiastical, which meant by then papal, power. Such ecclesiastico-political interpretations were, of course, far from the thought of the historical Augustine—almost as far as the anti-hierarchical and spiritualizing reinterpretation of his thoughts which is also to be met in the late Middle Ages. He supported the misunderstanding only in so far as his work shows the demonic forces of the 'City of Satan' manifest precisely in its political ambition, in the greed of states for power and glory, whereas a corresponding demonic perversion of ecclesiastical ambition has not yet come under consideration. Therefore the 'City of God' readily assumed in the eyes of posterity a Gregorian tendency. When speaking of political and ecclesiastical problems, the real Augustine is not yet thinking institutionally in medieval terms. In particular he does not recognize the idea of a 'Christian state', but only recognizes individual Christians, rulers as well as subjects, who then as persons in the state can serve justice and earthly peace, while at heart they remain humble citizens of the heavenly city.

On the other hand, in Augustine the church certainly appears as the city and citizenship of God which lasts through all time, although by no means everyone who is outwardly counted as in it belongs to it in reality. Yet in such connections Augustine is not thinking of the visible ecclesiastical organization. In the twenty-two books of the *City of God* it is scarcely mentioned. Only in the anti-Donatist writings is it of great importance, as is but natural. Otherwise it regularly recedes into the background so soon as the real religious meaning, the spiritual significance, and the true life of the church come under discussion. The church is Christendom, the community of believers in Christ in all the world, and in each single Catholic congregation, united in love by virtue of the power of the Holy Spirit. This does not mean, of course, that Augustine was indifferent to the external form of his church; rather is it a matter of course to him. Like all theologians of the early church Augustine was an episcopalian. He believed in the episcopal organization of the church, which had its source in Christ and the apostles. All bishops are equal in principle; they teach and administer their own congregations, and every Christian is obliged to render them obedience. Only if they 'err', or oppose the Holy Scripture itself, 'must we not agree with even the Catholic bishops'

(*Unit. Eccl.* 11, 28). This statement too is for Augustine a matter of course; he has not thought out the implications it might have if taken seriously. To him all canonical questions as such are basically uninteresting. The church lives through Christ, her Head, and all Christians are her members. The clergy are servants and, in the strict sense, priests, called to administer word and sacrament to the faithful, without their character as human beings having any decisive effect on their ministration. The whole congregation is the body of Christ, and experiences this particularly in the communal reception of His body and blood. 'If you yourself are Christ's body and His members, your mysterious nature appears on the Lord's table: you receive your own mystery.' The Holy Spirit makes the whole congregation into one bread. So 'then, be that which you see, and receive that which you are' (*Serm.* 272). Augustine is certainly very far from glorifying the church as a spiritual institution in its own right. She lives only so far as she continuously receives all things from her Head, by whom she is reconciled and united with God. The sinner is justified when believing in Christ, and receives also simultaneously with justification the Holy Spirit's renewing power of love. This event cannot be isolated. It happens only within the living fellowship of the Christian church, nevertheless the church does not save us, but Christ Himself through the church. We are 'nothing without Him, but in Him we are Christ Himself and ourselves' (*Psalm. Enarr.* xxx, 2, 3). The Head 'redeems His body', and the body then partakes in all blessings which the Head has won. Christ and His people cannot be separated; only as united with His body is He Himself the 'whole Christ'.

This work on the *City of God*, which was supposed to destroy the last bulwarks of paganism, ran parallel right from the beginning with a new controversy internal to the church, the repercussions of which can repeatedly be traced in the book itself. This is the so-called 'Pelagian controversy'. This quarrel occupied Augustine's thoughts more than all previous disputes, and he never came free from it until his death. He had taken it up

on his own account, but during its course he recruited comrades everywhere, and then put them into action. In order to
win the battle, he even became extremely active in the field of
church politics, contrary to his usual way. Year by year his
voluminous treatises were published, works which in attack and
defence increasingly reached deeper levels of the problem, and
envisaged ever more difficult and radical solutions—until finally
death took his pen away from an unfinished work, the *opus
imperfectum* against Julian. The controversy with the Pelagians
was Augustine's real struggle for the doctrine of the church.
The issue here was one of high theological hair-splitting problems, and of new answers which only became really pressing
by this controversy. It was not an issue of traditional controversial views regarding old differences and ecclesiastical positions, as in the battle against the Manicheans or Donatists. With
his teaching on the omnipotence and complete freedom of
divine grace, of which the hereditary bondage of human will is
the counterpart, Augustine sums up the whole of his theological
endeavours and of the development of his life. He has to admit
that at the beginning he was himself unable to formulate the
truth in its full meaning and with complete consistency, and
that his earlier writings, with which his adversaries now confronted him, left many things unclear and were more or less in
need of correction. In spite of this, the basic theme of God's
omnipotence and the sovereignty of his grace was firmly established from the outset. Already in his life confessions Augustine
had testified to it unmistakably, and now he realized it as his
sole task to establish the church's doctrine definitively in this
sense. This led finally to the affirmation of complete divine predestination, that is to say, the foreknowledge of God, which as
such must be at the same time a pre-determination and a pre-
decision. On this the whole of Christianity depends. Only from
this principle does it become incontestably certain that God
alone is, and must ever remain, the goal as well as the only
hopeful way for mankind, which is lost without Him, and
that any strength and endeavour which tries to operate

independently is necessarily perverted and directed against God. In consequence our own faith which effects salvation is also to be understood correctly only as God's gift and work. 'For in him and by him and to him are all things' (Rom. xi. 36). In the adoption of this Pauline confession, Augustine's philosophical theology and his conception of the Holy Scriptures converge. Apart from this belief there is for him no truth, and no true and real Christianity.

In the details also, Augustine developed his teaching on the basis of the Holy Scripture, and at the same time according to the logic of Platonic religious philosophy. This makes him theologically invincible; but at the same time pushes him far beyond the immediate data of the Bible, and also beyond Paul, and ties him down to positions difficult to defend. His opponents drove him further; in his own thinking he was not yet far enough ahead of them, and this explains many a weakness and rigour of the position he finally came to. Augustine did not wish to be an innovator; yet on the whole he had in fact no precursor in the claims for which he contended. Also he would hardly have found companions and successors had he not been, when the Pelagian controversy broke out, for a long time the spiritual master of the African church, the bishops of which stood behind him like one man. Despite his victory, Augustine, however, could not prevail in the long run without concessions, and just at this point his heritage has again and again caused difficulties and provoked new discussions. This is not only because this conflict really concerns an eternal opposition of factors, and faith and disbelief, pride and humility can in the Christian world also never come to a settlement. Nor is it due only to differences in practice, the complacency and readiness for compromise frequently blamed in the Catholic state-church, which he wanted to serve, and did serve. It is primarily a matter of the formal, logical insolubility of the problems, a systematic solution of which Augustine nevertheless tried to force by the methods of his time and school of thought. To this extent he was craving for something impossible of accomplishment, and the victories

he obtained remain in their theological results Pyrrhic victories
of logic, which never could end the war in which he was engaged. Nevertheless, the anti-Pelagian dogma marks a theological boundary which was reached once for all, behind which
Latin Christianity, taking everything into account, could never
fall back to the level of pre-Augustinian moralism and rationalism. It was now firmly established that in the realm of religion
everything primarily depends always on God and not upon
man. The conception of grace was from now on the central
idea of Latin theology. Western Christianity saw itself henceforward basically as a religion of grace. While Augustine continued to build upon older foundations in his teaching on the
church, the sacraments and God, he created something new
here, and he marks a new epoch in the history of theology and
of ideas.

Pelagius was an eminently moral and 'sanctified' personality.
At the start of the controversy Augustine himself repeatedly
attested this, and did not retract it even later, when the ambiguity and apparent deviousness of his opponent exasperated
him. British by birth, no priest but a zealous ascetic, Pelagius
found his intellectual field of action, like Rufinus, in Rome.
Here he carried on propaganda for his monastic ideals, won
disciples, and successfully preached against the laxity and immorality of Christian society. He also came forward as a theological writer, more independent and systematic than Rufinus,
and tried to effect a combination of the older Western tradition
and the ideas of the Greek, Origenist theology. There was,
indeed, in Rome at the time the beginning of the renaissance of
Origen's thought. A man quite orthodox, Pelagius argued
against the Arians, yet his most determined opposition was
directed against the Manicheans. Their dualistic fatalism infuri-
ated the moralist. The problem was how to enforce against
them the power and importance of the will, and to work out
the free responsibility of man for his own actions. For this
reason, Pelagius studied Augustine's anti-Manichean writings,
and particularly his important work *On Free Will*, which had

made the first attempt to unite the appeal to human freedom, inevitable in this connection, with the idea of grace. Pelagius too was far from regarding God's grace as of secondary importance or as unnecessary. As a skilled expositor of Paul he even stressed the doctrine that redemption comes about by faith *alone*, and by grace *alone*. But he considered this in relation to the liberation of man effected by baptism and forgiveness, and the freedom and self-determination of the will recovered 'by grace', in contrast to the bad 'habits' of pre-Christian humanity. While Augustine went further, and saw this liberated will itself as operative and determined by God's grace, Pelagius did not go beyond emphasizing the significance of man's free contribution as decisive for salvation. The systematic manner in which his practical activism was developed, and sought to combat the alleged perversity of any other doctrine of sin in the name of the liberated human nature, created good, was dangerous.

His criticism was originally directed not against Augustine, but against the understanding of Paul given by '*Ambrosiaster*', a writer unknown by his real name, whose commentaries then circulated under the name of 'Hilary'. It would be, he held, absurd to deduce from Rom. v. 12 a doctrine of the original sinful nature of all the descendants of Adam. The nature created good by God must remain unchangeable, and the assumption of a corporeal transference of guilt from generation to generation by procreation would, moreover, be Manichean and in contradiction to God's justice. Pelagius also spoke against Augustine's *Confessions*, which in Rome had become a fashionable book in the society of the 'religiously interested'. When objection was made to him from Augustine's prayer: 'Give what thou commandest—and command what thou wilt' (*Conf.* X, 31, 45), he passionately opposed such quietism. It was always his concern to show the lazy what human nature should and in fact could accomplish. The reference to God who 'creates from persons who do not will those who do' (*Op. Imperf.* III, 122) 'by helping him whom He commands, so that he can also do the good' (*Grat. et Lib. Arb.* 31), accordingly appeared as a complacent excuse.

Fleeing from the Visigoths in 410/411, Pelagius sought refuge in Africa. Probably intentionally, he avoided an encounter with Augustine. He feared a superior adversary, and, like so many moralists, was perhaps of the opinion that dogmatic controversies are in any case unproductive, and merely cause discord. From Africa he travelled on to Jerusalem, and soon gained a reputation and good friends in the East, where nobody took offence at his teaching. Meanwhile in Africa his pupil Caelestius, who was less cautious and also theologically more superficial, had one-sidedly and pointedly drawn out the consequences of the Pelagian teaching on freedom and when he applied in Carthage for the office of priest in 411, he was therefore solemnly rejected as a heretic, and excommunicated. The prime factor in most people's mind was that Caelestius did not accept the 'remission of sins' in infant baptism, and anti-Donatist Africa was, of course, particularly sensitive about any innovations in baptismal teaching. Yet for Augustine this condemnation bore a wider significance. Whoever asserted the 'innocence' of new-born babies, i.e. declared the natural, unredeemed man to be sound and free to do all good, was in his opinion denying the basic relationship in which all men stand 'since Adam', and rendered salvation by Christ superfluous. This meant opposing the idea of 'grace by which the ungodly is made righteous, and by which we are Christians at all' (*Retr.* II, 52). Augustine now sent his own disciple Orosius to the East with a letter of introduction to Jerome, in order to obtain a condemnation of Pelagius there. But these efforts failed completely. Pelagius tried to elude them, and maintained particularly that the teachings under discussion did not represent 'dogmas'. By reason of their whole way of thinking and tradition the Greeks were unable to see in the questions of anthropology and the doctrine of grace under consideration anything more than an obstinate quarrel about trivialities and commonplaces. They acquitted Pelagius. In Africa this decision produced indignation. With the active participation of Augustine, new synodal decrees were here issued, and in addition to this they constrained Pope Innocent I expressly to condemn the new heretics. When his successor, the Greek Zosimus, tried to revoke the decision, they renounced obedience to him, instigated the imperial government against the Pelagians, and finally coerced even the pope to endorse the condemnation and make it generally known (418).

Only when the cause of the Pelagians in church politics was lost did their most important spokesman, Julian, Bishop of Eclanum in Apulia, step into the foreground. Augustine considered that without him the Pelagian scaffolding would forever have remained without a master-builder. Julian was the only opponent Augustine encountered during his lifetime who was more or less his equal, and at times one has the impression that Augustine looked upon this indefatigable nuisance with a secret and reluctant sympathy. 'A self-assured young man' of good family, like Augustine a brilliant dialectician and stylist, yet more elegant, carelessly unconcerned and reckless in his polemic, Julian remained fundamentally a man of the world, fully content with himself and with the type of Christianity he had constructed, a rational and life-affirming Christianity. As the manifest enemy of grace, Pelagius was hardly understood by Augustine, and was in any case depicted one-sidedly. The picture of Julian, however, is clear and quite unmistakable. He was more than just a theological opponent of Augustine. In him a declining life-spirit tried for the last time to voice a cause for which there was no longer to be any place in the Augustinian-medieval church. As a theologian Julian spoke for the convictions of classical enlightenment. He was a popular philosopher in a Christian costume, the last defender of that Stoic 'dignity of man' which believed in God, yet did not fundamentally need his help, and which relied simply on one's own nature, even though this 'nature' is called 'creation'. The difficulties which Augustine came across in his self-examination never really worried Julian, because he did not know them. Thus the whole theological exposition of the terms grace, original sin, and the

alleged perversion of man's being, itself appeared to him perverse, or at least utterly superfluous. Such things refute themselves by their own absurdity. Why should Adam's descendants
have to suffer to all eternity for Adam's not too tragic guilt?
How can sin in any way 'be hereditary' through procreation?
And what kind of reason is it which for the future punishes the
sinner with inevitable sinfulness? In what sense is it just to punish a sinner, if freedom for doing good has actually been lost?
Like every 'enlightened' thinker, it was easy for Julian to proceed 'logically', and to disclose the obvious discrepancies and
contradictions of his adversary. He did this with moral passion
and with pleasure! The consistency of his system had but one
defect, that it did not correspond with reality. But this was in
Julian's opinion exactly the matter in question: whether Augustine had indeed arrived at the reality of man, or whether his
whole teaching on sin and grace was based instead on one vast
'complex'. From his own presuppositions he simply could not
understand how Augustine's conception of the totality of life
recognizes the forlorn state of fallen mankind in the famous
incident of stealing pears, a 'harmless' boyish prank reported in
the *Confessions*, or indeed even in the helpless whimpering of
the baby.

On one essential point Julian separated himself even from his
own friends. Pelagius had naturally seen something wicked and
dangerous in sensual and sexual desire. After all, he was a monk!
Yet how can this be allowed if, on the other hand, the 'nature'
of man is declared to be unchangeably good? Sexual lust, *concupiscentia*, does belong to human nature: without it the generation and continuance of mankind would not even be conceivable. Julian had been married, and refused to surround the sphere
of the sexual with the tabu of the half-prohibited, the tempting,
the blasphemous. The sensual urge as such is not evil; of course
it has to be controlled, and must be rationally mastered, but in
itself it is simply natural and therefore also good. He who teaches
the reverse must be still in principle a Manichean, who denies
the goodness of creation, consigns the corporeal to the devil,

and so, of course, cannot take seriously the 'freedom' of man. There is no middle way here. One is either a Christian in Julian's sense, or a Manichean heretic. This accusation, advanced ever and anew, was for Augustine especially embarrassing, for it was not simply fabricated. There really was an obvious spiritual connection between Augustine's theology of grace and his former Manicheism. The arguments Julian introduced against him had earlier been used by himself against the Manicheans! Therein lay the extraordinary difficulty of his position, which constantly drove him to new and subtle distinctions. For Augustine also had no intention of giving up creation and freedom. Freedom was to him an ineradicable element of undefiled human 'nature'. By the Fall, however, the state of human nature had changed in such a way that now, in spite of its 'freedom', it is no longer able to liberate itself from its bondage to sin. Augustine realized that, regarding his terminology, he was in somewhat of an impasse with this conception of a bound freedom. The problem was to define grace in such a way that freedom was not abandoned, and, on the other hand, to define the freedom of the will in such a way that the all-embracing effect of grace was nevertheless neither reduced nor limited.

Seen as a whole, his teaching on *concupiscentia* caused Augustine the least trouble, despite difficulties in detail. Here he remained the ascetic he had always been. That sensual concupiscence had something to do with sin was for him beyond question. He spoke here out of experience, and had only to repeat the reminiscence of his own conversion-story. The involuntariness and uncontrollability of the sexual drive, and the shame connected with it, prove at least this much: that since the Fall the constitution and the psychological order of man are disturbed. Augustine developed the grotesque idea that in paradise Adam would have possessed, if he had not fallen, the faculty to procreate children without tumultuous desire by moving his organs in complete freedom and at will, like arms and legs. Yet this does not mean that the present predominance of sensual impulse has to be given a 'Manichean' explanation, by

assuming an evil substance. Evil as such is for Augustine still a
negative quantity, even though this nothingness expresses itself
as a manifest power in perversion and confusion of nature and
the will. On the other hand, it remains really difficult for him
to explain how the transmission of original sin to all children of
Adam could be conceived of. To be sure, they were all 'in'
Adam when he ate the forbidden fruit, and in so far they participated in his sin. Yet the real abode of sin is the human spirit,
by which Adam in disobedience and pride set God's government at naught. Augustine does not venture to maintain a
generation of the soul analogous to physical generation, which
Julian would have liked to chalk up as a new heresy. It is just
because his teaching on original sin does not exhaust itself in
the sensual connotation that it is so difficult for Augustine to
define its nature. Sin was doubtless existent from the beginning.
It adhered to man 'by contagion and not by decision' (*Op.
Imperf.* IV, 98). Nevertheless it does not derive only from his
sensual nature, but dwells precisely in the spiritual, willing ego,
and determines him completely.

The decisive thing to be recognized, which mattered everything to Augustine, is that we are helpless when entirely dependent upon ourselves, and that God's grace must do no less
than everything in order to save us. This does not mean that
man does not possess any freedom of will at all, but only that
this will is of itself always inclined to sin, and is never in a
position to change its inclination. God's grace, therefore, cannot
be moved by our good volition, but exactly the reverse: 'The
human will does not achieve grace through freedom, but rather
freedom through grace' (*Corr. et Grat.* 8, 17). When the human
will redeemed by Christ finds its way back to faith, to hope, and
to love, then it is truly set free. Here emerges a new and deeper
concept of freedom. For Augustine freedom is no longer defined
as the capability of arbitrary choice, but as the condition of
determination by the good, and by God. Because He alone can
be good, God is not therefore Himself unfree, but rather, on
the contrary, free in an absolute sense. 'Our freedom consists

in that we are subject to the truth' (*Lib. Arb.* II, 13, 37); the 'being a servant' of righteousness 'itself is the true freedom' (*Enchir.* 30). 'Thus only are we truly free, when God takes us in His fashioning hands, i.e. when He forms and creates us—not as men (for this He has already done), but to the end that we may become good men, and that is what His grace now does' (*Enchir.* 31). Consequently, there is something like an 'effected' freedom. The perfect freedom and humanity of man is just what is effected by God and yet remains freedom which man affirms, co-operates with and adopts in his own volition. 'Hence we will; but God works in us that we will. Thus we act, but God also works the action in us' (*Don. Pers.* 13, 33). The problem of co-ordinating grace and freedom—a novel problem not understood by Julian and also never considered by the entire Greek theology—is solved by Augustine in such a way that he no longer adjusts freedom and grace one to the other, but views them as a unity wherein grace is always the dominating element, and human will the subordinate element controlled by God. This by no means excludes, in fact it includes the notion that the liberated human will itself now actually do the good work, and to this extent also can earn 'merits'. It does not, however, have itself to thank for these merits. They are from God's grace living in the man, totally excluding all pride and 'glorying in one's works', and thereby making him entirely humble. 'When God crowns our merits', Augustine explains time and again, 'He crowns only His own gifts' (*Conf.* IX, 34), for grace alone creates merit, and before grace there is no human merit: 'What hast thou that thou didst not receive?' (I Cor. iv. 7).

But if this be so, how does it come about that this freedom of the redeemed does not fall to the lot of everyone, that so many are lost, and even that Christians who really have believed and lived in Christ's love can subsequently fall away and perish? To this there is only one answer: it is a matter for God alone, who certainly never in any circumstances wills what is evil, but can at His free discretion grant, refuse, or retract the divine grace without which none is able to do that which is

good. This is the ultimate proof that His grace really is nothing
other than grace, and that salvation 'is not of him that willeth,
nor of him that runneth, but of God that showeth mercy'
(Rom. ix. 16). 'For, just as the eye of the body, even when
completely sound, is unable to see unless aided by the brightness
of light, so also man, even when most fully justified, is unable
to lead a holy life, if he be not divinely assisted by eternal light
of righteousness' (*Nat. et Grat.* 26, 29; Oates, 1,540). In Augustine's usage predestination is the final testimony to God's glory,
and to the unconditioned sovereignty of His grace. Yet why has
God damned those not elected? 'Why except that He willed it?
As to why He willed it, "Who art thou, O man, that repliest
against God?" ' (*Ep.* 186, 23; *FC*, 12, 207). We must humbly
rest content with this answer already given by Paul (Rom. ix.
20)—and we must know at the same time that God remains
good and just in all things, even when we do not understand
him.

Augustine, however, would not acquiesce entirely in this last
ignoramus to which he confesses. Particularly in defending himself, time and again he tried to reach beyond it, and in some
way to make visible or show to be reasonable the incomprehensibility of God's decree. The question of God's righteousness
and of man's guilt is to find an answer at least to this extent,
that, not the predestination of the elect—for this is grace and
nothing else—but the rejection of the reprobate can still be
counted as 'merited'. For this purpose Augustine once again
refers to 'Adam' 'in whom' all have sinned in advance. For
Adam still really was 'free' for good or evil; only 'a penal cor-
ruption closely followed thereon, and out of (original) liberty
produced necessity (of evil)' (*Perf. Iust.* 4, 9; *LPNF*, 5, 161).
And because he voluntarily decided for disobedience and revolt,
he and his posterity were therefore justly damned by God.
Indeed, God is inexplicable in his mercy but not unjust in his
condemnation. For modern feeling it is, of course, extremely
unsatisfying to see how Augustine tries to solve the difficulties
of his theological interpretation of existence by throwing the

blame on 'Adam'. The vain fantasy of a 'freedom of choice', which with respect to present man he had rightly denied to Julian, now appears again for man in his original state. In order to remove moral and logical objections the myth which interprets Adam symbolically is rationalized in a way which must cause even greater offence. If we wish to follow the train of Augustine's thinking, it appears in fact more consistent to let Adam's fall also be determined by God's decision, and thus—as the theological formulation has it—to teach a 'supralapsarian' predestination. But is such a terrible consequence still tolerable to the religious mind? As we can see, Augustine, at any rate, could not or would not find it so.

There is no denying that on the whole predestination plays an essentially different role in Augustine's thought from that which it plays in the Biblical texts to which he refers. To be sure, with him also it ministers to God's glory as we have seen, yet the comforting and uplifting character it displays with Paul is here largely lost. Only with Augustine did the idea of predestination attain the gloomy inevitability which made it 'the horror of Christian thought in all ages' (Heinrich Barth). How does this come about? The answer leads us to the ultimate weakness of the Augustinian theology, a weakness which merely culminates in the doctrine of grace. In primitive Christianity likewise the salvation of man depended on God's election alone, and to this the impenitence and condemnation of the ungodly necessarily corresponded. Yet this election never took place in this connection in an abstract incomprehensibility, but always through Jesus Christ as God's incarnate Word. In the encounter with Christ human doubt has no room for play: there is opened an assured way in which faith may and must tread. 'He is righteousness to every one that believeth' (Rom. x. 4)—he is allowed to regard himself as of the elect, and from this view the theological speculations lose their relevance and justification. Now, of course, Augustine also wants to maintain the central position of the Saviour, and testifies to it with emphasis: 'This way has never been lacking to the human race ... no one has ever been liberated, nor is being liberated, nor ever will be liberated, except by this way' (*Civ. D.* x, 32, 2; *FC*, 7, 184). But this Christ and His grace are in Augustine nevertheless not exclusively united to the proclaimed word. Christ as God's eternal truth attains to a much more general and almost timeless significance, and his actions become limitless. The theology of grace therefore largely follows its own theological and philosophical logic. It turns into an independent principle of thought which can no longer be clearly applied in the range of the particular and the individual. The question of a personal assurance of salvation remains explicitly unanswered in Augustine's theology.

From this standpoint it is no doubt theoretically possible to play off the idea of predestination against the concrete community and medium of salvation, i.e. against the church. If God's grace follows its own incomprehensible laws, then the church cannot possibly consist purely of the elect. In these circumstances, who can know whether he really belongs to their number? Augustine observed with sorrow the effect of his own teaching on grace: it threatened to entice men into false security, and this is exactly what it was intended not to do. Yet earnestly as he entertained such thoughts, in order to quench all spiritual pride, Augustine never turned them against the concept of the church as such, or against the certainty of ecclesiastical salvation itself. He wants her means of grace and her fellowship to be taken seriously and received in confident joy. To draw the opposite conclusion, along idealistic or sceptical lines, would no longer be Augustinian. The sole object of Augustine's teaching on grace is to rebuke the pride of man who is imprisoned by himself and who deceives himself. A piety developed by the sinner for himself, and thus not received in humility from God, is in his eyes pagan and demonic however Christian its appearance. For it rejects Christ and the Holy Spirit precisely at that point where one needs them the most: in one's own inner self, in the overcoming of egotism and the delusion of our ungodly self. The redeemed and therefore truly

18

human man finds his centre and his 'freedom' no longer in himself, but as it were outside himself. The fountain of his life lies in God. His self-consciousness and self-confidence are replaced by confidence in God, who arouses faith, hope, and love. The 'idea of man' current in antiquity is thereby struck at the root, and religion likewise changes its meaning and idea. It no longer means the perfection of man, who inaugurates a relation with the higher powers for the sole purpose of securing or perfecting his own existence. It means rather that God, the Lord of the whole of reality, has become completely Lord of man also, and in a new sense. God is really present for man only when he permeates also the innermost man, i.e. his will, and when he becomes man's all in humble love.

The older Augustine grew, the more passionately and completely he devoted his life to his church and his congregation. This was the home of the revealed love of Christ and of mutual assistance. Here the Holy Spirit operated, and the truth of God was preached and lived for the whole world. Here he felt himself to be in the outer courts of his God. Augustine was concerned that the holiness and miraculous power of Christianity should remain no abstract thought but become visible, attractive and convincing in appearance. He welcomed the circumstance that now, when martyrdoms were an event of the past, monasticism supplied new saints. The emerging cult of saints and relics was ardently promoted by him. His teaching on grace offered the necessary theological justification for this. If it be God who works all grace and all miracles in His believers, then all the veneration one renders to them leads likewise back to God, and does not impair but rather augments his honour. Even more characteristic is Augustine's interest in concrete miracles, such as happen particularly at the tombs of the martyrs. It could be seen from them that the proofs of the Spirit, and of the power which once distinguished primitive Christianity had not been withdrawn from the contemporary church, and the Holy Spirit was still at work in it. Nothing more is to be seen of the cool reserve with which the young Christian philosopher once observed these phenomena. At that time Augustine had thought that 'since the Catholic church had been established and diffused throughout the whole world' miracles had become superfluous; God had stopped them 'lest the mind should always seek visible things, and the human race should grow cold by becoming accustomed to things which when they were novelties kindled its faith' (*Vera Rel.* 25, 47; *LCC*, 6, 248). Now he could report an abundance of miracles which were supposed to have happened in his lifetime alone, and in his own town, especially in the chapel with Stephen's relics. He concerned himself to list them authentically, he had these records read in the services, and he could not understand that such unheard of things were received so calmly by the congregation, and were so quickly forgotten. Augustine was of a surprising and almost sentimental naïvety and credulity. This great speculative thinker showed hardly a trace of criticism with regard to all historical questions. In this respect he put no impediment in the way of the Middle Ages, with their fondness for miracles.

If one reads the biography devoted by Possidius to Augustine, his revered teacher and example, the latter appears as the model of the faithful bishop and pastor, the man who paved the way for the monastic movement in Africa and contended as the faithful defender of the Catholic truth against heretics to right and left. Yet in the whole book there is no mention of a single theological question as such. It is instructive that Augustine could be seen and described like this at close quarters; but this picture of the man offers too little—not only in our opinion, but also in the opinion of Augustine himself. Augustine knew what he was. He did not wish to be merely a pious custodian of the orthodox tradition, but felt himself to be through and through a doctor of the church, pointing the way it must go. This was the highest responsibility he had to bear and meet. The remarkable monument of this intention is his *Retractationes*, i.e. 'revisions' of his earlier writings, which he had planned for a long time and began to dictate three years before his death, yet finishing only the revision of the 'books' properly so called, not that of the letters and sermons. Augustine was aware of the fact that his writings were read and heeded all over the world. Yet how much there was that could be compiled from them, which, though not exactly false, was nevertheless somewhat distorted and in need of correction. Even now as an old man, Augustine did not consider himself infallible. But he knew he 'wrote by advancing in knowledge, and advanced by writing' (*Ep.* 143, 2). He was concerned with stating publicly that 'even I myself have not in all things followed myself' (*Don. Persev.* 21, 55) and since he could not now withdraw the books in circulation, nothing else was left for him but to publish his 'corrections' in a new book. According to this, what he had written could be 'read with benefit. Some things have to be pardoned, or, if people will not pardon them, they should at least not adhere obstinately to what is wrong in them' (*Retr.* prol. 3).

These acts of self-accusation and—on the whole rarely—of self-defence are, of course, an interesting source for studying the 'progress' of Augustine's principles and convictions. Some corrections concern only external and small oversights, particularly in quotations which could be rectified without much ado. The retraction goes deeper in relation to a number of statements, especially in the books of his youth, in which Augustine had given too full scope to his rhetoric, and had used bombast and pagan flourishes which had been better avoided. His judgement upon pagan mythology, literature, and education has hardened. Augustine strives for a religious purism which previously was alien to him. Most instructive is his self-criticism in actual dogmatic questions. It touches especially his teaching on creation, and his eschatology. The Neo-Platonic contempt of the corporeal, earthly, and visible contradicts, as Augustine now realizes clearly, the historical and concrete thinking of the Bible. The latter must be taken more strictly and more literally in its utterances. In this short and thoroughly moderate book one can detect no literary vanity, no evidence that Augustine has immodestly taken himself too seriously. Augustine is not concerned with his fame after death, but with the church's truth, i.e. with the correctness of the teaching for which he stood, and with its protection against possible error and misinterpretation. It depends really on this. He who does not see this objective dogmatic striving of the old Augustine has not comprehended the direction of his development.

The schoolmaster of former times had become the doctor of the church. He was concerned with the organization of his intellectual property, and with correct perception and the accurate use of knowledge which, however, does not by itself make a man 'wise'. He was concerned with the distinction of the essential from the non-essential. Whoever hears Christ, the one true teacher, and does not add anything of his 'own', avoids the useless babble and superfluous talk against which the Bible gives warning. Yet even though it sometimes becomes extensive, and extremely circumstantial, the presentation of what is requisite must not be regarded as mere babble—'by no means!' (*Retr.* prol. 2). Already in Cassiciacum Augustine had designed the plan of an encyclopedic work which was to deal, after the pattern of Varro but in the spirit of Christianity, with the seven traditional branches of 'Learning', the *artes liberales* of medieval times. At that time he did not get beyond the description of grammar and rhythm. As he complained, the acceptance of his ecclesiastical office made further realization impossible. Later, however, he took up the work again more thoroughly. At the time when he began the *Retractationes*, his new Christian teaching on education was completed. It is the four books on *Christian Learning*, *De Doctrina Christiana*.

Until then the church had not possessed such a work. Its basic significance reaches far beyond its detailed content, which in part is only in rough draft, yet important even so. The problem of secular education and the schools had uninterruptedly occupied the church since the end of the second century. It could not be avoided, in so far as the Christians could not do without higher education. The schools, and the whole educational tradition of the environment, however, were pagan and in their classical curriculum could not be divorced from pagan mythology and philosophy. The external Christianization of the empire did not at first change anything here. We can see this from the conflicts in which Jerome was involved, as well as from his amateurish attempts to present Jerusalem as the Christian Athens, and King David as the Christian Pindar or Horace. With Augustine the situation had now changed. More than any of his predecessors Augustine was at home in classical education and culture, but he did not need to 'suppress' them forcibly, because he had overcome them inwardly, in himself. He thus ventured upon the project of a new education, determined throughout in the light of its goal, which should select from the knowledge existing hitherto that which appeared useful, and be content to lay aside what it could use no longer. As there is only one philosophy and one wisdom, that is the philosophy of Christ which has overcome and replaced all pagan philosophies, so there is henceforward also only one true way of knowing, and one 'Christian learning', which serves the Christian wisdom. This 'learning' is the knowledge of the Bible, and most of all the art of correct interpretation of everything the Bible says and the accurate proclamation of its truth. Augustine's work was published at first as a kind of manual 'for those persons who interest themselves in the Holy Scripture', primarily therefore for the young clergy and preachers of the Catholic church. It shows them what knowledge they must obtain in order to do justice to their spiritual task. It indicates, in traditional ways throughout, that the knowledge of grammar, rhetoric, etc., required up to then, including even the knowledge of music, still remains necessary if one now wishes to understand and to proclaim the Scripture alone, in place of the classical authors. Subsequently, Augustine develops the principles of interpretation (hermeneutics), and of preaching (homiletics). Yet the knowledge he demands in this way is nevertheless no mere professional knowledge for theologians and churchmen. In his view it is the 'Christian' learning as such on which everything depends for all, and beside which there is nothing in the last resort essential. For the Bible is the book of truth; it is the whole and is sufficient for all.

The new element in this position is the methodological consistency with which perception of the Biblical truth is simply made the centre and basis of knowledge and of the spiritual life. In this Augustine operates like the first 'medieval' thinker, which in other respects he certainly never was. On the other hand, his unconditional acknowledgment of the Bible, and of its significance for the entire life of faith, is in itself by no means original. In this he is in complete accord with the entire early church. The Bible is God's book, inspired and dictated by His Spirit and deserves unlimited confidence. While bishops may err, one must 'in no manner doubt or dispute whether anything is true or false, once it is established that it is written there' (*Bapt.* 2; 3, 4). This verdict is valid in principle even with regard to the accessory data and statements contained in the Bible; it is not limited to the assertions 'significant for salvation'. Characteristically, however, this does not prevent Augustine—like so many believers in the Bible—from handling it in practice, if need be, with comparative freedom. Completely without prejudice he takes account of errors of translation or copyists' faults, and in certain cases even with later corruptions. He emphasizes that God, or His prophets and apostles, naturally had to accommodate themselves to the understanding of their hearers, and in case of obscure passages he referred to the clearer ones, or to the whole of Scripture, which indeed will always serve the true love of God and neighbour as taught by the church. Allegory also naturally plays its part, opening the possibility of turning to a higher or multiple meaning of the Scripture, and so reaching an acceptable result in every case. Augustine also took pains with the philological, archaeological, and chronological details—precisely for this purpose the exegete needs the different 'sciences', but on the whole he was no philologist like Jerome, and even disapproved of his labours on the original Hebrew text. Augustine looked for that which was theologically essential and decisive, and in doing so also time and again hit upon the correct content. 'Let us therefore hear the gospel, just as if we were listening to the Lord Himself present. . . . For the precious truth that sounded forth from the mouth of the Lord was both written for our sakes, and preserved for our sakes, and will be recited for the sake of our posterity, even until the end of the world. The Lord is above; but the Lord, the Truth, is also here' (*John tr.* XXX, 1; *LPNF*, 7, 186). So the horizon of the Scripture grew broader from within. It is for him who can hear the truth and who leaves idle curiosity aside. It is truly the book of books, containing everything, and furnishes answers to all the questions which really matter to us.

The notion of education centres around this, and the extent of significant knowledge is correspondingly reduced. This is done with full awareness of what this reduction to essentials means. One may say that in this also Augustine meets the need of his age. Late antiquity was the time of normative textbooks and standardized education: these generations were no longer carrying intellectually the superfluity of riches of a culture that had grown old. Now finally all its wisdom and knowledge was placed at men's disposal in a single book, and from this book one realizes again why a certain amount of knowledge and traditional education still remained indispensable. Christianity had intensified the impression of the sterility and 'scholastic' emptiness of the old grammatical and theoretical instruction. An ascetic withdrawal was now simultaneously justified and limited by Augustine. 'One thing is necessary', and but little is enough in order to do justice seriously to this one thing. The 'arts and sciences' are no longer there for their own sake; only as disciplines supplementary to the Bible do they have a right to exist. A 'knowledge for the sake of knowledge', which does not know and envisage any more of the ultimate goal of man, cannot serve truth, but ministers only to the ambition and vanity of scholars. 'Knowledge puffeth up, but charity edifieth' (I Cor. viii. 1). It is not accidental that this attitude of Augustine reminds us of the state of mind of the aged Plato; yet his concept of love leads him beyond the latter, and takes away the sullen undertone from his instruction. One need only remember too the new preaching of the church, which was so relevant to life, and for which there was no counterpart in the realm of secular education, in order to understand that the Augustinian ideal of education by no means remained fruitless; it lived and shaped life. To be sure, it is an ascetic ideal, carrying all the dangers that such a strictly limited plan also involves intellectually at all times. Augustine did not sense these dangers. In his youth, he had traversed in full freedom the whole range of intellectual experience, only in the end to find 'all the depth of the riches both of wisdom and knowledge' in Christ and His word. From this point he started with determination. He desires to preserve only the essential, and to avoid all the by-paths of intellectual play which turn it into a game. All détours are wrong ways. The result of an abundant life is made without more ado the basis and firm rule for all. Augustine did not ask whether such a thing is possible. To him the straight line between two points is unquestionably the 'shortest way'. He founded his instructions on the sole basis of theology, yet this foundation once again reveals the whole Augustine.

The love of man must not remain fixed upon this and that. It has its aim in the eternal and unchangeable things, i.e. in the last resort in God, and only secondarily in what can be loved for God's sake. By giving the command to 'love Him "with all thy heart, and with all thy soul and with all thy mind"' (Matt. xxii. 37), God has taken up our whole life and 'left no part of our life which could be empty and, as it were, give place to desire to enjoy any other thing. Whatever else comes to our attention to be loved is to be carried along to that place to which the whole torrent of our love rushes.' This applies also to love of our neighbour, and to the affirmation of the self; the love of God 'suffers no trickle to be led off from itself by whose diversion its own volume might be lessened' (de Doctr. I, 22, 21; FC, 4, 42). God remains the sole object of man's ultimate devotion. All love of the creature, which we may 'use' according

to His will, is subject to this reservation. It is by the Christian
reservation of unconditioned obedience and joyful surrender
to the one Creator and Lord that we are withdrawn from the
dominion of 'this world', and have become 'free' as His redeemed. But, as always with Augustine, this is combined with
the reservation of the intellectual man, that is to say, the
Platonic pride which does not really acknowledge the lower
this-worldly existence as the object of its concern and love. The
spirit of man stems from God. God and his eternal truth are for
this reason the only truly worthy aim of his striving, inquiry,
and love. Augustine's love of God always displays something
of the impetuous pressure of a passionate lover, who feels as a
betrayal of his love any thought that leads away from the beloved object, or is not directly taken up and maintained for its
sake. It possesses nothing of the innocent security of children
as they play under the supervision of their mother, and are
therefore both completely with their play and entirely with
their mother. The ascetic feature of this piety is even more
strongly expressed in Augustine than it was in the Middle Ages
which he influenced so strongly, because, as already noted, he
neither tolerates nor knows any separation of theology and
philosophy, wisdom of God and the wisdom of this world. The
worldly things and sciences thus lose their relative independence
and intellectual autonomy. All things are only a thoroughfare
to life in God—and God is the real and immediate meaning of
life, and can nowhere be evaded or somehow edged away to
the periphery.

It is misleading to interpret Augustine's theology as a *com-
plexio oppositorum*, as a combination of mutually opposing elements. True, the Christian Augustine was a Platonist, because
the Platonist had become a Christian. But in his thought and
life, he was always concerned only for the exclusiveness and
completeness of his faith which he perhaps formulated most
precisely in his teaching on grace, but which he never lost sight
of and never denied. This theology of the unconditioned love
of God in its many-sidedness cannot be adopted and applied in

a new intellectual and historical environment, without undergoing change, in the course of which intellectual difficulties and tensions are bound to appear. But this characteristic it shares with all living intellectual systems, which never live or have their truth for themselves, but seek to touch living reality and are therefore never completely closed. In his historical setting Augustine can be understood only as an historical personality, and in what he wished to say and did say he is quite unmistakable.

The end of Augustine's life was passed under the shadow of the Vandal invasion, the horrors of which the aged bishop felt and experienced more deeply and painfully, as his biographer remarks, than most of his compatriots; 'for in much wisdom is much grief: and he that increaseth knowledge increaseth sorrow' (Eccl. i. 18). Whether he realized that this was the beginning of the decline of the Western empire nevertheless remains uncertain. Up to the last minute he sought to admonish and encourage the imperial officials and officers to carry out their duties energetically. He absolutely forbade the clergy to leave their congregations. Only when all had fled, would they be allowed to follow. He himself took care of the refugees who crowded besieged Hippo. He had the golden vessels of his church melted down in order to alleviate the misery, and continued 'incessantly, vigorously, and courageously' to preach the word of God. In the third month of the siege, Augustine, who was then 75 years old, contracted a fatal disease. He caused the penitential psalms of David to be pinned up on the wall in front of his bed. He accounted himself to be a penitent, and wept and prayed. Ten days before the end, he asked his friends not to visit him any more. They were to enter his room only when he needed in any case to receive the physician, or was taking food or medicine. Augustine wished to be alone, and remained so until the hour of death, when all hastened up in order to unite their prayers with his. He was fully conscious,—all the members of his body 'intact'—and retained until the end clear eyesight and good hearing. He had not made a will, because, as Possidius says, he, the poor man of God, possessed no property which he could have bequeathed. Yet 'he always ordered the church's library, with all the books, to be carefully preserved for posterity' (*Possid.* 31; *FC*, 15, 123). It was in large part made up of his own works. As a matter of fact, when the city was later taken and burned, his friends succeeded in saving the books. Whoever reads his writings, says Possidius, realizes that Aurelius Augustinus 'lived uprightly and wisely in the faith, hope, and charity of the Catholic Church', and will draw corresponding benefits therefrom. 'However, I think,' he adds, 'that greater profit was derived by those who were able to hear and see him speak when he was present in church, especially those who knew his life among men' (*Possid.* 31; *FC*, 15, 124). The personal fascination in Augustine's nature is no modern invention or discovery. He appears to have retained it even in extreme old age.

CHAPTER VII

BOETHIUS

THE century after Augustine's death was rich in theological writers, but poor in outstanding personalities. Though the intellectual impulses which Augustine had given to his time produced further effects, the spiritual level to which he had lifted every theological question could not be maintained. The external political and economic conditions were not conducive to the overcoming of a definite decadence, and furthered the decline. The Germanic mass migration pressed forward irresistibly. In the West it swept over almost all the provinces of the old empire, and the enormous efforts which had to be made in resistance and reconquest exhausted the over-taxed strength of the populace. Despite this, no permanent restoration and pacification was achieved. During this time monasticism spread widely in the church. Especially in Gaul, its thought became theologically productive. The radicalism of the Oriental ideal was here combined with the moralistic, rationalistic, and organizational tendencies of early Western Christianity. The ascetic conception lost the comprehensive and living significance it had attained with Augustine. Piety came into tension with his teaching on grace, and at the same time combined with the claims and expectations of a hope of salvation to be mediated by means strictly ecclesiastical. The 'semi-Pelagian' controversies were the expression of these unresolved tensions in the wake of the Augustinian theology. The difficulties which arose could not be solved within the circumscribed ambit in which the questions were raised, and were never really settled.

The transformation of the social order, as barbarians and Germans took over the old Mediterranean culture and social structure, meanwhile began to reach and influence the church too, but the changed situation was not yet realized as a task and a new opportunity for activity. It is true that here and there leading men adapted themselves skilfully to the new circumstances, but in general they still felt themselves to be Romans, citizens, and representatives of the empire, of its old judicial order and of its culture. While the Western imperial régime ceased to exist (476) and new, Germanic states sprang up everywhere, men still clung to the fiction of a continuing *orbis Romanus*, the Roman world and sovereignty. It was the churchmen who continued to look to the East, where the orthodox emperor reigned, who had to protect the church. The Germanic vassal peoples and their kings were not Catholic Christians, but adhered to the 'Arian' confession, and were for that reason also not accepted as real rulers. Even the theological literature of the fifth century still breathed the spirit and character of 'antiquity'.

The decadence of this period was by no means uniform and general. Under the rule of the Ostrogoth King Theodoric (493-526), Italy at least experienced once again a long period of peace and a revival which was also to the advantage of the church and of cultural life in general. To be sure, the military and political power lay exclusively in the hands of the king and his German followers; but Theodoric allowed the traditional order of civic life to exist, and indeed he enjoyed being considered a patron of the classical traditions. He did everything lying in his power to reconcile ancient society with his prudent and beneficent rule. The emperor had recognized him. The consuls for the year were now appointed as of old by consent between the two courts. The city of Rome in particular, with her senate, and her ancient practices, offices, and games, once again enjoyed a golden age.

Boethius, the man with whom we conclude the line of Latin church fathers, was at home in this world. Apart from Augustine, there is no other Christian teacher to whom the church of the Middle Ages went so consciously for instruction as

Boethius. He has been called both the last Roman and the first
of the Schoolmen. Boethius was in fact both, for as a Roman
he felt called upon to teach the true philosophy to the whole
Latin-speaking world, and he did this in the 'scholastic' spirit
of his time. Yet although he was a Christian, and even composed theological writings, he would hardly have allowed himself to be called a 'Father of the Church'. For this he stood too
much apart from all ecclesiastical activity in the narrower sense,
and not only externally. Boethius had his roots in the older
humane, intellectual and religious traditions, and was faithful to
them to a far greater degree than Augustine, the African Christian and 'philosopher'. In spite of his time and its manners,
Boethius remained at heart a classic, the last Greek philosopher,
and, just because he knew this, a Roman aristocrat and citizen.

All political turmoil and change could not interrupt the con-
tinuity of public life in the city of Rome. After the emperor had
left the nominal capital of the empire, its old aristocratic character had even grown stronger, and the Byzantine caste-feeling
and bureaucracy furthered this development. A small, exclusive
circle of immensely rich landed families, privileged, and the
bearers of very ancient names, still had in its hands the control
of current business and bore the burden of a revered tradition
and representation with solemn pride through the changed
times. This noble Roman society no longer possessed serious
political significance, yet to the mind of the inhabitants of the
empire there was still a glamour and historical dignity about
these consuls and senators which seemed incomparable and irre-
placeable. Taken all in all these last Romans showed themselves
not unworthy of their position and their high name. They not
only willingly took over all the burdens of their position; they
also cultivated higher education, particularly Greek, which
otherwise had almost no home in the West, and they took care
of educational institutions and libraries. We are largely indebted to them for the preservation to later times of the classical authors. Some also showed a keen interest in the church, for
in the course of the fifth century the last families who had so

long resisted became Christian without exception. Catholicism was from now on as much a matter of course as once the acceptance of pagan tradition had been, yet pride in the old tradition and the feeling of a duty to it was nevertheless preserved.

Boethius is the greatest representative of this late Roman society, and its strict, noble and somewhat inbred culture. He was born about 480. The *gens Anicia* to which he belonged had first begun to rise in the social scale under the later republic, and then, under the empire, had attained to extraordinary wealth and influence. Many consuls and two emperors belonged to it, and it was related by birth or marriage to all the leading families of the city. Boethius never experienced material want, or struggle for recognition or position. Once he listed among the annoying disadvantages, which can make a man's life a burden, low birth in the first place, and lack of a suitable fortune in the second (*Consol.* II, 4, 13). Fortuna had granted him both! His father, the elder Boethius, had been consul, and had held various municipal offices. If he is to be identified with a Boethius mentioned as a prefect in Alexandria, he would even have served the Eastern emperor directly at an earlier period; but this cannot be confirmed. The younger Boethius, Anicius Manlius Severinus Boethius junior, was still a child when his father died. He was received into the house of his relative Quintus Aurelius Memmius Symmachus, later his father-in-law, the great-grandson of that Symmachus who on one occasion had stepped forward in the name of the senate in favour of the subsidies for the pagan cult, and had been rejected by Ambrose (p. 105 f.). Symmachus was not only the guardian of the rich heir; he also became his mentor and friend, who introduced him to the world of higher education, literature, and philosophy, in which Boethius was later so much at home. Boethius dedicated various writings to him, and time and again confessed that he was indebted to this man for almost everything. Symmachus must have been an important personality. He wrote a (lost) Roman history in seven books, had a thorough knowledge of Greek, and was known in East and West as a brilliant speaker. He became prefect of the city, consul, and head of the senate. He was also honoured by Theodoric, although—perhaps indeed because—after Odoacer's overthrow he had come forward in the senate against the expulsion of the senators appointed by him. Yet Symmachus was reserved in his attitude to the new German lords. He was satisfied with his acknowledged position among his peers, and in occupying himself with philosophical and other studies. In this respect, too, Boethius became his pupil.

Boethius must have developed with amazing rapidity. He was, it is said, an indefatigable reader, a kind of infant prodigy 'whom industry had already in his boyhood changed into an adult, despite his youth' (*Ennod. Ep.* 7, 13). Delays and impediments did not exist for him. As the confidant of his father-in-law, with whom he agreed in all essential matters, he soon enjoyed the happiness of independent research which, as he expressed himself, was at the same time 'spiced by the sweet pleasant flavour of love' (*Hypoth. Syllog.* praef.). His marriage with Symmachus' daughter Rusticiana, who bore him at least two sons, was likewise happy. Even at the close of his life, when, at length overthrown and condemned, he tried to see through the vanity of all earthly good, he had to confess that he had never personally experienced the reputed disadvantages of marital life, and the trouble which wife and children may cause to a man (*Consol.* III, 7, 5). The outward course of his life also developed just as a man might wish. Soon from all sides fame and admiration were showered upon him. Boethius was esteemed a perfect speaker in Greek as well as Latin. He not only knew the works of literature, but was also completely familiar with the practical scientific disciplines which one 'ordinarily uses without real knowledge'—music, mathematics, and the technical arts; he had explored them, as Cassiodorus assures us, 'at the spring of science itself' (*Cassiod. Var.* I, 45). Boethius himself praised the beautiful library of his palace, adorned with mosaics and ivory (*Consol.* I, 5, 6) in which he used to work and philosophize in peace (*Consol.* I, 4, 3).

Yet one must not therefore imagine Boethius as an eccentric

19

recluse. He also entered with self-assurance and as a matter of course upon the usual career of the Roman aristocrat, for whom all doors were open. Before he was 30 years old, we find him already honoured with the most illustrious titles, which often 'remain denied to old men' (*Consol.* II, 4, 7). He was senator and patrician, and undoubtedly also held other high posts of honour. He was once commissioned by Theodoric to investigate certain payments, regarding which there had been loud complaints as to the weight of the coinage. Another time he successfully applied himself to secure a remission of taxes for the province of Campania, which had been afflicted by a bad harvest. In the year 507 the king asked him in the most flattering terms to procure a sun-and-water clock which the Burgundian king was to receive as a gift; and, as an expert in music, he was to find a singer and player of the zither for the Frankish king Clovis. (The letters are worded by Cassiodorus, Boethius' cousin, who was at that time Theodoric's right-hand man at court in all administrative questions.) In 510 Boethius was finally appointed consul, and without a colleague, the highest honour which traditionally could fall to the lot of a Roman. (The expenditure one had to make in this position for games, gifts and the like, was estimated a little later, in Justinian's time, at more than twenty hundredweight of gold.) Yet all these were functions which did not satisfy Boethius, and which he sought to perform more or less incidentally. He had long ago found his true lifework in the intellectual realm, i.e. 'in the complete study and treatment of all branches of philosophy', which meant to him the highest consolation and enjoyment of life (*Hypoth. Syllog.*, Migne, LXIV, 831 B). The methodical planning and steadfastness with which he pursued this aim, without ever letting himself be dissuaded or confused, is astounding, and typical of his scholarly character, and his firm, calm nature.

Boethius was conscious of the importance of his studies; they seemed to him imperative, an urgent, practical necessity. For he observed the disadvantage which Latin education still showed when compared with the Greek East, and felt that the gap was

then threatening to widen. The Latin world still lacked the
capability for a real, scholarly study of philosophy, such as
appeared to be the advantage of the Greeks. His literary work
was to answer to and correct this. As consul he emphasized that
this task of instructing the people was very appropriate to his
high office, and that he therefore wished to remain faithful to
it so far as his duties gave him time. The Roman statesman of
the time had a different calling from that of old. Even as the
man of time past subjected and made all states subservient to the
one city by military power, so there now remains 'nothing left
to do' but to further the moral life of the Roman common-
wealth, and for this purpose Greek wisdom and knowledge is
especially appropriate. It has indeed always been in accord with
the Roman nature to adopt and imitate the noble and worthy
traits possessed by other peoples (*in Categ. Arist.* II, praef.). The
traditional phrases on the *civitas Romana* as mistress of the world
must not be taken too seriously. Boethius knew very well what
was really becoming of the glory of Rome in the contemporary
world, and how insignificant had become the proud offices
which the city was able to confer (*Consol.* III, 3, 15). Yet Rome
should remain the capital of the world at least intellectually.
'We must see that we develop ourselves better and more effectively, not in the sphere where we cannot even distinguish ourselves from the brutes, but in the reflection of heavenly virtues
by noble action and speaking for eternal glory' (*in Isag.
Porphyr.* A. II, praef.). This is an unusual re-interpretation and
sublimation of the old Roman *virtus*, and sounds somewhat
doctrinaire. But Boethius thus did in fact grasp the last possibility which time 'had left' to the old custodians of Roman
greatness, and this decision was not without moral greatness
and genuine historical understanding. It is easy enough to mock
him. We still possess a spiteful epigram (*Carm.* II, 132) with
which the later Bishop Ennodius of Pavia, himself one of the
meanest flatterers and position-hunters of his century, tried to
take revenge on Boethius. The old military glory, he argues,
was forgotten today, the Roman pride was gone. Boethius had

substituted the distaff for the sword, and lived only for drinking
and pleasure. But behind this aspersion merely stood the fact
that Boethius had ignored, at first politely, and then coldly, the
repeated begging letters of the unctuous poet, who wanted to
be given a house in Milan. We may simply ignore this, as
Boethius himself did.

When Boethius spoke of the wisdom of the Greeks which the
Romans should learn and appropriate, he was thinking, in a
word, of the latest, Neo-Platonic form of classical philosophy,
the systematically arranged teaching of a comprehensive understanding of truth, encompassing God and the world. Yet he did
not essay these heights without more ado. It was first necessary
to give a *propaedeutic* introduction. This consisted of the disciplines of the ʻ*Quadrivium*ʼ, to which he was the first to give its
name, that is to say, the fourfold method of education in the
propaedeutic sciences: arithmetic, music, geometry, and astro-
nomy. Only so could one arrive ʻin the various branches of
philosophy at the highest perfectionʼ (*Inst. Arithm.* I, I). Accordingly, Boethius first dealt with arithmetic. The book is
dedicated to Symmachus, and represents essentially an abbreviated Latin revision of the *Introduction to Mathematics* composed
by the Greek mathematician Nicomachus of Gerasa in the
second century A.D. Then follows a handbook of music, in
reality rather an admonitory *Protrepticus* for these studies, and
an introduction to the problems of acoustics and harmony. The
rational relationship of music to numbers, the moral effect
which was to be expected from such perceptions within an
introductory *instrumentum philosophiae*, have but little in common with musical problems in the modern sense. This book
also relied primarily on Nicomachus, but discusses other authors
also, and, above all, regards the great Ptolemy as the decisive
authority. We can trace the influence of Alexandrian Neo-
Platonism and its tradition of learning. The geometrical and
astronomical manuals—all but a few remains of the geometry
—are lost.

The high-flown dedicatory epistle to the mathematics is in

marked contrast with the severe and nobly restrained style displayed by Boethius in his later writings, and shows him still to
be an apprentice. He certainly did not win his lasting importance as a teacher of the *Quadrivium*, but as the great translator
and interpreter of Greek philosophy, particularly of the logical
writings of Aristotle. The *Dialectics* seems separated from the
traditional context of grammar and rhetoric, and is already to
be considered as the beginning of real philosophical education.
In a famous preface to his commentary on the Aristotelian
theory of judgement, Boethius expressed himself regarding the
over-all plan of his work as he then envisaged it. Of course, he
says, there has been up to the present no lack of excellent men
who have taken pains to make known more intimately to the
Latin-speaking world the things about which he is concerned,
yet they did not preserve a satisfactory arrangement of the
material, and did not present the philosophical disciplines step
by step in the necessary sequence. This was now to be undertaken. Boethius wished to provide an *Organon* of the whole of
philosophy in the Latin language, in which translations and
explanations should mutually support one another. 'I wish', he
says, 'to translate the whole work of Aristotle, so far as it is
accessible to me',—a complete Aristotle was therefore even
then no longer to be obtained without more ado,—'into the
Roman idiom and conscientiously offer his complete utterances
in the Latin tongue. Everything Aristotle ever wrote on the
difficult art of logic, on the important realm of moral experience, and on the exact comprehension of natural objects, I shall
translate in the correct order. Moreover, I shall make all this
comprehensible by interpretative explanations. I should also like
to translate all Plato's Dialogues, and likewise explain them, and
thus present them in a Latin version. When this is accomplished,
I will furthermore not shrink from proving that the Aristotelian and Platonic conceptions in every way harmonize, and
do not, as is widely supposed, completely contradict each other.
I will show, moreover, that they are in agreement with one
another at the philosophically decisive points. This is the task

to which I will dedicate myself, so far as life and leisure for work
are vouchsafed to me. I know that this will be as useful as it is
laborious, and that it needs the assistance of those (powers)
which are ever alien to envy and jealousy' (*in Arist. de Interpret.
B. II praef.*).

This formalized summary bears, exceptionally for Boethius,
a character still pagan, but must not on that account be taken as
a concealed anti-Christian confession. Here is, indeed, a gigantic
task—a truly scholastic *Summa* of the whole of philosophy,
which can only be conceived as one, and which is to be erected
on the basis of the classical texts of the two greatest philosophers! The systematic goal, a complete harmonization of the
Aristotelian and Platonic systems, is not original; it accorded
with the systematic programme of the Neo-Platonic tradition.
In this Plato determined the ideological framework and structure, Aristotle is considered more as the teacher of logic, in the
narrower sense. (Yet this is an area for which Boethius had a
special liking, and to which he attributed again and again the
greatest scientific importance.) Here, however, the work was
actually to be done according to a uniformly designed outline
and presented in literary form. In view of the dimensions of
such a plan one may well ask whether it could be carried out
at all by a single individual; but if it could, then Boethius was
the right man to do it. His clear vision, and the sure energy of
his dedication to the task, once he had taken it up, show a certain grandeur. Boethius was untiring. Nobody, he suggests in
the passage quoted, who has once experienced the happiness of
work can ever give it up again, and 'whoever is discouraged
would have lost his courage already'. With the same imperturbability as the great theologians and dogmatists of his epoch,
the philosopher also believed in the objective reality and the
eternal meaning of the systematic perception of truth. And as
they built upon the revelation and tradition of the church, so
Boethius likewise confided in the 'invincible authority' of the
old teachers and masters—*veterum virorum inexpugnabilis auc-
toritas* (*Syllog. Categ.* II praef.).

It cannot be established for certain how far Boethius actually came in the realization of his plan. Preserved are—after elimination of various false medieval writings of 'Boethius'—a commentary upon the teaching of categories, and two commentaries on Aristotle's theory of judgement (*de Interpretatione*): a brief one in two books for beginners, and a comprehensive and scholarly one in six books for advanced readers who wish to understand the problems in their whole complexity. The commentaries on the Aristotelian analytics, topics, and physics are lost. On the other hand, the *Introduction* (*Isagoge*) to Porphyry on the theory of judgement, indispensable in the opinion of Boethius, is doubly preserved in two editions, of two and five books respectively. In the older commentary, the earlier translation of Marius Victorinus is still taken as a basis; in the second, more detailed commentary Boethius furnished his own, more literal, translation. There was, moreover, a wordy commentary on Cicero's *Topics* (the doctrine of arguments and proofs for speakers) which has only come down in part and which itself was intended to interpret Aristotle's *Topics*. Finally, Boethius published five independent monographs on logical problems. He was especially proud of his examination of hypothetical judgements, a treatise in two volumes (*de Syllogismo Hypothetico*), because this subject had not been treated by Aristotle, nor by the Greeks at all adequately up to this time, and by the Latins not at all. Otherwise his dependence on the Greek models is mostly clear enough: Boethius frequently offered not much more than Latin paraphrases of the writings of his predecessors. Nevertheless, one must not just regard him as a mere plagiarist and compiler. A derogatory judgement on his philosophical independence and significance has definitely changed in his favour in recent research, in the same way as the judgement upon that medieval Scholasticism which depends upon him. Boethius receives serious consideration in modern logic, partly for his own sake.

At all events, the historical importance of what Boethius created by his translations, commentaries, and his own researches is indisputable. He did more than anyone to establish the medieval reverence for Aristotle; and Aristotle remained known to the Latin West only so far as he had translated him. In their literary arrangement, also, his commentaries became the model for the medieval commentaries on Aristotle, and through the adoption of his translations Boethius created the philosophical terminology of all the Middle Ages. In this way he is also 'the father of our logical terminology' (Ernst Hoffmann). The famous *quinque voces* used so diligently by Scholasticism had its source in him. This is the *schema* of definitions: genus, species, differentia, property and the added term accident. A basic theme of the entire medieval theology, the 'disputation on universals', concerning whether the universals possess more or less of real existence, took its rise from a passage in his commentary upon Porphyry. This originated, in the final analysis, in the combination of Platonic and Aristotelian elements of thought, i.e. in a Neo-Platonic dogma which through the mediation of Boethius was determinative for the whole Aristotelianism of the early and high Middle Ages.

Anyone comparing today the Aristotelianism of Boethius with the genuine Aristotle has his eye immediately caught by yet another difference in the whole style of thought of the two men. The inner and free-ranging zest with which Aristotle approached and so effectively developed his problems, has in Boethius given place to quite a different kind of organization, arrangement, and systematization, precise and often rather pedantic in operation. Philosophy has become academic, 'Scholastic'. Characteristic is the value Boethius everywhere attaches to an accurate and fixed terminology, in consequence of which the meaning of a word once established can never vary, or appear in a new light. He likewise considered it a serious deficiency in a system if 'gaps' existed anywhere. He was always pressing after completeness, and was tireless in making references and pinning things down. Again and again he expatiated on the appropriate arrangement of the material, on the methodical development of the examination, and on the correct form of instruction. To be sure, this corresponded to the general tendency of this late Roman period, but it also stood in an inner relationship to the specific concern of his whole enterprise. Boethius saw himself as the schoolmaster of the West. He wished to educate his fellow-countrymen at last to a scientifically based course of studies, and for that purpose it was imperative that everything be presented as unmistakably and precisely as possible, so that every serious student might immediately find his bearings and be sure of his way within the philosophical course. For this reason too translations must be so reliable that reference to the Greek originals could for the future be dispensed with. Boethius emphatically admonished his readers not to consider his elaborate expositions superfluous or of secondary importance. 'Since I have not shrunk, despite the immense labour, from writing such a voluminous work', the readers should be willing at least to read it at leisure, and not to pass judgement upon it prematurely (*in Aristot. De Interpret. B. VI praef.*). Boethius was concerned with superseding the usual rhetorical half-education. He knew that he would meet with resistance, and he anticipated personal criticism. But the high calling of his scholarship must not be dragged through the mire.

Boethius still gave the form of a dialogue to the first version of his commentary on Porphyry. The scene of the conversation, continued for two winter nights, is set in the solitude of a villa in the mountains, and is charmingly depicted. In his later works Boethius renounced such pleasant settings. Furthermore, the elegantly worded prefaces in which he sometimes says a little about his intentions are kept quite brief, and then as a rule pass over almost immediately into the scholarly presentation with a short 'But now to the subject-matter', or some such phrase. We can see with Boethius that he was a master of all the fine points of rhetoric; but they are not essential to him. Not only are 'moral questions more important than rhetorical skill' (*in Cicer. Top.* I praef.), but Boethius also did not wish to play to the gallery by misusing logical examination for the sake of rhetorical show-pieces, but above all to attain lucidity. 'If this

turned out well, then I have attained my purpose perfectly—
even if the form of my discourse perhaps seems to be very un-
polished' (*Syllog. Categ.* I praef.). With Boethius this is not, as
so often, another rhetorical phrase. The style of his philosophical treatises is certainly chosen with care, and to that extent not
formless, yet at the same time it is also of an unsurpassable objective sobriety which has no place for aesthetic irrelevancies.
This is the more impressive, because Boethius, as we shall see,
was in reality also a rhetorician, and indeed a poet, and when he
wished could very well display his abilities in this area. In this,
however, the Platonist did not follow the example of the Platonic dialogues, which certainly were not even for Plato the
whole of his instruction. Even less has his manner anything
in common with the literary method of instruction used by
Cicero, whose philosophical essays he nevertheless knew and
esteemed, and in one case, as we saw, even commented upon.
Yet according to the preface it was only out of friendship for
the rhetorician Patricius who had commissioned it, and to whom
it also was dedicated, that he had undertaken this work,
primarily for the benefit of dialectics.

For the decade following his consulate hardly anything is
known about Boethius' life. The greater part of the works just
reviewed were probably written within this period. In retrospect it appeared to Boethius as a period of happiness, which
allowed him to proceed almost undisturbed upon the course
on which he had entered. Had it been granted to him to continue on it, the major work as he envisaged it might actually
have been completed. The change in his life was due to politics.
It was first to carry him to the highest peaks of fame and success,
only then to throw him down and ruin him in a sudden turn
which none had foreseen. All at once it became obvious how
artificial and uncertain were in reality the political assumptions
upon which Theodoric had built his whole régime, and upon
which also rested the fortunate peace which Rome and Italy
had until then enjoyed. In this connection ecclesiastical relations
also now attain a certain importance.

We have already mentioned that Roman society in the sixth century had, like the whole empire, become Christian, indeed Catholic Christian. Arianism was in Italy exclusively the religion of the caste of Gothic over-lords, and Theodoric himself did not attach any great importance to the occasional obliteration through conversion or assimilation of the confessional distinction which was thereby established. On the other hand it was not unwelcome to him that before the beginning of his reign Catholic communion between West and East had also been interrupted, and could not be restored for thirty-five years. In 484 the doctrinal divergence on the Christological question had led to the breach between Rome and Constantinople, in consequence of imperial church politics. The stubborn maintenance by the pope of his condemnation of the Byzantine Patriarch Acacius, who was then in charge, had converted the so-called 'Acacian schism' between the two capitals also into a question of prestige. So long as this quarrel was not settled, the pope and the whole Catholic church of Italy had no interest in returning to the direct dominion of the emperor, and adhered with all the greater loyalty to their new Gothic over-lords. On the other hand, those circles which were still interested in the unity of the empire deplored this dissension on political grounds. The majority of the senate, and Symmachus and Boethius too, probably belonged to them. In the fourth century, the Anicians had become Christians before other aristocratic Roman families, and Boethius naturally wanted to be regarded as a good Catholic. This does not, however, mean that he was bound to approve papal actions in every respect. The intransigence of the Roman see, which made it difficult even for the secret adherents of orthodox doctrine in the East to remain in communion with it, was perhaps the occasion of the first theological treatise Boethius had written, probably in 512. It is dedicated to John, a deacon, and in a thorough treatment discusses the Christological heresies of Eutyches and Nestorius, i.e. the two extreme and equally erroneous viewpoints on the question which was in dispute at that time: namely, how the relationship of Christ's one Person to His two natures, the divine and the human, was rightly to be understood. Boethius alludes only lightly in his introductory dedication to the current disputes, it is true, and he avoids dealing with the fierce controversies of church politics. He contents himself with rationally elucidating the complex logical problems which had arisen. Yet it seems that he wished in this way to make a contribution to peace, or at least to work for a theological reconciliation. This, at any rate, would fit in well with his political intentions as well as with his general intellectual attitude. As a matter of fact, his Christological researches did prepare the solution which was later to meet with general acceptance.

Some years later, the official peace between Rome and Constantinople was concluded (519). This was primarily to the credit of Justinian, the nephew of the reigning Emperor Justin, who obviously had not really understood the great political importance of the ecclesiastical union. Nevertheless, the theological tensions were not completely resolved. In the so-called 'theopaschite controversies' the contrasted points of view threatened to revive; only they now came to expression no longer only in a purely Christological form but as a question of the possibility of a Person within the Trinity being capable of suffering. This caused Boethius to take up from now on the Trinitarian problems too. He dealt with them in three smaller tracts, one of which is dedicated to Symmachus, the two others again to John. His restraint in the face of any public dispute, his exclusive concentration upon systematic questions as such, are even more strictly observed here than in previous treatises. The work *Why is the Trinity Only One God And Not Three Gods?* dedicated to Symmachus, carries this reserve so far that it expounds the questions in dispute with a terminology partly novel, and in such an over-subtle, seemingly contradictory, and intentionally complicated way that it discourages any unqualified reader immediately, and is intended to do so. This esoteric style gives the impression that Boethius did not intend in his writings to intervene in the actual discussion, and himself to bring about a decision. We must leave it open whether he was at all interested in the immediate effect of his tracts, or whether he was perhaps only stimulated to develop the systematic possibilities almost as a game for their own sake. On the point at issue, however, he actually took under his protection the threatened 'theopaschites', who had also appealed to the senate, against their adversaries in the Roman church. He thus found himself again in the camp of those who were interested in a settlement and in peace, not the least of whom was the Eastern emperor himself. The whole circle around Symmachus had always maintained a close, or in the political jargon of our day, 'cordial' relationship with the emperor's court.

The danger of the new situation could not possibly remain hidden from Theodoric. The restored peace of the church removed an essential guarantee of his own régime! Henceforth the Catholics again saw in the emperor their orthodox overlord, and the Goths therefore could again be regarded as a hostile army of occupation, heretics about whose dominion no one was concerned. It thus became more important for Theodoric to emphasize his good relations with the emperor, and, as a matter of fact, the latter also met his wishes to the extent that he recognized his son-in-law in due form as the successor to the royal throne, and on his part seemed to support the permanent existence of the Gothic dynasty. But simultaneously his diplomatic activity in ecclesiastical and patriotic circles of the West was increased. This resulted in a new honour for Boethius, probably proposed by the emperor, which represented something most unusual, and was welcomed by the whole pro-Byzantine aristocratic clique. For the year 522, Boethius' two sons, Flavius Symmachus and Flavius Boethius were jointly appointed consuls. Both were still boys so that the honour in reality fell more to their father. Soon afterwards, however, Boethius himself was appointed *magister officiorum* by Theodoric, i.e. supreme head of all court and government offices, and by this responsible position was brought into his immediate presence. This promotion of a Roman went beyond the framework of titular honours. It took on political significance, and in this was all the more extraordinary. For Boethius, however, it was the first step toward catastrophe.

Boethius would not have been an Italian had he not felt and enjoyed to the full the glory of the consulate of his two sons. Even during his last imprisonment he remembered this incomparable 'peak of happiness'. No misfortune of the days that followed, his 'philosophy' told him, is to be allowed to, or ever can obscure the light of that day 'when thou sawest thy two sons being both Consuls together carried from their house, the Senators accompanying them, and the people rejoicing with them; when, they sitting in the Senate in their chairs of state, thou making an oration in the King's praise deservedst the glory of wit and eloquence. When in public assembly, thou, standing betwixt thy two sons, didst satisfy with thy triumphant liberality the expectation of the multitudes gathered together' (*Consol.* II, 3, 8; *LCL*, 185). Boethius was perfectly equal to this situation. Entering upon his new office was something quite different. With this he left his former course of life, and entered upon a dangerous area. Until then Boethius had in every way kept away from real political life. He was hardly prepared for it, and in his whole nature was certainly not made to be a courtier. What had led him in spite of everything to this fatal step? Boethius later passionately protested that vulgar ambition had played only the remotest part. The acceptance of the office had appeared to him as his duty. In fact he may have been of the opinion that it was not open to him to decline the appointment at this moment. In Theodoric's court, influential forces were at work which did not approve of his policy of settlement. Feelings towards the Italian population had grown considerably more hostile: a general prohibition from carrying arms was issued for all non-Gothic subjects. Friction also occurred in church affairs. When Theodoric nevertheless now decided to call a representative of the old Roman tradition and of the idea of the Roman empire to an authoritative position, should Boethius have refused, even if he could? Actually, he had no choice. Boethius was much too much a Roman at the decisive moment to decline political responsibility, forgetting his name and tradition, and to retreat to the secure life of a wealthy private scholar, content with the mere semblance of a public reputation. Why, he asks, should government always be left only to the careerists and criminals, who then misuse it to the detriment of their fellow-citizens? Had not Plato rather taught him 'that commonwealths should be happy, if either the students of wisdom did govern them, or those which were appointed to govern them would give themselves to the study of wisdom' (*Consol.* I, 4, 5; *LCL*, 143-145). One dimly senses behind these declamations also a painful and personal motive for the disastrous decision: 'I desired to practise that by public administration which I had learnt of thee (philosophy) in private conference' (*Consol.* I, 4, 7; *LCL*, 145); 'I longed for the opportunity to perform deeds—why should my manhood turn grey and wither?' (*Consol.* II, 7, 1). Viewed like this, Boethius' fate attains a truly tragic character. It was precisely his sense of duty which united with his most secret desires, and thus enticed him to a step in which he deluded himself about the possibilities of his time no less than about his own capacity to prevail in it.

There is no doubt that Boethius at first fully possessed Theodoric's confidence, and also repeatedly enjoyed his support against his Gothic advisers. At any rate, in several cases, partly however in the earlier period, Boethius successfully prevailed over the 'covetousness' of the barbarians, as he called it. He was able to prevent the appointment of a certain Decoratus because he mistrusted the character of this parvenu. (After his downfall Decoratus, however, was immediately promoted *quaestor palatii*.) On the whole, the difficulties with which Boethius had to contend probably came from the very beginning more from the circles of his colleagues who had suddenly to accept as their chief this prominent Roman who had come from outside. His reserved and republican pride, his personal feeling of superiority, and his quite disturbing inclination to judge and decide all things from the point of view of moral principle certainly did not win him friends at the court. Furthermore, there was the difference of political conviction and tradition. Boethius was undoubtedly determined to serve the king with loyalty; yet the recognition of the Gothic régime was in his eyes itself always an act of resignation, a bitter necessity in view of the general political decline. There was nothing left but to resign himself to circumstances as they were, and to make the best of things for the sake of the empire and its culture. On the other hand, the other officials and advisers of Theodoric had quite another attitude. They had risen with him, admired his successes and his astute rule and perhaps even from the standpoint of Italian nationalism gave him preference over a Byzantine dominion. At all events, there was no sympathy with the ideals of restoration held by the Roman high aristocracy; all that was desired was accommodation with the new lords. So Cyprian the *referendarius*, one of the chief opponents of Boethius, had his children trained in the Gothic use of arms and made them learn the Gothic language. This whole clique must have felt itself provoked and neglected by the new course which the appointment of Boethius seemed to inaugurate, and accordingly hampered his activity.

However, this certainly would not have been enough to overthrow him, if a general reaction had not taken place at the same time. The policy of reconciliation towards the Eastern emperor had in reality already collapsed at the moment when Boethius assumed office. Byzantium was evidently playing a double game, even though it did not openly express itself against Theodoric. The Vandals in Africa suddenly threw themselves on the side of the emperor, and all Goths in that country were murdered or put to flight. The Franks invaded adjacent Burgundy, and only a remnant of that kingdom could be saved at the last minute by Theodoric's intervention. Also the question of succession had again become completely uncertain through the unexpected death of the heir to the throne. Moreover, there was the unfavourable shift in the ecclesiastical situation in Italy itself —the possibility of a Byzantine Catholic reconquest began to appear. It is easy to understand that the elderly Theodoric followed the developments with anxiety, that his disposition grew morose, and that he saw adversaries at work everywhere. 'The King', wrote a later historian, 'held the Romans capable of evil intentions . . . and believed false witnesses more than the Senators' (*Anon. Vales* XIV, 87). And although, as the Greek Procopius assures us, he was in reality no tyrant, and was for that reason respected by both Goths and Italians as a legitimate ruler, he committed in this mood 'the first and last crime' of his life. Boethius, whom 'malicious people' envied, was the victim (*Bell. Goth.* I, 1, 34, 39).

In August of the year 523 Pope Hormisdas had died. Under his pontificate the Acacian schism had been terminated; but he personally always remained a faithful adherent to the Gothic régime. So it must have been extremely unwelcome to Theodoric that the successor of Hormisdas was Pope John I, whose election represented a clear victory of that group whose sympathies were Greek and who looked to the imperial church. He was possibly the same John to whom, when still a deacon, Boethius had dedicated his theological monographs. The Roman post which went at this occasion to Constantinople was censored, and a letter of the senator Albinus detected which, perhaps written in the name of the whole senate, produced suspicion. Besides a report of the election it perhaps contained still further information about the ecclesiastical and political situation, and in the tone of traditional devotion and loyalty expressed all too openly a wide agreement with all imperial wishes. The letter may have appeared to the senders as harmless and correct. On the governmental officials, however, it made the impression of high treason. The ambiguity lay in the odd constitutional situation which on the one hand allowed the empire to remain, and to be represented by the one emperor, but which, on the other hand, had also subordinated the Roman senate, proud of its nominal independence, to the Gothic king. The confiscated papers were submitted to Boethius, who checked them and then decided to let the whole matter

20

drop. He knew his colleagues in the senate, and shared or at
least understood their attitude, and, on the other hand, he was
doubtless afraid of arousing the misgivings of the barbarians if
he specially called their attention to this correspondence not
intended for their eyes. Yet this procedure was too bold. Happy
to be able now to pull his rival to pieces, Cyprian went to the
king on his own account. He represented the whole occurrence
to him in the most dangerous light, and was believed. Albinus
was at once summoned before the royal consistory. Boethius,
who attended, could perhaps have still intervened and prevented the worst. But it seems that, offended in his pride, he
made instead an unfortunate attempt to justify his behaviour up
till then, and to treat the matter even now as a trifle. It is said
that he explicitly declared that, if they found Albinus guilty, he
would be, too! The whole senate would stand united with him
in this matter; Cyprian's accusations were a slander! With this
the case was immediately pushed to an extreme. The *referendarius*, who felt himself to be a dutiful official, and was by no
means prepared to let himself be insulted as an informer, now
had to assume the offensive. Further documents, forged as
Boethius maintained, were adduced whereby he himself was
charged with illegal actions on behalf of the senate, and with
treasonable intent. And now decisions followed in rapid succession. Boethius was indicted, suspended from office, and then
sentenced by a royal court to exile, to confiscation of his fortune, and to death. A last hope from the senate, which had to
endorse the sentence, came to nothing. Threatened themselves,
the senators approved it without objection, to the bitter grief
of the fallen Boethius, who felt this failure to be perfidy and
treachery. Nobody dared oppose the enraged king. However,
the sentence was, as so often in such cases, not carried out for
the time being. Boethius was merely interned in Pavia, so that
a favourable turn of events was not yet impossible. Then some
new deterioration of the situation seems to have taken place.
In the autumn, perhaps in October of the following year, he
was executed, most likely also in Pavia. Symmachus, too, was

now put on trial, and he followed Albinus and Boethius to
death. At last even Pope John fell into disgrace because he had
not performed some action of church politics in Constantinople
to Theodoric's satisfaction, and died in prison.

Thus Boethius' fall produced a sequence of dreadful measures which darkened the last years of the life of the great Gothic
king. The good terms between Goths and Romans upon which
the existence of his government had relied were broken. The
subsequent restitution of the family fortune of Boethius' sons
by Queen Amalaswintha, and the amnesty also for his widow,
who under Totila had demolished statues of Theodoric, could
not remove this impression. With Justinian's attack soon after
Theodoric's death (526), the thirty years 'struggle for Rome'
began, in which not only the rule of the Goths, but also the
old tradition and culture of the country disappeared for ever.
Henceforth, there was no ancient aristocracy, no Roman senate,
no consuls, and no philosophy; the 'Dark' Ages were beginning.
With such a background Boethius' fate automatically takes on
an awesome and glorious light. Boethius felt himself to be a
martyr of higher culture and reason, of justice and freedom, and
of the upright attitude of the old Romans at the hand of barbarians, and so described himself to posterity. This view is at
any rate more correct than the later legendary re-interpretation
of his death as a martyrdom for Catholic orthodoxy. The confessional question played no role at all during his trial. On close
examination, his case nevertheless appears in a more or less
doubtful light, at any rate susceptible of more than one interpretation.

Apart from a few brief allusions, our picture of Boethius'
fall comes exclusively from himself, and that only in an interpretative and rhetorically idealizing style appropriate to the
special aims of his last work. The extensive and factual defence
address to the king there mentioned has been lost. What we
have is naturally an extremely one-sided account. In spite of all
the complaints and protests which Boethius raises, and despite
the similar position adopted by Procopius, we can hardly view

his conviction as a miscarriage of justice. Naturally, it was a political trial, in which the question of guilt is always difficult to decide, yet the proceedings employed seem to have been correct, and we hear of no direct attempt to bring influence to bear. The unfavourable estimate, together with the atrocity legend of a sadistic form of execution, stems from a later time when, in the misery of the last struggles, the Gothic rule had long since forfeited all sympathy. At first public opinion seems to have fluctuated (*Consol.* I, 4, 44). It is interesting that during the trial Boethius was also accused of resorting to the '*sacrilegium*' (the adjuration of demons and witchcraft), for the purpose of obtaining office surreptitiously,—things which he himself was, of course, perfectly right in repudiating as unworthy of a philosopher. Philosophy itself, he thinks, is calumniated and accused in his person. It seems that his scholarly studies had a sinister and strange effect upon outsiders—in the eyes of the crowd Boethius was perhaps already something like 'the sorcerer' Virgil or Doctor Faustus. All this alone, however, was not decisive. The decisive thing was the suspicion of political conspiracy in which Boethius seemed to be involved with Albinus and probably some other senators. Boethius was accused of having 'hoped for Rome's liberty', and of wishing to protect the senate on his own. The manner in which he reacted to these double reproaches is quite characteristic. 'What freedom can still be expected, after all? If only it had still somehow been possible!' For then no plot would ever have been discovered through him (*Consol.* I, 4, 27). But he must not be charged with such political shortsightedness. On the other hand, the reproach that in his actions he had kept the senate's welfare in mind cannot in his opinion be esteemed as an accusation at all; it was his duty as a Roman to protect the senate. It is for Boethius still a far higher and holier institution than the whole governing power of the barbarian king. We do not know what real actions and intentions hid behind this general declamation; it can hardly be a matter only of his lax treatment of the Albinus affair. But that such an attitude and spirit in a leading official appeared as treason from the Gothic point of view is understandable. Perhaps Theodoric wanted to make a clear example by the execution of Albinus and Boethius. This was cruel, perhaps not completely just, and in any case an error politically, but the sentence should not be regarded as an act of sheer caprice and barbarity. Boethius was no politician, and for that reason at the decisive moment he was unable to take in hand the dangerous game into which he found himself and play it successfully to the end. In his opinion he was no traitor, and certainly never meant to be, when he indignantly took refuge in his clean conscience. But he had not served his king with that faithfulness and singlemindedness which the latter could expect from him, and to which he was otherwise accustomed from his vassals. Boethius failed through the inner contradiction between the confidential position he assumed and the ideals which he wanted to serve at the same time, and thus he was bound to perish. To himself his tragic fate appeared in a different and more basic light. Had he not in any case let himself be tempted, when the glory of executive action appeared to him higher than his philosophical calling? It had been a weakness to yield to that desire. Certainly it was the kind of weakness which 'can mislead just those who have elevated natures, when they are not led to the last stage of virtue and perfection' (*Consol.* II, 7, 2). This 'last step' Boethius reached only in imprisonment, and here he then established for posterity, as though a penitent, the ideal image of his true personality and his philosophical faith. It made him unforgettable, and it still lives on.

If we can imagine Boethius leaving the world without addressing this last word to it, he would indeed have occupied a secure place in all histories of philosophy and of doctrine. Humanly speaking, however, his name would not signify more than that of any commentator of late antiquity, or compiler of the Neo-Platonic school. He would be for us an able expert on Aristotle, who had occupied himself with certain logical and scholastic problems—and nothing more. We should never have known of what freedom of feeling and spirited expression this man was at the same time capable, and what spiritual fire in reality burned in his reserved inner self. The sole evidence for this is his last work, *The Consolation of Philosophy*, *Philosophiae Consolatio*. This, too, is a philosophical writing, but at the same time a work of art and a book of confessions which can fairly claim a place beside the *Confessions* of Augustine. Like the latter, it has been endlessly imitated but never equalled, because in its spiritual and personal content it remains unique. And even though the *Consolatio* does not equal the *Confessions* in originality, it surpasses them in the refined elegance of its artistic execution and in the bright clarity of its perfect composition. Boethius conceived this work in the painful situation of a condemned man, and wrote it in a few months—not exactly in 'prison', as the medieval interpreters and illustrators thought, but still without the luxury of his usual surroundings, without his books and other resources, without friends and converse, in complete solitude. When this is taken into consideration, his achievement almost borders on the miraculous.

Boethius began work on the *Consolatio* when the sentence on him was already passed. To be sure, he still did not reckon, it appears, with the worst; he did not know anything about the indictments with which his father-in-law was probably already then charged, and he perhaps still hoped for pardon. Yet there is no mention of all this in his book. Instead of dwelling upon tormenting surmise, Boethius resolutely turned his back on the world which had betrayed him. In the presence of philosophical truth he will account for his situation as it had now developed, and speak about what remains to him imperishably and for ever. The five books of the *Consolatio*, like Augustine's *Soliloquies*, are a great monologue, or rather just as in that work the soul holds a dialogue with 'reason', so here he holds one with philosophy herself, the teacher who had educated him in early youth, and who was the only one who had kept faith with him. The friendly 'muses' of former times can certainly share his pain, but cannot help. In the introduction, Boethius describes his mood of perplexity and loneliness, when a tall, strange figure suddenly enters his room. She carries books in the one hand, a royal sceptre in the other, and wears an odd home-spun gown. Boethius immediately recognizes her—she is Philosophy. Late antiquity had a predilection for such personifications, and Boethius also goes somewhat far in interpreting the allegorical details of her appearance; yet, all in all, his description retains something immediately clear and of gripping vivacity. With a glance of flaming anger the goddess banishes the 'muses', those vulgar 'whores of the theatre', from the bed of their pupil. Boethius is ill; he must not be weakened further by the sweet poison of melancholy excitement. But strict as her utterance sounds, Philosophy is not cruel. She, too, bends down as a Saviour over the suffering disciple, tries first only to soothe and strengthen him, and thus leads him slowly from his inner confusion once again to his senses. She awakens anew by her questions and answers his remembrance of the true good things of life, and finally guides him back into the realm of perfect freedom and understanding in which his soul finds repose. The dialogue is arranged according to these stages of the process of recognition. Formally, it stands of course in the Platonic tradition, but in some passages approaches the style of a philosophical hortatory writing, as the defence of the accused assumes the form of an address to the court, etc. . . . Boethius evidently aimed at bringing into play the most varied literary forms one after another, and at producing with each a tiny piece of art. This is likewise true of the thirty-nine poems which enliven the discourse: there are at least eleven poetic metres which are not found elsewhere.

At the beginning Boethius still tries to justify despair over his fate, and in this way finds an opportunity to defend himself, and correspondingly to show the baseness of his opponents. But philosophy shows him how wrongly he acts in being enraged at the change of fortune, which had formerly spoiled him, and never was obliged to fidelity. Gradually by her questions he is brought to see the worthlessness and vanity of all external good

things, wealth and luxury, glory and all success. The true possession consists only in the inner treasures of the spirit and of
truth, and of true moral attachment to these values. A lover
of philosophy ought not to complain, but rather be proud, of
being allowed to suffer for his mistress and his love. Those who
find satisfaction in the earthly strain after mere phantoms of
happiness; they are like topers who in their intoxication have
forgotten the way and are unable to find their true home. There
is one sole highest good for which all strive unknowingly, a real
power, beauty, goodness and perfection, which is sufficient in
itself and alone can give satisfaction. This is the great One who
unites and harmoniously sustains the variety of the universe and
is called 'with a name familiar to everyone'—God (*Consol.* III,
12, 8). He, 'the Father of all things' is to be called upon in prayer
according to the example of Plato (*Tim.* 27 c), if we wish to
discover the highest happiness and good (*Consol.* III, 9, 32 f.).
The popular philosophy of seeking consolation in resignation
is now thrust into the background. Boethius feels freer and turns
his gaze upward and forward. Now he partakes in the conversation on his own account, and correctly carries it further to the
delight of his teacher. He perceives the uniform law of the world
which animals, plants, and even minerals and crystals, follow in
maintaining their being, and for which men also fundamentally
yearn when they are striving for happiness. This law of ordered
being does not tolerate any exception. 'Thus evil is nothing,
for he cannot do it who can do anything' (*Consol.* III, 12, 29).
The world is God's, and seen from the perspective of almighty
God everything is necessarily set in its proper place. The world
is the best and most perfect of all worlds.

What then was the misery which had befallen Boethius? How
was the undeniable truth of the thought now grasped to be
harmonized with the experience of the reality of injustice and
disorder in the world? The answer to this question is given in
the fourth book, with a detailed theodicy developed in the
Platonic spirit. In reality the wicked are not happy but unhappy.
Because of what they are doing they fall into nothingness, and

together with their good existence they lose their real existence.
The good man, however, preserves it and gains a richer and
more secure happiness the greater the determination with which
he sees through the vanity of all which at first tried to tempt and
distress him, and the more firmly he attaches himself to the true
and highest good, in which he is saved. God's indestructible
order secures that every man in the world draws upon himself
his reward or punishment, as he deserves. Everything depends
on having his eyes firmly fixed upon the eternal, divine reality.
It is this to which the old story of Orpheus is meant to testify:

> But you this feigned tale fulfil,
> Who think unto the day above
> To bring with speed your darksome mind,
> For if, your eye conquered, you move
> Backward to Pluto left behind,
> All the rich prey which thence you took,
> You lose while back to hell you look.
>
> (*Consol.* III, 12, 52 ff.; *LCL*, 297)

From this point the fifth book leads to a last and difficult problem. How is the leading principle of moral compensation com-
patible with God's omnipotence? Does not his 'providence'
annihilate man's freedom, on which all morality depends?
Here, too, the right solution consists in the correct way of seeing
things. We must be clear that God's Being exists in eternity,
i.e. not in the dimension of the transient, earthly time in which
our activity takes place. That which unfolds to us as past, present, and future, lies before his view as if it were eternally
present. For that reason the decisions of his 'providence' are not
really prior to our free actions, but can correspond to them
precisely at any given moment. It is therefore by no means
pointless to ask for Him, and to continue to strive with all our
strength for the good. This is the sum total of all the considerations which 'Philosophy' draws at the end: 'Neither do we in
vain put our hope in God or pray to Him; for if we do this well
and as we ought, we shall not lose our labour or be without
effect. Wherefore flee vices, embrace virtues, possess your minds

with worthy hopes, offer up humble prayers to your highest Prince. There is, if you will not dissemble, a great necessity of doing well imposed upon you, since you live in the sight of your Judge, who beholdeth all things' (*Consol*. V, 6, 46 ff.; *LCL*, 411). After Boethius, who evaded no difficulties, has followed his philosophical path to the end in strict consistency, he concludes the work with a direct appeal, moral and religious.

The *Consolatio* is anything but a naïve work. This is true of its content as well as of its form. Boethius consciously wrote it in his own defence, as an apology, and the picture of his personality which he portrays is therefore consciously stylized. We recognize this, for instance, from the manner in which he declares with a noble pride at the end of his political vindication that he must renounce any self-praise—it would violate too much the 'secret' of an upright mind (*Consol*. I, 4, 33). Then in the next paragraph he testifies expressly through the mouth of Philosophy that he has been too modest, and has not given his objective merits their due praise (*Consol*. I, 5, 7). Every detail in the structure of the writing and its arrangement of thought, too, is carefully considered. The *Consolatio* is a book for educated men; it is deliberately and consciously such. The refinement of its methods, its organization, its emphases, and its connections, the Greek quotations that are thrown in, and the countless reminiscences and echoes of older literature would even at the time be wholly clear only to the most learned reader. They make the book today an ideal field for the exercise of linguistic detection and of feeling for style. It is a typical book of late antiquity, in which originality is almost always expressed only as 'an originality of the synthesis of traditional elements' (Wolfgang Schmid). Yet while lesser spirits were bowed under the burden of the gigantic heritage, and with their artificial products appear only grotesque, pedantic, or ineffectual, Boethius remained inwardly one with the whole treasure of tradition, and freely and naturally works out its intellectual and literary possibilities as an artist and a master.

If we come from the reading of the scholarly commentaries

we are at first surprised how strongly the Platonic elements
dominate the *Consolatio*: they are constantly expanding, and in
the end control the field alone. Not only the ideas, however,
but also the spirit and mood of the book are largely Platonic, or,
more precisely, Neo-Platonic. In the sensitivity, rhetoric, and
directness of his religious feeling Boethius surpasses Plato. A
new and passionate accent gives to the whole dialogue an almost
dramatic charm, because the psychic development of the ques-
tioner and the speculative unfolding of objective truth under
the conversational guidance of 'Philosophy' again and again
fall into line. In the same way the poetic insertions, the 'hymns'
of the dialogue, are by no means artificial embellishments. By
reflecting and purging the emotions, by first introducing the
ideas, and then summarizing them and carrying them forward,
the hymns are indispensable for the understanding of the intellectual movement in the framework of the whole. Boethius was
indeed not 'original' even as a poet, but above all the custodian
of a heritage. When we hear that in earlier days he once produced a '*carmen bucolicum*', an idyllic and perhaps also allegorical pastoral poem of the kind then popular, we need not
particularly deplore the loss of these verses. But the poems of
the *Consolatio* are undoubtedly more than skilled experiments
in various types of poetry, although they are this too. Boethius
reveals himself here as a true lyric poet of ideas. Indeed, apart
from its beginnings in Seneca and others, he is perhaps the
typical representative of this kind of poetry in its Latin late
form. Since it corresponds to his whole nature, it is real poetry.
This is true of the hymn to Orpheus already mentioned, and
the great prayer in the third book. It is also true of the elegy
in the first book, since Boethius sees order and beauty everywhere in nature, whereas harmony and justice are missing in
man's world alone:

> O Thou that joinest with love
> All worldy things, look from Thy seat above
> On the earth's wretched state;
> We men, not the least work thou didst create,

With fortune's blasts do shake;
Thou careful ruler, these fierce tempests slake,
And for the earth provide
Those laws by which Thou heaven in peace dost guide.

(Consol. I, 5, 42 ff.; *LCL,* 159)

Who was the man who composed these prayers? In what sense was he a theologian as well as a philosopher? And was he a Christian at all? This is a question which is often asked, and which still finds no uniform answer. To it we must turn in conclusion.

It is surely a strange state of affairs that the same person whom the Middle Ages venerated as a 'Father of the Church' and a saint, in his last writing, composed in the presence of death, receives 'Philosophy' as his consoler, and nowhere mentions Christ the Saviour of the Christian. This cannot be set aside as a formal question, and explained simply from a traditional feeling for style, in that he wished to avoid speaking of Christ in a philosophical dialogue. In subject-matter also all reference to unequivocally Christian teachings and conceptions is missing. This is the more striking as the *Consolatio* is through and through a book of a religious, and indeed of a devotional, tone, and the 'Philosophy' who here speaks reveals herself as an outspokenly pious philosophy. By what she teaches she desires only to remind Boethius of the truth which he had all along known, believed, and stood for. There is actually no contradiction in the *Consolatio* of what he has written elsewhere, so far as we can judge. This rules out the possibility that we have to reckon with a surprising *volte-face,* which Boethius might have experienced during his last imprisonment, due either—even this view has strangely enough been held—to a subsequent 'conversion' to serious Christianity, or to a final abandonment of his former theological conviction in favour of a now consciously pagan philosophy. In reality Boethius never faltered in his belief in what he thought to be the truth.

At one time there was a common tendency simply to declare Boethius a pagan on account of his *Consolatio,* and to regard his theological treatises as medieval forgeries. Since they are, however, guaranteed by the explicit testimony of Cassiodorus, such a superficial solution of the problem is now out of the question. A formal paganism is impossible for this reason alone, that in the sixth century a non-Christian would never have been appointed to the highest offices of state. On the other hand, the theological writings do not yield as much for his personal faith as we might expect. We have already spoken of their inception and their strict dogmatic character. Boethius restricts himself to the formal exposition of certain Christological and Trinitarian problems, and proceeds according to the acknowledged rules and principles of logic in the same manner 'as is customary in mathematics and the other sciences' (*Opusc.* III praef.). These are indisputable for him. He does not seek, in the words of Anselm, to 'believe in order to understand' in the Augustinian sense, but vice versa seeks rather to penetrate faith with his rational understanding. Only so can he make it credible scientifically in its full, responsible meaning. This certainly does not exclude the fact that from the beginning Boethius acknowledges the 'Catholic faith' to be valid, including the condemnation of all heretics, and that for his part he also knows and cherishes Augustine's writings—especially his book on the Trinity. For his own examination of this topic he expresses the hope 'that the seeds of the writings of Saint Augustine' may have produced some fruit in it (*Opusc.* I praef.). The reserve which Boethius tried to maintain, as we have seen, toward all ecclesiastical party quarrels must not be interpreted as a secret scepticism. Yet just as he desires to know only one philosophy, and in this realm accordingly despises all quarrels of the schools, he probably acknowledged the teaching of the church as a given form of the truth, which only lacks to some extent strict philosophical perfection. He scarcely took note of the Biblical writings, and in any case never referred to them for the substantiation of his statements. He starts in his intellectual labours with the great philosophers, and here he finds spiritual exaltation and his real religion. How many philosophers after him have behaved in just the same way, and nevertheless have

felt that they were good Christians! Boethius could do so all
the more confidently, for he nowhere gave offence with his
opinions, and found acceptance for his theological treatises even
with the clergy, so far as they understood them. So far as we
know, the *Consolatio* was also criticized by no one, and was for
centuries read with joy by all Christians.

We here see how close Neo-Platonic philosophy and post-
Augustinian Christianity had now come to one another in the
West also. Christianity was no longer felt to be anti-philo-
sophical, and Platonism pagan. There existed between the two
a far-reaching community of religious temper and outlook.
This also came to full expression in Boethius. All obvious
'pagan' elements of belief have disappeared from the *Consolatio*. The classical gods appear at most as poetical personifications. Strict monotheism is in absolute control, and in Boethius
especially has a decidedly theistic colour: God hears prayer and
as the Father rules the world. No less decisive is the ascetic
feature of his thought. Personally Boethius was no ascetic, but
the depreciating evaluation of earthly good things, in itself a
stock feature of the whole ancient literature of consolation,
assumed a deeper meaning in the light of Neo-Platonic religi-
osity, and reminds one of Augustine. The human spirit must
not cleave to external things. It is really at home only with God,
i.e. in the spiritual vision of God and his eternal perfection.
From this point of view even the proud memories and political
virtues of Rome lose their splendour. Measured by the ultimate,
even they are vain and empty, the outflow of a senseless thirst
for glory. Withdrawal from the political ideal of life is no less
justified in principle, and goes even beyond that of Augustine's
Civitas Dei. Suffering, however, gains in moral significance, and
attains a positive value: 'I think that Fortune, when she is opposite, is more profitable to men than when she is favourable'
(*Consol.* II, 8, 3; *LCL*, 221). However, the question is focussed
remarkably in the innermost area of metaphysical questioning:
the entire last book of the *Consolatio* deals with man's freedom
in its relation to God's omnipotence. Boethius is here hardly

dependent upon Augustine. At any rate, he still conceives the
problem of freedom as a problem of the universal order, not
of the inner experience of man himself, and in so far remains
in the line of the traditional philosophical discussion. As a
matter of fact, in this he only touches on the great theological
theme of his century, that is, the question about predestination.

However, the decision regarding Boethius' Christianity cannot be made on the basis of such general contacts with the
history of ideas—any more than by a mere demonstration of
his church membership, and his dogmatic and theological
literary work. The *Consolatio* itself directs us to ask the question
about his faith in a more serious way; for surely in theme it is a
book on man's eternal salvation, and even more, on his deliverance in the presence of a world that is hostile to him and outwardly destroys him. How does the oppressed human being win
back his freedom in this extreme danger? The answer can only
run: by philosophy, i.e. by the calm and reasonable consideration of that which proves itself eternally true and lasting beyond
the confusion of the moment, the whole of the well-ordered
world, the freedom of the moral self, and above both, sustaining and uniting everything, the omnipotence and kindness of
the one God himself. Boethius begins his consideration with the
cosmos. He realizes how ridiculous and insignificant are his
petty earthly miseries, and likewise all the glory of monarchs
and their seeming world-empires in reality, when measured by
stellar space, and all human deeds, when measured by eternity.
Yet this discovery only makes a man happy and free because
the eternal order and justice exist and operate also in man's
spirit. Only this is necessary, that he really recognize them, and
resolutely follow their orders. Then he will see God himself, the
'true sun', who penetrates everything with his light (*Consol.*
V, 2, 14). In this light he will ultimately perceive all existence
as good, and everything which is real as rational. This perception
renders the philosopher happy, reconciles him with his lot, and
gives his moral self a lasting foundation in the truth and in God.

Such a teaching on salvation is not Christian. It has thrust aside everything which occasions the miseries of the Christian, the sufferings and historical struggles 'of this Age', the demonic power of evil, and the impossibility ever to overcome it by his own strength. For Boethius all these things do not possess ultimate importance. He certainly takes them into consideration, but merely in order to expose them in their nothingness, and to dissolve them theoretically by his philosophical examination —they are 'thought away'. For this reason all the elements which for the Christian establish salvation are lacking in Boethius. He does not need any help and revelation from outside, no historical change and renewal in time, least of all any real conversion of his human person. The gloomy 'physical' passions which at the beginning of his dialogue confused his mind and his moral attitude are precisely not his actual essential ego. And this ego can never really become lost to him—it can at most be forgotten, and go astray in 'inebriation'. Yet philosophy leads him back to himself, and thus man again attains existence in himself. Boethius believes in himself, in his reason, and in his moral freedom. The whole significance of what in his thinking corresponds to 'predestination' amounts to the protection of this freedom and the maintenance of the moral order which justly distributes rewards and punishments. By contrast, Augustine's teaching on predestination was the ultimate consequence of his doctrine of grace, and the expression of an 'absolute' ethical dependence of sinful man upon God, which is at the same time his happiness. Augustine became a Christian as a Neo-Platonist; Boethius as a Neo-Platonist and Christian theologian remained basically a pagan. That is why philosophical faith is here sufficient to itself. It is pious mediation and poetic reverence of the one divine principle rather than 'faith' in the strict sense, which expects everything from God's intervention and builds life on his firm promise. Boethius needs neither word nor Spirit nor mercy, neither church nor fellow-Christians in order to be what he is. It is therefore no accident but entirely appropriate that his last confession does not speak about Christ.

Boethius still enjoys a local cult in Pavia. It is, as it were, symbolic that his relics and those of Augustine are together here in the very same church, San Pietro in Cieldoro. The last two Latin church fathers of rank each in his own way brought to an intellectual conclusion an epoch of Western church history, and of all history. Yet in their conjunction the old tension still lives between the aspiration for virtue and humility, reason and faith, philosophy and theology, and between pagan and Christian antiquity. The Greek philosophy which, for Augustine, became the bridge for the understanding of Christianity as gospel in opposition to all moralism and rationalism in his church, conversely in Boethius led to the mistaking of Christianity for a higher form of pagan humanism and religion. Shortly after Boethius theological work was in abeyance for centuries. Gregory the Great (d. 604) and Isidore of Seville (d. 636) were only stragglers of the classical epoch, and lived spiritually in a changed world, educated no longer in an ancient but in a medieval fashion. When intellectual life revived in the Carolingian empire, pains were taken to comprehend the Golden Age of the church fathers as an inner unity. This in reality it had never been, and it did not conclude with a ready solution, but with an open question.

CHRONOLOGICAL TABLE

395	Division of the Empire	395	Augustine Bishop of Hippo Regius
		397	April 4, death of Ambrose
410	Alaric conquers Rome		
		419-420	Death of Jerome
429	Vandals in Africa		
		430	August 28, death of Augustine
476	Odoacer deposes Romulus Augustulus		
493-526	Theodoric	510	Boethius Consul
484-519	Acacian schism		
		524	Death of Boethius

LIST OF ABBREVIATIONS

ACW   *Ancient Christian Writers*, ed. by J. Quasten, J. C. Plumpe, and W. J. Burghardt (Westminster, Md., London, 1946 ff.)

ANF   *The Ante-Nicene Fathers*, Edinburgh edition, rev. by A. C. Coxe (Buffalo, 1884–1886)

CC   *Corpus Christianorum, Series Latina* (Turnholti, 1953 ff.)

CSEL   *Corpus Scriptorum Ecclesiasticorum Latinorum*, ed. by the Wiener Akademie der Wissenschaften (1866 ff.)

FC   *The Fathers of the Church*, ed. by L. Schopp, G. Walsh, and R. J. Deferrari (New York, 1947 ff.)

LCC   *The Library of Christian Classics*, ed. by J. Baillie, J. T. McNeill, and H. P. Van Dusen (London, Philadelphia, 1953 ff.)

LCL   *The Loeb Classical Library* (London, Cambridge, Mass.)

LPNF   *A select Library of Nicene and Post-Nicene Fathers of the Christian Church*, first and second series, ed. by P. Schaff and H. Wace (Oxford, New York, 1886–1905)

ML   *Patrologia Cursus Completus, Series Latina*, ed. by J. P. Migne (Paris, 1844 ff.)

Oates   *Basic Writings of Saint Augustine*, with an introduction and notes by W. J. Oates (New York, 1948)

BIBLIOGRAPHY

Whenever the translations of quotations from individual church fathers have been taken from extant English editions, an abbreviation of the title has been added to the reference (cf. List of Abbreviations opposite). Otherwise the German translations of Professor von Campenhausen have been translated into English, with reference to the original sources. In many cases the second procedure has proved preferable, for the author's translation of quotations seemed to convey the thought of the particular church father more clearly. At the author's request, the translator has enlarged the following bibliographies for the use of English readers, and assumes the responsibility for this portion of the book as well as for the Index.

INTRODUCTION

A few general references to the literature may be appended here, as in *The Fathers of the Greek Church*.

Since 1866 the Wiener Akademie der Wissenschaften has been engaged in producing a critical edition of all the Latin Church Fathers in its *Corpus Scriptorum Ecclesiasticorum Latinorum* (*CSEL*). So far, 75 volumes have been published. Since 1953, the *Corpus Christianorum* (*Series Latina*) (*CC*) of St. Peter's Abbey in Steenbrugge (Belgium) has appeared beside it, making more rapid progress. Besides these, the comprehensive collection of J. P. Migne, *Patrologia Cursus Completus, Series Latina* (*ML*) (Paris, 1844 ff.), extending to the time of Innocent III, still has to be used. It is now being completed with critical supplementary volumes (*Supplementum*, 1958 ff.) by A. Hamman.

E. Dekkers and E. Gaar, *Clavis Patrum Latinorum* (Sacris Erudiri III, Steenbrugge, 1957²), provide a survey of the whole material (with titles, catalogue of the best editions, and critical supplements added). A large selection of English translations is found in *The Ante-Nicene Fathers* (*ANF*) (Edinburgh edition, rev. by A. C. Coxe, Buffalo, 1884–86); P. Schaff and H. Wace, *A select Library of Nicene and Post-Nicene Fathers of the Christian Church* (*LPNF*), first and second series (Oxford, New York, 1886–1905); J. Quasten, J. C.

317

Plumpe, and W. J. Burghardt, *Ancient Christian Writers* (*ACW*) (Westminster, Md., London, 1946 ff.); L. Schopp, G. Walsh, and R. J. Deferrari, *The Fathers of the Church* (*FC*) (New York, 1947 ff.); *The Library of Christian Classics* (*LCC*), ed. by J. Baillie, J. T. McNeill, and H. P. Van Dusen (London, Philadelphia, 1953 ff.); some translations in *The Loeb Classical Library* (*LCL*) (London and Cambridge, Mass.).

The most substantial history of the literature of the ancient church is that of O. Bardenhewer, *Geschichte der altkirchlichen Literatur* (Freiburg, 1913²–1932), in five volumes. In the *Handbuch der klassischen Altertumswissenschaft*, newly edited by W. Otto, the Latin Christian literature has been treated by G. Krüger (III³, Munich, 1922; IV, 1-2, Munich, 1914–20). Concise but excellent information is given in the summary presentation *Leben, Schriften und Lehre der Kirchenväter* (with further references to literature) of B. Altaner, *Patrologie* (Freiburg, 1960⁶; English tr., *Patrology*, by H. C. Graef, Edinburgh, London, New York, 1960). Available in English are particularly: J. Quasten, *Patrology I-III* (Westminster, Md., 1951, 1953, 1960); and E. J. Goodspeed, *A History of Early Christian Literature* (Chicago, 1942).

The following standard general histories of the ancient church should be mentioned: K. Müller, *Kirchengeschichte I, 1* (Tübingen, 1941³, in association with H. v. Campenhausen); H. Lietzmann, *Geschichte der alten Kirche I-IV* (Berlin, 1953²/³; English tr., *A History of the Early Church I-IV*, by B. L. Wolff, London, New York, 1937–51, 1953²); and the first four volumes of the collective work *Histoire de l'Église* (Paris, 1934 ff.), edited by A. Fliche and V. Martin (Vol 1: J. Lebreton and J. Zeiller, *The History of the Primitive Church*, tr. by E. C. Messenger, London, New York, 1942–47); and its continuation: J. R. Palanque, G. Bardy, and P. de Labriolle, *The Church in the Christian Empire*, tr. by E. C. Messenger, London, New York, 1949–52. Another translation from the French into English: L. Duchesne, *Histoire ancienne de l'Église I-III* (Paris, 1906–11²⁻⁵; English tr., *The Early History of the Christian Church I-III*, by C. Jenkins *et al.*, London, New York, 1908–24). In English: B. J. Kidd, *A History of the Church to A.D. 461* (Oxford, New York, 1922); and the *Cambridge Ancient History*, vols. 11 and 12, ed. by S. A. Cook *et al.* (Cambridge, 1936–39). A short but very good introduction to the history of the ancient church (with select readings) is to be found in R. H. Bainton, *Early Christianity* (Princeton, 1960).

The most important accounts of the history of doctrine in the early church in the German language are: A. v. Harnack, *Lehrbuch der Dogmengeschichte I-III* (Tübingen, 1932[5]; 1909–10[4]; tr. by N. Buchanan *et al.*, *History of Dogma*, 7 vols., London, 1894–99); R. Seeberg, *Lehrbuch der Dogmengeschichte I-II* (Darmstadt, 1953[4]; English tr., *Text-book of the History of Doctrines*, by C. E. Hay, Philadelphia, 1905). F. Loofs, *Leitfaden zum Studium der Dogmengeschichte I-II*, ed. by K. Aland (Halle, 1959[6]); the Roman Catholic *Handbuch der Dogmengeschichte*, edited by M. Schmaus, P. Geiselmann and H. Rahner, has been appearing since 1951 in thematic rather than chronological order. Translated from the French into English is: J. Tixeront, *Histoire des dogmes* (Paris, 1930[11]; *History of Dogmas*, tr. by H. L. B., 3 vols., St. Louis, 1923 ff.). English works are: A. C. McGiffert, *A History of Christian Thought* (2 vols., New York, London, 1932–33); J. F. Bethune-Baker, *An Introduction to the Early History of Christian Doctrine* (London–Cambridge, Mass., 1933[5]); D. L. Neve, *A History of Christian Thought* (Philadelphia, 1946); and J. N. D. Kelly, *Early Christian Doctrines* (London, New York, 1958); cf. also Ch. N. Cochrane, *Christianity and Classical Culture* (Oxford, New York, 1940).

When quoting the writings of the fathers, I have frequently made tacit use of older translations. I beg my predecessors not to consider this a plagiarism. In other instances too it would have been possible in innumerable passages to name older authors whom I have followed consciously or unconsciously. I prefer, however, to take my stand with Cervantes, who in the prologue of his *Ingenious Gentleman Don Quixote de la Mancha* expressly renounces marginal citations, footnotes, and other noble things of this kind 'partly because I do not consider myself clever and learned enough, and partly because I am too lazy to hunt up in other authors what I can perfectly well say without them'.

Ch. I—TERTULLIAN

The critical edition of Tertullian's works in the *CSEL* is not yet entirely completed; the most recent and complete edition was published in *CC* (Turnholti, 1954). There are in addition the numerous editions of individual books, among which the edition of *De Anima* by J. H. Waszink, with its detailed commentary, should be especially mentioned (Amsterdam, 1947), as well as C. Becker's Latin-German edition of the *Apologeticum* (Munich, 1961[2]). Many of his works are

found in English translations in *FC, ACW, ANF, LCC*, and in indi-
vidual editions. Besides these, the excerpts and interpretations of A.
Neander in his *Einleitung* to the writings of *Antignostikus (Geist des
Tertullianus*, 1849²; tr., *Antignostikus, the Spirit of Tertullian*, by J. E.
Ryland, London, 1851) are still helpful and worth reading.

A real biography of Tertullian, such as that once attempted for
instance by E. Noeldechen (1890), can hardly be written. We know
of him and of his history practically solely from his works, which are
not sufficient for this task. Newer general presentations come from
P. Monceaux (in the first volume of his *Histoire littéraire de l'Afrique
chrétienne*, Paris, 1901), A. d'Alès (*La Théologie de Tertullien*, Paris,
1905), R. E. Roberts (*The Theology of Tertullian*, London, 1924), and
others. A brilliant characterization is given by K. Holl, *Tertullian als
Schriftsteller* (Berlin, 1897, *Gesammelte Aufsätze III* (Tübingen, 1928–
1932), 1 ff.). For Tertullian's literary style particularly compare—
besides various special examinations—E. Norden, *Die antike Kunst-
prosa II* (Leipzig, 1959³), 606 ff., 943 f., as well as the profound study
of his setting by H. Koch in Pauly, *Realencyclopädie V, A* (Stuttgart,
1934), 822 ff. Important aspects are treated, among others, by J.
Lortz, *Tertullian als Apologet I-II* (Münster, 1927–28); A. Labhardt,
Tertullien et la philosophie (Mus. Helv. 7 (1950), 159 ff.); J. Morgan,
The Importance of Tertullian in the Development of Christian Dogma
(London, 1928); C. de L. Shortt, *The Influence of Philosophy on the
Mind of Tertullian* (London, 1933); H. Karpp, *Schrift und Geist bei
Tertullian* (Gütersloh, 1955); on the penitential question, see H. v.
Campenhausen, *Kirchliches Amt und geistliche Vollmacht in den ersten
drei Jahrhunderten* (Tübingen, 1953), 243 ff.

Ch. II—CYPRIAN

The abundant and, to some extent, also complicated transmission
of the letters and writings of Cyprian makes a critical edition very
difficult. The edition of Hartel in *CSEL* (1868–71), out of date and
from the beginning deficient, is today still not yet entirely superseded. There is no lack of translations into modern languages, for
instance into English in *ANF, ACW, FC, LCC*, and in *Patristic
Studies* of the Catholic University of America.

Among over-all presentations of Cyprian should be mentioned:
E. W. Benson, *Cyprian, his Life, his Time, his Work* (London, New
York, 1897); P. Monceaux, *Saint Cyprien, évêque de Carthage* (Paris,

1914²); J. Ludwig, *Der hl. Märtyrerbischof Cyprian von Karthago* (München, 1951); especially the chapters dealing with Cyprian in H. Achelis, *Das Christentum in den ersten drei Jahrhunderten II* (Leipzig, 1912) 387 ff.; and H. Lietzmann, *Geschichte der alten Kirche II* (Berlin, 1953²), 229 ff., 261 ff. (tr. *The Founding of the Church Universal* [*A History of the Early Church*, vol. II, London–New York, 1938], 298 ff.). The best expert on Cyprian's writings, which he treated time and again in his essays, was H. Koch: especially in his *Cyprianische Untersuchungen* (Bonn, 1926), and *Cathedra Petri: Neue Untersuchungen über die Anfänge der Primatslehre* (Giessen, 1930). On Cyprian's conception of the church and its ministry, see H. v. Campenhausen, *Kirchliches Amt und geistliche Vollmacht in den ersten drei Jahrhunderten* (Tübingen, 1953), 292 ff.

Ch. III—LACTANTIUS

A critical collective edition of the prose works of Lactantius was, in his day, produced by S. Brandt in *CSEL* (1890–97). Some special editions of particular works are now to be added to it, especially that by J. Moreau (with commentary) of *De Mortibus Persecutorum* (Paris, 1954), by H. Kraft and A. Wlosok of *De Ira Dei* (Darmstadt, 1957), and by M. C. FitzPatrick of *De Ave Phoenice* (Philadelphia, 1933, with an English translation). The *Epitome* is translated by E. H. Blakeney (London, 1950), the *Death of the Persecutors*, by D. Dalrymple (Edinburgh, 1782), selections of the *Institutes*, by T. W. Radius (Grand Rapids, Mich., 1951) and in *ANF*.

The standard biography was written by R. Pichon, *Lactance* (Paris, 1901). In addition, see P. Monceaux, *Histoire littéraire de l'Afrique chrétienne III* (Paris, 1905), 287-371. Useful recent examinations of the biography of Lactantius are to be found, among others, in: S. Prete, *Der geschichtliche Hintergrund zu den Werken des Laktanz*, in *Gymnasium* 63 (1956), 365-382; J. Stevenson, *The Life and Literary Activity of Lactantius*, in *Studia Patristica I, Texte und Untersuchungen*, 63 (1957), 661-677; J. Moreau and H. Kraft in the introductions of their editions, mentioned above; A. Wlosok, *Lactantius und die philosophische Gnosis* (Heidelberg, 1960).

Ch. IV—AMBROSE

The edition of Ambrose's writings in *CSEL* is now approaching its conclusion. A selection of English translations is available in *FC*,

LPNF, and the *Patristic Studies* of the Catholic University of America. The best edition of the Latin hymns is found in W. Bulst, *Hymni Latini Antiquissimi LXXV, Psalmi III* (Heidelberg, 1956). The best German biography, by Th. Förster, *Ambrosius, Bischof von Mailand* (Halle, 1884), is today out of date. The most comprehensive account was written by F. Homes Dudden, *The Life and Times of St. Ambrose I-II* (Oxford, 1935); cf. also P. de Labriolle, *Saint Ambroise* (Paris, 1908²; English tr., *The Life and Times of St. Ambrose*, by H. Wilson, St. Louis–London, 1928). For his ecclesiastical politics mention should be made of H. v. Campenhausen, *Ambrosius von Mailand als Kirchenpolitiker* (Berlin–Leipzig, 1929), and J. R. Palanque, *Saint Ambroise et l'Empire romain* (Paris, 1933); for his dogmatic views L. Herrmann, *Ambrosius von Mailand als Trinitätstheologe* (*Zeitschrift für Kirchengeschichte*, 69 (1958), 198-218).

CH. V—JEROME

The most fascinating part of Jerome's literary work, the letters, are critically edited by I. Hilberg in *CSEL*, 54-56 (1910–18) and more recently by J. Labourt in the *Collection des Universités de France* (Paris, 1949 ff., with French tr.). Since the *CSEL* edition is making only slow progress, Jerome is still generally quoted from Migne (*ML*, 22-30). A selection in English is provided by *FC, LPNF, LCL, LCC*, and individual editions.

The German biography by G. Grützmacher, *Hieronymus I-III* (Leipzig, 1901–08), is obsolete since F. Cavallera's book, *Saint Jérôme I-II* (Louvain–Paris, 1922). This work has remained basic for all later accounts. For particular topics, mention should be made of P. Monceaux, *Saint Jérôme—sa jeunesse* (Paris, 1932; English tr., *St. Jerome, the Early Years*, by F. T. Sheed, London, 1933); W. Süss, *Der hl. Hieronymus und die Formen seiner Polemik* (*Giessener Beiträge zur deutschen Philologie*, 60 (1938), Hepding-Festschrift), 212-238; M. Villain, *Rufin d'Aquilée : La Querelle autour d'Origène* (*Recherches de Science religieuse*, 27 (1937), 5-37, 165-195); the collection of essays by F. X. Murphy, *A Monument to S. Jerome* (New York, 1952), with contributions by G. Bardy, L. Hartmann, J. R. Palanque and others; and the relevant essays by A. Vaccari, *Scritti di Erudizione e di Filologia II* (Rome, 1958). For Jerome's relationship to the Greeks, see P. Courcelle, *Les Lettres grecques en Occident* (Paris, 1948), 37-115; for his dependence upon classical Latin writers, see H. Hagendahl, *Latin Fathers and the Classics* (Göteborg, 1958), 89-328.

Ch. VI—AUGUSTINE

Augustine's works were completely edited by the Maurists (Paris, 1679–1700) and have been reprinted repeatedly, as in Migne (*ML*, Paris, 1841 f.) and now also in a new Latin-French edition (Paris, 1949 ff.), partly also already in *CC*. So far *CSEL* has edited little more than one half of the writings and is already superseded by many new special editions of particular books. These are as innumerable as the translations. In larger collections they can be found particularly in *ACW*, *FC*, *LPNF*, *LCL*, *LCC*, and the *Patristic Studies* of the Catholic University of America.

Whereas Possidius believed (chap. 18, see p. 219) that hardly any scholar could read all the works of Augustine, this is even more true of the literature on Augustine, which is boundless in every respect. It is continuously brought together in the periodical *Augustiniana* (Louvain, 1951 ff.) and the *Revue des Études Augustiniennes* (Paris, 1955 ff.). In addition we shall mention here only the papers and transactions of the Paris Augustine Congress of 1954 (*Augustinus Magister I-III*, Congrès International Augustinien, Paris, 1954, 3 vols.) and the report on *Die Augustinliteratur seit dem Jubiläum von 1954*, by R. Lorenz in *Theologische Rundschau*, 25 (1959), 1–75. An excellent and comprehensive bibliography of the literature on Augustine has been recently provided by C. Andresen in *Zum Augustin-Gespräch der Gegenwart* (*Wege der Forschung V*, Darmstadt, 1962). I have not myself been able every time to indicate where I have followed other authors (and sometimes also their translations). In what follows, I single out—more or less at random—some works as particularly important or easily accessible, and completely leave aside the systematic-theological examinations.

No comprehensive biography has been written since LeNain de Tillemont's *Mémoires pour servir à l'histoire ecclésiastique XIII* (Paris, 1702). The literature on Augustine's conversion is particularly abundant. I mention : J. Nörregaard, *Augustins Bekehrung* (Tübingen, 1923); R. Guardini, *Die Bekehrung des hl. Aurelius Augustinus* (Freiburg, 1959[3]; English tr., *The Conversion of Augustine*, by E. Briefs, London, Glasgow, Westminster, Md., 1960); P. Courcelle, *Recherches sur les Confessions de saint Augustin* (Paris, 1950); J. O'Meara, *The Young Augustine* (London, 1954). F. van der Meer, *Augustine de Zielzorger* (Utrecht, 1947; English tr., *Augustine the Bishop*, by B. Battershaw and G. R. Lamb, London–New York, 1961), gives a superb description of Augustine as a bishop. A. v. Harnack in his

Lehrbuch der Dogmengeschichte II, *2* (Tübingen, 1932⁵), 59–236 (English tr., *History of Dogma*, by N. Buchanan *et al.* (London, 1894–99), vol. V, p. 3-13, 61-240) provides an interpretation of his personality which is still readable and, despite its modernizations, in many aspects congenial. There is a valuable collection of essays on his thought and personality in *A Monument to St. Augustine* (London, 1930). In his excellent sketch, *S. Augustin et l'augustinisme* (Paris, 1955; English tr., *St. Augustine and his Influence through the Ages*, by P. Hepburne-Scott, New York, 1957) H. I. Marrou also touches upon the history of Augustinianism (though the consideration of the Reformation and Protestantism is inadequate). K. Holl's essay on *Augustins innere Entwicklung* (Berlin, Leipzig, 1922, reprinted in *Gesammelte Aufsätze III*, Tübingen, 1928) presents a magnificent study of a deep-seated hostility to Augustine. Regarding Augustine's monasticism see A. Zumkeller, *Das Mönchtum des hl. Augustinus* (Würzburg, 1950); for his teaching on the Trinity: E. Benz, *Marius Victorinus und die Entwicklung der abendländischen Willensmetaphysik* (Stuttgart, 1932); on the *Civitas Dei*, W. Kamlah, *Christentum und Geschichtlichkeit* (Stuttgart, 1951²), F. G. Maier, *Augustin und das antike Rom* (Stuttgart, 1955), J. O'Meara, *Charter of Christendom, the Significance of the City of God* (New York, 1961); for his teaching on grace: H. Barth, *Die Freiheit der Entscheidung im Denken Augustins* (Basel, 1935), and J. Burnaby, *Amor Dei, A Study of the Religion of St. Augustine* (London, 1947², 226 ff.); on Augustine's education and position in his time, see the great work of H. I. Marrou, *Saint Augustin et la fin de la culture antique* (Paris, 1958³) with his appended 'Retractatio' of 1949, and R. Lorenz, *Die Wissenschaftslehre Augustins* (*Zeitschrift für Kirchengeschichte*, 67 [*1955–56*], 29-60, 213-251).

Ch. VII—BOETHIUS

The learned philosophical writings of Boethius have still substantially to be used from the reprint of an old edition in Migne (*ML*, 64). The *Commentary on Cicero's Topics* was published by J. C. Orelli and I. G. Baier in *Ciceronis Opera V, 1* (Zürich, 1933), those writings on the *Quadrivium* which have been preserved were published by G. Friedlein (Leipzig, 1867), the *Porphyry Commentaries*, by S. Brandt in *CSEL*, 48 (1906). The theological *Opuscula* are best found in H. F. Stewart and E. K. Rand (Cambridge, 1936³), together with the text of the *Consolatio*, the last edition of which was excellently produced by L. Bieler in *CC* (*Series Latina*, 94, 1957). The *Consolatio* has been repeatedly translated into English; a translation of the theological *Tractates* (by H. F. Stewart and E. K. Rand) is found in their 1936 edition. The introduction (by F. Klinger) of the German translation of the *Consolatio* (by K. Büchner, Leipzig, Dietrich'sche Verlagsbuchhandlung, no date) is worth reading. L. Cooper has produced *A Concordance of Boethius* (Cambridge, Mass., 1928).

The literature on Boethius deals for the most part with particular historical, philological and philosophical questions. The best survey of his life and work is that of M. Cappuyns, article *Boèce* in the *Dictionnaire de l'Histoire et de Géographie Ecclésiastique IX* (Paris, 1937), 348-380. For the biographical and historical connections, see particularly J. Sundwall, *Abhandlungen zur Geschichte des ausgehenden Römertums* (Helsingfors, 1919), and E. Stein, *Histoire du Bas-Empire II* (Paris, 1949), 107 ff.; also H. M. Barrett, *Boethius, Some Aspects of his Times and Work* (Cambridge, 1940); for the literary questions, P. Courcelle, *Les Lettres grecques en Occident* (Paris, 1948), 257-312; K. Dürr, *The Propositional Logic of Boethius* (Amsterdam, 1951); and for the theological writings, V. Schurr, *Die Trinitätslehre des Boethius im Lichte der 'skytischen Kontroversen'* (Paderborn, 1935). As to Boethius' classification within the history of ideas, see also E. Hoffmann, *Pädagogischer Humanismus* (Zürich, Stuttgart, 1955), 117 ff.

INDEX OF PROPER NAMES

25. L